They Fight Like Devils

They Fight Like Devils

Stories from
Lucknow During the
Great Indian Mutiny, 1857–58

D.A. KINSLEY

SARPEDON
New York

Published by
SARPEDON PUBLISHERS
An Imprint of Combined Publishing

Copyright © 2001 by D.A. Kinsley

ISBN 1-885119-76-3

For sales or rights inquiries please contact Combined Publishing,
476 West Elm St., Conshohocken, PA 19428

Cataloging-in-Publication data is available from the
Library of Congress.

First edition, first printing.

PRINTED AND BOUND IN THE UNITED STATES OF AMERICA.

Contents

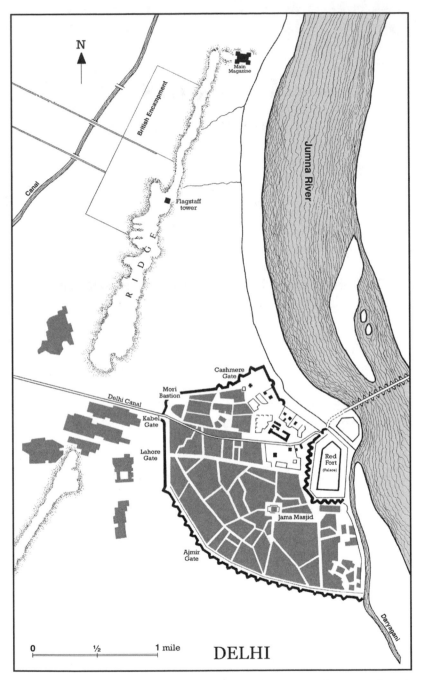

The British siege, or rather beleaguerment, of Delhi in the summer of 1857. Lacking the strength to surround the city, the British built up their forces along a ridgeline to the north, and on September 14 successfully stormed the city's gates.

Introduction

In no war of modern history was there such desperate combat as that which occurred during the war of the Indian Mutiny, or Sepoy Rebellion, of 1857–59. This was particularly the case in the sieges and campaigns of Lucknow, the main center of armed conflict for nine months, in which small numbers of men struggled against immense opposition. Their triumph over adversity captured the popular imagination on both sides of the Atlantic, as evidenced by Tennyson's "The Defence of Lucknow" and Whittier's "The Pipes at Lucknow," and the fact that flags were flown at half-mast in the United States when it was learned that one of the greatest heroes of Lucknow—General Havelock—had died. (During the U.S. Civil War, white cloth covers with neck flaps for military caps were known as "havelocks." Also, seven U.S. towns were named "Havelock" and six "Lucknow," not to mention the number of "Delhis.")

The causes of the Mutiny were primarily the enactment of military regulations and procedures that many "sepoys" or native soldiers of the Bengal Army regarded as violations of their customs and beliefs. But the precipitating factor was the introduction of paper cartridges that disaffected sepoys and others alleged were sized and lubricated with the fat of cows and pigs, the touching of which was disgusting and defiling to those who considered the cow a sacred animal and the pig an abomination. (The allegation originated in the arsenal at Calcutta, and it was later discovered that Indian contractors had fraudulently supplied cheap beef fat instead of expensive mutton fat. They were possibly bribed to do so by Russian secret agents because a lot of rubles turned up in the Calcutta Exchange at that time, giving credence to the theory that the Mutiny was the czar's revenge for the Crimean War.) Worst of all, the powder end of the cartridge had to be

1

bitten off in order to pour the powder into the barrel before reversing the cartridge and ramming down the bullet end.

The resultant revolt in the Bengal Army also incited a rebellion by Indian civilians who were opposed to the new reforms of the East India Company, that commercial enterprise which governed and garrisoned British India for the Crown. The Company's and the Queen's regiments of "Europeans" (as all non-Indian troops were then called) were outnumbered by at least ten to one, had to fight for their very existence, and might have been annihilated but for the help of loyal sepoys and the thousands of Indian and other Asian volunteers who joined them. This made the conflict a civil war between Indians of opposing customs and beliefs, with the Europeans as an enabling force, and such wars are always the worst. Little or no mercy was shown or expected by either side, because mutiny and rebellion were capital crimes and the guilty became desperate criminals. Until amnesty was finally proclaimed for the remaining rebels, it was in fact a "war to the death."

After several months of discontent in the Bengal Native Army, the Mutiny erupted on the Sunday evening of May 10, 1857, at Meerut, a large military station forty miles east of Delhi. Eighty-five of the Indian garrison had just been court-martialed and jailed for refusing to receive the new cartridges; most of their fellow soldiers revolted, stormed the jail and freed them, amidst considerable bloodshed, and then marched off to Delhi. The European garrison at Meerut was taken by surprise—most were preparing for church parade—and due to the incompetence of the old and ailing general in command, who thought that staying put was a better tactic than pursuit, the mutineers were able to escape.

It was said in Russia and Asia that "he who holds Delhi holds India," because of its strategic location between the three hostile frontiers. And so, to guard against invasion by Russians and Asians, Delhi was the most fortified city in British India—having the largest arsenal and surrounded by seven miles of defensive walls and towers. But, in May of 1857, confidence in the loyalty of the Indian Army was such that Delhi had no European troops in its large garrison. Also, Delhi was formerly the capital of the Mogul (or Mongol) Empire of India; and this total lack of European troops was in deference to Sirajooddeen Bahadur Shah, the last of the Mogul emperors, who was now an old and powerless dependent of the Honourable East India

Company, which had appropriated his decayed empire and dignified him with the courtesy title "King of Delhi."

Consequently, when the mutineers from Meerut arrived at daybreak on Monday the 11th of May, and most of the Indian troops of Delhi joined them in revolt, the city with all its resources easily fell into their hands, and it was soon the rallying point of thousands of other rebels. Bahadur Shah was proclaimed "Emperor of India," but he was little more than a figurehead; for the powers behind the throne were his two eldest sons and eldest grandson—Meerza (Prince) Moghul Beg, Meerza Khezzer Sooltan, and Meerza Aboo Bukht—and his general in chief, Bukhtawer Khan, who was formerly a "soobahdar" or captain in the Bengal Native Artillery and who was assisted by several European and Eurasian "renegades."

Delhi thus became of utmost political and military importance to both sides; and to retake it as soon as possible was then the imperative task of some three thousand European and loyal Indian and other Asian troops, with forty guns—less than half of which were of siege caliber. These were mobilized and on the move within three weeks to oppose a force ten times their number, with five times as many guns—most of which were of heavy caliber. But it would take them more than three months to accomplish the task, under the most grueling conditions. (Too late to prevent the Great Panic of 1857, because European and American financiers had millions invested in the new East India Railway and other potentially doomed projects in British India.)

The besiegers were too few to surround the entire city, so had to dig in on and behind the two-mile-long rocky ridge that diagonally overlooked the mile-wide stretch of woodland that skirted the northern wall of the city. The rebels therefore had free access to the Jumna River on the east and could come and go as they pleased from the west and south, and they gave their opponents no rest. Their heavy artillery thundered day and night from the bastions, raking the ridge with shot and shell; and they launched continual sorties of from five to ten thousand men, usually at several points of the ridge at once, which required nearly every man of the Delhi Field Force to repel them. So, while the rebel attack forces could relieve one another, those they attacked got little or no relief, but were almost constantly on the move to reinforce one threatened position or another. Thus, the besiegers actually became the besieged; and only when adequate reinforcements and munitions arrived, and casualties and desertions reduced the rebel garrison, were they able to deliver an effective bombardment and storm the shattered defenses. Even then, however, it took a week of hard fighting from street to street and house to house before the city was recaptured.

As if that weren't enough, it was the worst time of the year for military operations. In June, hot dust-laden winds and blinding sandstorms swept the exposed British position, where the temperature rose to above a hundred degrees Fahrenheit in the shade. And in July and August, torrential rains flooded the trenches and turned the camp into a stifling quagmire. Those on picket duty were alternately drenched and scorched, and the continuous tension and anxiety also contributed to causing the ailments that put a third of the Delhi Field Force on the sick list or in the grave. Moreover, the rotting corpses of rebels and carcasses of draft animals that dotted the terrain attracted and bred plagues of insects—especially flies, which swarmed in millions all over everyone and everything, making eating and sleeping extremely difficult. And nights were disturbed by the squabbling of carrion birds and beasts, and by the unrelenting activity of bloodsucking bugs. (The most assiduous of the noninsect nuisances were the kites, or small hawks. On one occasion, when a field surgeon cut off a soldier's crushed big toe and cast it aside, a kite that was circling overhead instantly swooped down, snatched it up and flew off with it, much to the amazement of the surgeon and the soldier. In fact, these birds were so aggressive that they even snatched food from men's plates and had to be fought off along with the flies and stink bugs and other insects, who committed suicide in hot soup and tea and coffee.) But just as these torments were generally endured with grim humor, so the constant clatter and thunder of weapons soon became as natural as the stench of gunsmoke and decay.

The left flank of the Delhi Field Force was protected by the mile-wide river, the rear by the deep and steep-banked Jumna Canal; but the right was exposed and particularly vulnerable, overlooking as it did a mass of suburbs with walled gardens and fortified houses full of enemy sharpshooters. Sorties were constantly launched to clear out these "hornets' nests," but although a couple of the closest suburbs were eventually occupied by the attackers, those nearest the city remained under control of the rebels, who reoccupied them soon after they were driven out. The heavy fire from the city walls and towers prevented any permanent occupation by the attackers, just as it prevented them from clearing away the noisome remains—too numerous even for the scavengers to dispose of. (Those who had served in the Sikh Wars and in the Crimea said that they had never been under such heavy fire or in such a pestilential hole before, and they even admitted that some of the rebel artillerymen outmatched them in accuracy and rapidity of fire.)

The fact that continual mass attacks on the right flank of the Delhi Field Force did not succeed in turning that flank and driving the defenders off the ridge may be attributed to the remarkable endurance of the small body of Gurkhas (or Nepalese soldiers), Indians, and Europeans that was posted in Hindoo Rao's House, a mansion near the southern end of the ridge and once occupied by a native nobleman. Every effort to demolish and storm this outpost failed. The magnificent structure was pockmarked and honeycombed by missiles, the ground around it strewn with dead rebels and shrapnel; but the defenders never deserted it, though they lost heavily and had to be constantly reinforced, and poured out a steady fire from the sandbagged doorways, windows, and veranda, from the loopholed parapets of the flat roof, and from the rifle pits and the field-gun battery in an earthwork outside. And for every man they lost, they killed at least ten of their assailants. Still, they barely held their ground. After the first series of continuous assaults on the ridge, lasting thirty-six hours, the European defenders of Hindoo Rao's House were so exhausted that most of them didn't care if they lived or died; and were it not for the hardier Gurkhas and Sikhs, who were game to the last, they would have let the enemy overrun them and put them out of their misery. But they eventually became inured to the almost daily ordeal.

Although the "besiegers" were well entrenched and protected in several other buildings on the ridge, the "besieged" still had an advantage in the immense cover provided by the thick vegetation below the ridge and the rocks and shrubs and gullies on the slope, enabling them to get within effective range as they swarmed up the hundred to two hundred yards of incline. But the Sepoys were armed mostly with smoothbores, and these old "Brown Bess" muskets were no match for the new Minié and Enfield rifles carried by most of their opponents and which could be deadly accurate up to more than a thousand yards—at least four times the effective musket range. And besides, the expanding "manstopper" Minié bullet was a killer or crippler wherever it struck a man. ("The Minié is the king of weapons," wrote war correspondent William Russell of *The Times*, noting that it killed over ten thousand Russians in twelve months during the Crimean War.) And as soon as the attackers were driven back, the attacked would rush from cover in pursuit and cut down as many of them as they could. This was done by the Gurkhas with their "kookries" or longknives, which had broad curved blades measuring a foot long—broader at the point than at the handle, having the cutting edge on the concave side, and capable of hacking off the head of an ox and slicing a man in two from crown to crotch at one blow. The pursuers would continue the slaughter until driven back themselves by the fire from the city's walls. Nevertheless, the "besiegers" never gave an inch of their original position; and only once were their own defenses penetrated by the enemy.

It happened in the second week of July, when a squadron of rebel cavalry passed some outlying pickets of their opponents by pretending to be loyalists, then made a dash for the Bengal Horse Artillery lines in an attempt to incite the loyal native gunners to desert with their guns. But the gunners refused to budge, and the intruders were given a warm reception of bullets and grapeshot. Nevertheless, they succeeded in scattering an inlying picket of the Queen's 6th Dragoon Guards, cutting loose and driving off a number of artillery horses, and cutting down several Indian teamsters who tried to stop them. (Among the raiders were several female cavaliers, known as "ordé begnian" or "army queens," who were such fierce fighters that they put many a man to shame. Women also served in the rebel batteries and performed other hazardous tasks.)

An entire troop of the rebels was actually taken on singlehandedly by Lieutenant James Hills, whose half-battery was threatened by its sudden approach. Mounting at once and drawing his sword, he charged at the foremost troopers, cutting down several of them before his horse collided with another and threw him to the ground. He had no sooner regained his wind and his feet than he was confronted by several opponents, who rode at him with a yell. Having dropped his sword in the fall, he drew his revolver and shot at his assailants, who turned and fled; but he had no sooner retrieved his sword than he was attacked by a man with a lance. Knocking the lance aside with his blade, he shot the man down, then was confronted by a swordsman. Hills tried to shoot him, but his pistol either misfired or was empty; so he threw it at the man's head and lunged at him with his sword. His foe dodged the missile, and the blow of Hills' blade was softened by the man's thick leather shoulder pad. The man then parried Hills' second stroke and instantly dealt him a stunning blow on the head that knocked him to the ground. (Although he got a nasty gash, his turban-wrapped leather helmet saved him from getting a split skull.) Dismounting, the rebel would have finished Hills at once but for Major Harry Tombs, Hills' commanding officer, who arrived on the scene afoot just in time to shoot the rebel down with a single-shot pistol at a distance of thirty paces. Tombs then had to draw his sword and rush forward to defend Hills from another attacker. But by then, Hills was on his feet, parried the man's blow, and cut him across the neck; whereupon Tombs ran him through and finished the fight. For this daredevilry, Hills was awarded the Victoria Cross; Tombs was merely commended. As for the intruders, they were chased back to Delhi with a loss of half their number as well as their leader.

Failing to dislodge their opponents from the ridge, the rebels made several attempts to cut off their communications. But these were summarily dealt with by "flying columns," which were sent out to drive the disruptive forces back into the city. The first such expedition, which occurred in the first week of July, nearly ended in disaster for a detachment of Her Majesty's 61st Regiment. When it was learned that a large body of rebels had attacked and plundered a British supply depot north of Delhi, the ill-fated defenders of which were too few to resist, a small task force was sent out to intercept the victors—which it did just in time, routing them after a brief encounter and recapturing all of their plunder. While the rest of the force returned to camp, two companies of the Queen's 61st were left behind to escort the casualties. These were being attended to and then loaded onto carts, and the unoccupied soldiers were resting on the tree-shaded bank of a shallow stream, when there suddenly appeared a brigade of enemy sepoys, which halted, deployed, and fired a volley, causing the surprised men of the 61st to take cover behind the trees and the bank. At the same time, one of their officers mounted frantically and galloped off to recall the departed horse artillery, which returned in the nick of time. The imperiled infantrymen were almost out of ammunition and prepared to sell their lives dearly with the bayonet when the guns arrived, were unlimbered and ranged and loaded in a matter of seconds, and drove the menacing enemy off with a few rounds of shrapnel.

When it was learned in mid-August that a large rebel force was en route to seize another and larger supply depot at Rohtuk, northwest of Delhi, a small task force of Indian cavalry under Captain William Hodson (the chief of native scouts and spies, and commander of Hodson's Native Irregular Horse) was sent to head the enemy off. But heavy rains and muddy roads delayed their progress, and they found the enemy already occupying Rohtuk and determined to hold it. To attempt to storm the place would have been disastrous, so Hodson resolved to draw the occupants out. Advancing his men almost to within musket range, he pretended to reconnoiter and then ordered them to withdraw—slowly and steadily. This had the desired effect. Rebel horsemen streamed out of the main gate with swords flashing; and behind them swarmed hundreds of footmen, brandishing their weapons and beating drums and blowing trumpets to keep up a defiant clamor. Hodson let them come to within a hundred and fifty yards, then shouted, "Threes about and at 'em!"

"Threes about! Form line! Draw swords! Charge!" shouted his subordinate officers, and in seconds they were at the enemy with a wild cheer. The rebel cavalry broke and scattered, then the infantry, which could not outrun the pursuers and were cut down in droves; and with the arrival of reinforcements from the loyal Raja of Jeend, Rohtuk was restored to the British line of communications.

Hodson and his "sowars," or mounted troopers, then proceeded to clear the entire district of rebels. When he learned from one of his spies that a number of them had taken refuge in a village between Rohtuk and Delhi, he surrounded the village and demanded their surrender. With a few exceptions, they refused to comply, and barricaded themselves in a large house. So Hodson's sowars broke into the house and drove them up onto the flat roof, where some furious hand-to-hand combat occurred, ending in all of the resisters being cut down. The few who had surrendered, including their leader, were condemned by drumhead court-martial and immediately executed by firing squad. "Desperate times call for desperate measures," Hodson later declared; and his Sikh orderly, Nehal Singh, added pointedly: "Jub ghur agcluggunté, billao ka moot nah dhoondé" (You don't look for a pissing cat when your house is on fire).

The most decisive of the counteroffensives occurred in the last week of August, when it was learned that a rebel force of some six thousand men with thirteen field guns was en route to intercept the convoy of twenty-two siege guns and twenty-two thousand rounds of ammunition that were destined to dismantle and breach the defenses of Delhi. (These "messengers of doom" were from the arsenals of the Punjab, that vast province northwest of Delhi, from which most of the reinforcements and supplies were coming, thanks to the indefatigable efforts of the Chief Commissioner, Sir John Lawrence, and his subordinates and supporters.) A force of only twenty-one hundred Europeans and Asians (with sixteen horse-artillery guns) trudged all day for sixteen miles through drenching rain and knee-deep mud and waist-deep water to head off the obstructive force, which was found encamped and deployed in a strong position. Despite their fatigue, the flying column bombarded and then attacked this position at once on the left flank—taking the entire array by storm from left to right, capturing all the guns and supplies, killing about eight hundred and wounding countless more of the enemy, and driving the rest back to Delhi—with a loss of only twenty-five killed and seventy wounded. The munitions convoy arrived safely in the first week of September, when final work began on emplacing the four breaching batteries.

It was a feat unsurpassed in modern war. For all of a month, under cover of darkness, relays of troops cleared the way and dug the approach trenches to within half a mile (and, on the left, to within two hundred yards) of the northern defenses of Delhi. Then, for all of a week, the batteries were constructed and the heavy guns dragged over the ridge and emplaced under a storm of fire from the north wall and towers. Several hundred men lost their lives in this perilous task, but it was worth the sacrifice. And it was accomplished none too soon, because the enemy immediately began to extend their entrenchments outside the wall and to erect flanking batteries on their left; and had they completed these countermeasures, they would have obstructed their opponents' operations. As it was, the Delhi Field Force was hard pressed to keep from being outflanked; and the heavy price paid for "sticking to one's guns" was commemorated by one artillery officer who, having the top of his head torn off by a shell fragment, miraculously survived to have the missing part of his skull replaced by a steel plate engraved with his coat of arms and a brief account of the mishap. But he could not replace the missing part of his brain. (Another officer, whose jaw was shattered and his teeth knocked down his throat by a small roundshot, prized the pieces as trophies as soon as they passed out of his body. He, however, did not survive.)

After three days and four nights of continuous bombardment by four batteries of heavy artillery, the batteries on the three bastions of the north wall were demolished and three practicable breaches were made in the walls adjoining them; and at daybreak of September 14th, the city was stormed. There were three assault columns, one support column, and one reserve column, totaling about 5,950 men. The assault columns, numbering only twenty-eight hundred, would attack simultaneously from their shelters at a distance of less than half a mile from the city.

At a signal from Brigadier John Nicholson, who commanded the assault as well as No. 1 Column, a covering party of two hundred skirmishers of the Queen's 60th Royal Rifle Corps dashed forward with a cheer, lined the garden walls and the road embankment a short distance beyond the northern defenses of Delhi, and kept up a steady and rapid fire at the rebels who lined the ramparts and thronged the breaches. These skirmishers were immediately followed by a demolition party of the Bengal Engineers, whose hazardous duty it was to blow in the main gate of the north wall, which was protected from artillery fire by an iron-plated barrier. Then, at another signal, the assault began.

No. 2 Column, numbering 850, advanced in column of fours at the double to storm the breach in the wall to the right of the Water Bastion, at the northeast corner of the city. Charging up the ramp that led to the ditch surrounding the city walls, the wildly cheering stormers slid and tumbled twenty feet down the outer slope of the dry ditch and raced twenty-five feet across an obstacle course of shattered masonry to the other side, where the men of the ladder party placed their bamboo scaling ladders for the ascent to the ledge at the base of the walls, which were twenty-four feet high. Till then, thanks to the covering fire of the Royal riflemen, the stormers suffered few casualties; but they now encountered some fierce resistance as they clambered up the ladders, because the riflemen had to hold their fire for fear of hitting them. Yet there was no stopping them as the enemy hurled stones and curses down on them, and the foremost officers emptied their revolvers in response as they scaled frantically. A slope of red sandstone rubble from the breach made the last ascent slightly easier; and the stormers quickly scrambled up to and through the breach, where there was a brief struggle with the few who awaited them inside. Hacking and jabbing, swords and bayonets soon finished these determined defenders, whose comrades had fled along the rampart or into the city, where they were pursued and disposed of with a vengeance.

The stormers of the second column swiftly cleared and occupied the nearby area, then moved half a mile westward inside the north wall and along the rampart (clearing the way as they went) to join No. 1 Column, numbering a thousand men, which stormed the breaches on the left side of the Cashmere Bastion and its adjoining wall on the left, clearing the ramparts in the middle of the northern defenses.

In the meantime, the demolition party of No. 3 Column had done its job at the Cashmere (or main) Gate. Commanded by Lieutenants Duncan Home and Philip Salkeld of the Bengal Engineers, the small detachment of European engineers and Indian sappers and miners advanced at the double under cover of the Royal riflemen and a thick haze of fog and gunsmoke. Each carried a twenty-five-pound bag of gunpowder. When they reached the outer edge of the ditch, they saw that the wooden drawbridge (although still down) was so shattered by cannonfire that little more than the support beams remained; and this required some fancy footwork to cross, which slowed them to a precarious extent. Several of the sappers and miners hesitated, fearful of falling into the ditch; and Sergeant John Smith, who was bringing up the rear, threatened to shoot them if they did not go on. At that moment, Salkeld came running back to see what was wrong and barked at Smith, "Damn their eyes! Shoot them! shoot them!" That had the desired effect, and the shirkers went on—with Smith behind them, pointing his carbine menacingly. Fortunately, they and their comrades crossed the ditch safely and were not discerned by those on the ramparts and in the gatehouse until they reached the barrier on the other side of the bridge; and by then it was too late to pick them off from above, since such firing was kept down by that of the covering Royal riflemen. Once they were beyond the barrier and under the archway of the gate, they were beneath the range of those on the walls above. They had only to fear those inside the gate, who could open the wicket or side door just far enough to shoot at them through the window grating and from behind the outer edge without much fear of being hit by the British covering fire.

Lieutenant Home and three men were first to lodge their powder bags against the hinged side of the barred gate. It was huge, of thick iron-ribbed wood, with a wicket to the right. This side door to the gatehouse now creaked open, and from behind it several rebels began to take aim at the intruders. Home and the three others instantly jumped into the ditch, and so saved themselves; but those who immediately followed them were not so lucky. Sergeant Andrew Carmichael was fatally and Havildar (Sergeant) Madhoo Singh seriously wounded, but both managed to place their powder bags and drop into the ditch. Then came Salkeld, Smith, and Corporal Frank Burgess with six men and a native officer. The bags were placed, and Salkeld was about to light the fuses when he was shot in both legs and an arm; and handing the slow match to Burgess, he slid into the ditch. But the match had gone out! And just as Burgess asked Smith for another, he too was fatally shot; and both Havildar Tilluk Singh and sepoy Ram Lal were mortally wounded as they helped him the ditch. It was now left to Smith, miraculously unhit as yet, to ignite the powder—which he did at once, leaping into the ditch as the gate shattered off its hinges in a gust of brick chips and wood splinters. His only injury was a badly bruised leg. Bugler Robert Hawthorne of Her Majesty's 52nd Light Infantry, who had accompanied the party as signaler and had jumped into the ditch with Home, now sounded the "advance" several times; and with a cheer, the soldiers of the third assault column (numbering 950) advanced at the double and entered the gateway, where they found the mangled remains of its defenders.

By a quirk of fate, Home survived only to be killed later by a premature explosion while blowing up an abandoned enemy fort; and Salkeld died of his wounds. Either posthumously or in person, the rest also received their rewards: the Victoria Cross and the Order of Merit.

Having been joined by the first two columns at the Cashmere Gate, which was occupied by a detachment, the third column pushed on southward into the city while the other two rushed on half a mile westward to take and occupy the Moree Bastion at the northwest angle of the walls. They then advanced a quarter of a mile southward to the Cabool Gate, which was also taken and occupied; and this gate, according to plan, would be opened to admit No. 4 Column, numbering 1,850 men, which was to join them by advancing through and clearing out the western suburbs. Then, while this fourth or support column moved eastward into the city and eventually communicated with the third column, the first and second columns would push on a quarter of a mile further southward to the Lahore Gate, which opened onto the main street that ran directly through the center of Delhi to

the Mogul palace and citadel on the east end, overlooking the river.
Once this gate and its protective bastion were taken and occupied, the
second column would move on a mile southward to the Ajmere Gate,
at the southwest angle of the walls, then advance another mile north-
eastward through the city and communicate with the other columns;
while the first column would advance directly down the main street to
the palace, taking and occupying all important points en route. In this
way, the entire city would be cleared of rebels, while leaving their
escape routes open on the east and southeast sides so as to make the
work easier by preventing too much desperate resistance.

The stormers met with little trouble until they were in the city, and
then everything went wrong. No. 3 Column penetrated a mile southward, but had to withdraw to the area of its starting point at the
Cashmere Gate when it got no support from nor saw any signs of the
other columns. Besides, the momentum of its attack was lost in the
maze of alleys and courtyards and walled gardens, which were teeming with marksmen; and the disorganized and demoralized troops
sought refuge in bar rooms and brothels, and preferred plundering to
street fighting. The narrow passageway and adjoining routes along the
inside of the city walls were blocked by enemy artillery, and almost
every building was occupied by enemy snipers. Three times the guns
between the Cabool and Lahore gates were charged by the soldiers of
the first column, and three times the attackers were repulsed by blasts
of grapeshot and musket balls with the loss of a dozen officers and
nearly a hundred men. The 1st Bengal European Fusiliers were almost
annihilated, and not even the daredevilry of one of their junior officers
could embolden them to try again. Lieutenant Thomas Butler (known
as "Little Tommy" because of his size) charged a gun singlehandedly,
shot the three gunners while they were in the act of loading, then
waved and shouted to his comrades to come on. But they would not;
and he got a flesh wound in the right thigh for his trouble and had to
hobble back to safety.

Brigadier Nicholson also tried to rally the men of his column for
one last rush on the Lahore Gate, but they would not budge even for
him—nor for the commander of the Fusiliers, Major George Jacob,
who lay mortally wounded and in tears at their plight, muttering "Go
on! go on! Better dead lions than live dogs!"

"Come on, you sons of bitches!" Nicholson shouted, far in
advance, holding his sword above his head. "I never thought that

Europeans would quail before Asians!" Suddenly a mutineer leaned out of a nearby window and shot him point-blank under the right arm and through the lungs. It was a fatal wound, but he willed himself to live long enough to see Delhi retaken; and when he heard that the commanding general (Archdale Wilson) proposed ordering a withdrawal to prevent further losses, he gasped, "Thank God I have strength yet to shoot him if he does!" But the majority decision of the council of war was that "to retire would be to court disaster"; that once inside the city, the Delhi Field Force had no advantageous alternative but to "hold on like grim Death" and finish the job at all costs; otherwise, a crucial advantage would be lost, and with it the prestige and much of the power of the British Raj. So Wilson ordered up the reserve column, numbering thirteen hundred men, and the bloody work went on.

What aggravated the situation was that the men of No. 4 Column never showed up at the Cabool Gate. They met with such fierce resistance in the suburbs, where at least half of the rebel army had concentrated when the bombardment began, that they were forced to fall back by the overwhelming odds of almost ten to one, and the only thing that saved them from disaster was the timely arrival of the cavalry and horse artillery, who held off the pursuing enemy amid a hail of missiles. Proportionately, these rescuers lost more men than those they rescued; and the rebels held their position in the suburbs until after the city was retaken, at which time they joined the other retreaters.

The failure of the first and second columns led to the failure of the third, and the failure of the fourth affected all, so that at the end of the day the stormers held only a mile and a quarter of the city walls and adjacent areas—a fourth of the city—and it took them another day to recover from the shock and to reorganize. Sixty-six officers and 1,104 men had been killed or wounded—a fourth of the 4,650 who were actively engaged—but the work was resumed on the 16th, when the Bengal Horse Artillery came into action and cleared away the obstructive artillery beyond the Cabool Gate, and the men of the reserve column gave new life to their battered comrades. Deploying by battalions, they swept through the city, slaying all who stood in their way and sparing those who did not; taking cover when they saw portfires being put to the touchholes of guns that barred their way, then dashing out to kill the gunners after the storm of grape had passed. And though shot at from roofs and windows and from behind garden and courtyard walls, they broke into every enclosure where the enemy had taken refuge, blasting and hacking their way up to the roofs, where the last desperate struggles occurred and from which the dead and wounded defenders were pitched for the carrion birds and beasts to pounce upon them with a hideous clamor and dispose of them in a sanitary manner.

Taking the arsenal was easy enough—fearing explosions, the enemy abandoned it without a struggle—but holding it was hard for a short time when several hundred rebels suddenly reappeared, armed with fire arrows and fire spears, which they launched through the windows from behind the surrounding trees. While those inside the building stamped them out, those on the flat parapeted roof managed to wreak havoc among the attackers by hurling live howitzer shells down among the trees; and after scores of them were blown to pieces, the rest withdrew. This was all the more daring because these shells were old and fuses tended to disintegrate in the tropical climate, causing premature explosions; but fortunately, none of the shells went off in hand.

The palace and citadel—the last strongholds of the rebels—were also taken without a struggle, abandoned by all but a few desperadoes who were shot down immediately. The scouring did not stop for five days, until every enclosure was taken and every rebel either killed on the spot or routed out of Delhi; and on the 20th of September, the Union Jack flew in triumph over the palace of the recaptured city—at a total cost to the victors, since the siege began on June 8th, of 992 killed, 2,795 wounded, thirty missing, and several thousand victims of illness; and at a total cost to the vanquished of untold thousands. The task could not have been accomplished without the support of thousands of Indian soldiers and civilians, and at least half of the Delhi Field Force was composed of Indians and other Asians. But the odds against that force were such that it should not have succeeded at all. The fatal flaw in its favor, according to every contemporary Indian account, was that the rebels generally lacked competent leadership. Ironically enough, this was also true of their opponents. But sheer desperation often saved the day for them in the absence of an able commander; whereas the rebels, unless cornered, thought discretion the better part of valor.

What hurt the rebel cause most was the disorder caused in Delhi

by the Mogul princes, whose misconduct and misrule the old and ailing king was amost at a loss to stop. Finally, both he and his chief general threatened to surrender to the British unless the corruption and
oppression ceased, reminding the wrongdoers that such behavior had
led to the original fall of the Mogul Empire. But even when the warning was heeded, there was too much competition and too little coop-
eration between the various factions in Delhi to reduce the rampant
disaffection and demoralization among civilians and soldiers, many of
whom were compelled either to abandon the city or to prey upon each
other in order to survive. This alone discouraged others from joining
or supporting the rebellion, according to contemporary Indian
accounts. Also, it was more advantageous for people such as the Sikhs
to join and support the British rather than the Moguls; for although
the British had recently been forced to conquer the Sikhs because of
their aggressive attempts to extend their borders, the British (unlike
the Mogul conquerors) did not persecute them.

One of the martyred seventeenth-century leaders of the Sikhs, who
was taken by treachery and beheaded as a rebel by order of one of the
Mogul emperors, had rightly prophesied that his oppressed people
would avenge him and destroy the Mogul dynasty with the help of the
Europeans, who had just begun to establish themselves as traders in
India. And that was how a British mercantile company became a political and military power—by being forced to take sides in the Indian
civil wars in order to protect its economic interests. By siding with the
opponents of the Moguls, it eventually helped to disintegrate and then
proceeded to appropriate the Mogul Empire.

Bahadur Shah (the former "King of Delhi" and "Emperor of
India") surrendered on condition that his life be spared, which it was;
but he was convicted of sedition and deported to British Burma, where
he died in custody four years later. His general in chief escaped and
was never heard from again; but his two eldest sons and eldest grandson, who had ruled in his name, surrendered outside of Delhi to
Captain Hodson and a patrol of his sowars on condition that their
lives, too, be spared. They were reputedly guilty of so many crimes
that Hodson could promise them nothing, and proceeded to escort
them back to the city for trial. As they neared their destination, a
threatening mob of the princes' retainers (led by the chief eunuch of
the palace) surrounded and halted the escort, shouting "Tukht ya
tukhtah!" (A throne or a bier!; i.e., Victory or death!) They seemed

about to attempt a rescue when Hodson suddenly dismounted and shot the three princes to death as they sat in a carriage. That ended the threat, the mob melted away, and the fleeing eunuch was pursued and cut down by a sowar. "It was them or us," Hodson later said; "and had I hesitated one second, it would have been us! Necessity has no law." And his Sikh orderly, Nehal Singh, added proverbially: "Ek murra kootta naheen kat sukta." (A dead dog cannot bite.) For the Sikhs were particularly glad to be rid of the princes, whose ancestors had persecuted them, and thus they hailed Hodson as an instrument of divine punishment.

And so ended the Mogul dynasty and the saga of Delhi. But it was only the beginning of the war. Most of the rebels had escaped from the city and were heading southeastward for Lucknow, their second-greatest stronghold in north-central India and their last great refuge. Formerly the provincial capital of Mogul viceroys, who later became client-kings of the British Raj when the Mogul Empire crumbled, it was now a part of British India—the last king having been deposed for misrule and deported to Calcutta and his kingdom annexed by the East India Company in 1856. But one of his wives, Begum (Queen) Huzrut Mahul, remained in Lucknow. She led the revolt there, aided by Moulvie (Master) Ahmed Shah, a religious scholar and teacher with a large following. However, they soon split to form rival factions—the Moulvie then calling himself "King of Hindustan"—and the result was fatal to the rebel cause. When faced with defeat, the Begum threw a pair of women's drawers at her chief commander and told him to retire to a harem; and she herself eventually escaped to Nepal, where she was given asylum by (and reputedly became a mistress of) Maharaja Jung Bahadur, who was a staunch supporter of her enemies, but was allegedly seduced by her charms. And the Moulvie was eventually shot to death in a confrontation with a pro-British Raja named Juggennath Singh, who cut off his head for a reward of fifty thousand rupees. (After being publicly displayed in India, the trophy was sent to the anatomical museum of the Royal College of Surgeons in London.) His obituaries credited him with having created the greased-cartridge phobia and the rumor that flour, salt, and sugar were being contaminated with the powdered bones of cows and pigs in order to destroy the beliefs and customs of those who opposed the British Raj.

As soon as Delhi and its surrounding districts were reoccupied and pacified, flying columns were sent in pursuit of the fleeing foe. Several sharp encounters resulted, in which the pursued were routed. The most noteworthy of these occurred at Agra, 120 miles south of Delhi and 180 miles west of Lucknow, where the pursuers were taken by surprise while they were encamped outside the city—then, as now, famous for the magnificent Taj Mahal. Success had made the victors unalert, and all twenty-five hundred of them were turned out of their tents in their underwear by a storm of missiles from a much-larger force of enemy infantry, cavalry, and artillery. "To horse! to horse!" shouted the British cavalry officers. "To your guns!" shouted the British artillery officers. "Form square!" shouted the British infantry officers. "Prepare to receive cavalry!" And receive them they did, and counterattack they did, driving the rebels off with great slaughter. The ferocity of the fighting was evidenced by one British lieutenant, who received (and survived) over seventy saber cuts; while another subaltern, who sustained more than twenty sword wounds, was so defaced as to be unrecognizable.

How the war progressed beyond Delhi and Lucknow may be summarized thus:

In three months, Brigadier John Nicholson and his small brigade of mostly Indian loyalists had pacified the northwest (including the vast Punjab province) before reinforcing the Delhi Field Force in mid-August of 1857; and these operations included intercepting and annihilating a large brigade of mutineers en route to Delhi. In the northeast, Colonel James Neill and other flying-column commanders had relieved several small beleaguered garrisons and had defeated and dispersed thousands of rebels with only a few hundred men; the revolts in the west were crushed by local forces of native irregulars; the rebellion in Central India was eventually quelled in the spring of 1858 by an Indo-European army under Major General Sir Hugh Rose. There, the loyalty of the Bombay and Madras native armies prevented the disaffection from spreading to the south except in isolated instances, and the loyalty of most Indian leaders and their subjects prevented it from becoming a national uprising.

The British suffered a major disaster at Cawnpore, on the Ganges River south of Lucknow in June, while their main forces were necessarily preoccupied at Delhi. At Cawnpore the rebels forced nine hundred defenders, half of whom were women and children, to surrender after a twenty-day siege. The men were killed after having been promised safe passage on boats, and most of the civilians were confined in a house. On receiving news of a British relief column approaching the city, five assassins were dispatched among the women and children on July 15, killing them and throwing their bodies down a well.

At the vital, rebel-held city of Lucknow by that July, three thousand British soldiers and civilians and loyal Indians had come under siege on the grounds of the British Residency, with no hope of rescue until the issue at Delhi was decided.

Ultimately, in mid-November of 1857, all of the flying columns from Delhi converged on Lucknow, where they joined other forces for the last great struggles of the Sepoy War.

For the majority of illustrations in this book I am indebted to the National Army Museum, London. The line drawings, except for that of William Hodson, are from C. H. Mecham's *Sketches and Incidents of the Siege of Lucknow*; the painting of Lt. F. E. Farquharson is courtesy of the Black Watch Regimental Museum, Perth; and the painting of Col. John Ewart leading the assault on the Secunder Bagh is courtesy of The Argyll and Sutherland Highlanders Museum, Edinburgh.

The stories that follow are based upon the numerous letters, diaries, memoirs, dispatches, and oral accounts of Lucknow veterans that were printed (usually anonymously) in Anglo-Indian, British, and American newspapers, magazines, and books during and after the Mutiny. As was customary at the time, such writings were submitted gratis to one or more newspapers and magazines as a public service; and once published, they were considered public property and were freely reprinted (wholly or partially, with many revisions) in other periodicals and in histories of the Mutiny. The magnitude and variety of this literature required a selection and adaptation of the best sources; and the various narratives and versions of narratives of individual combatants have been collated and interwoven, and enhanced by much choice information from the other sources. In the remainder of this work, the voices of participants will be printed in Roman type and my brief introductory or explanatory remarks in italics.

RAJPUTANA
(modern Pakistan)

NEPAL

● Lahore

● Meerut
● Delhi

● Lucknow

INDIA
1857

● Calcutta

● Bombay

● Bangalore

Dehli
● Meerut

NEPAL

Agra
Cawnpore
● Lucknow

Gwalior
Allahabad

Jhansi

Though discontent flared at many points on the subcontinent, the Great Mutiny took place primarily in north-central India.

1

A PERFECT STORM
OF FIRE

*Oudh, one of the largest provinces of British India, was the home of
three-fourths of all the rebels. It was also the main recruiting ground
of the Bengal Native Army, supplying two-thirds of its 120,000 soldiers. And so Lucknow, the fortified capital, became the prime focus
and rallying point of rebellion.*

*In May of 1857, when the Mutiny erupted, Lucknow was defend-
ed by a small garrison of Europeans and loyal Indians—too small to
hold it against the massive array of mutineers that hemmed the
defenders into an equally small area of the city.*

*Lord Canning, the Governor General of British India, wrote that
"there cannot be found in the annals of war an achievement more glorious than the defense of the Residency at Lucknow."*

*The British Residency compound covered an area of thirty-three
acres on a low ridge overlooking the Goomtee River in the northwest
corner of Lucknow, and it contained sixteen large houses and gardens
with a low wall on one side and only an earthen parapet on the other.
Crammed into the cellars and outbuildings were 1,280 noncombatants, mostly women and children, who were plagued by rats and
roaches and other miseries. Their 1,720 defenders, who were eventually reduced to 980 (including sick and wounded), not only had as
many as thirty thousand rebels to contend with, but also the plague of
flies and other pests that "obstinately disputed every mouthful of food
and any attempt at rest," as one of the garrison put it. This infestation
was caused by the uncontrollable pollution and by the large number
of dead and decaying men and animals, the burying of which kept
every able-bodied man busy when not repairing defenses and per-
forming numerous other nightly fatigue duties. As for the daily fight-*

21

ing, this aspect of the ordeal was well summarized by Lieutenant John Ruggles of the 41st Bengal Native Infantry:

Our successful defense for almost three months of a nearly ceaseless position was pronounced by the engineers of the relieving force to be miraculous and characterized by General Outram, our new commander, as unequaled in history. From the 30th of June to the 25th of September, we were exposed to a heavy continued fire day and night. The enemy were within fifty yards of our defenses on every side, and we were unable to stir in any direction without running the gauntlet of their sharpshooters.

Besides this, we were continually harassed by their mines [tunnels], which weakened our defenses; and we were continually occupied in countermining, We had three regular attacks in which they came on in swarms on all sides, but were driven back with terrific loss by our handful of men; and we made no less than five sorties, in which we spiked two of the enemy's heaviest guns and blew up several of the houses from which they had kept up their most harassing fires. In spite of their perseverance, their numbers, their showers of shot and shell, we never yielded an inch of ground, though many of the houses were reduced to mere heaps of ruins.

Our defenses were scarcely deserving of the name. We were merely defending a certain number of houses , with the enemy in possession of the houses adjoining, the line of defense between us consisting only of hastily constructed ditches and barricades. Fortunately, we had a good supply of shot and shell and thirty guns, with a plentiful supply of wheat, peas, and rice.

But the wonder was, that after going through such fire as we did, any of us escaped. Often, men were knocked over right and left and in front of and behind me; and yet I was miraculously spared. And Captain Sam Lawrence of the Queen's 52nd Regiment, although he commanded one of the most dangerous posts and was a volunteer on every sortie and one of the biggest men in the garrison, escaped without a scratch; and yet the sick and wounded were constantly shot as they lay on the hospital floor, small dogs were hit by stray bullets, and even a pet parrot had its head shot off while walking on the floor of a house. Strange to say, also, that we became so accustomed to the unceasing fire that we felt uncomfortable when it finally ended.

The rebels had sixty pieces of artillery, with an unlimited supply of ammunition; and Lieutenant George Hutchinson of the Bengal Engineers noted that "we engineers calculated that in all those months never a second elapsed without a musket shot being thrown at us, and at times upwards of seventy per second, besides roundshot and shell totaling no less than twenty thousand. Every house was shattered, pitted, and riddled."

Captain Robert Anderson of the 25th Bengal Native Infantry, who commanded an outpost, observed that:

Whenever a man left his post he had to run through a shower of bullets, which cut up the ground and whizzed all about him; but he was just as likely to be hit as a fellow who was too proud to run. Bullets danced on the walls of our houses like a handful of peas in a frying pan. Shells came smashing right into the rooms and dashed our property to pieces, and metal splinters and bits of wood and brick and other debris flew in all directions. Roundshot tumbled down huge pieces of masonry, filling the rooms with clouds of dust and grit, while grapeshot rattled against the stockades and thumped into the earthworks and plowed up the ground all about us.

Another of the garrison remarked that "the musketry fire was kept up so thickly and persistently that the carrion birds, attracted by the carcasses of horses and bullocks, fell dead from the surrounding trees; and the scavenger dogs were dropped dead in their tracks before they could feed. And so we were deprived of Nature's sanitation crews."

The chief leader of the demolition sorties was Captain George Fulton of the Bengal Engineers. This, in his own words, is an example of his work:

One night, we sneaked out of our lines to a nearby house. I had only a penknife, slow match, and portfire in my hands and was accompanied by two other European officers and a dozen men carrying powder bags. We expected to find the house empty; but Lieutenant Hutchinson, who was first in, suddenly startled us by firing his revolver and calling out: "Here are twenty of them!"

Our men fell back a pace or two, but I seized a musket from one of them and ran forward. They followed; and I then put them in position to guard the doors and windows while I twitted the enemy with not showing their faces, as I did, but standing behind the front door with only their firearms showing. The chaff had the desired effect on one of them, who dashed out and fired at me point-blank, but missed. I shot him down on the spot. The rest of them bolted out the back door as I gave the word "Charge!" but four of them were bayoneted and shot as they tried to get away . We then blew up the house . Great fun and excitement in a small way.

The "fun and excitement" were over for Fulton on September 14, as related by Lieutenant Frederick Birch of the First Bengal Native Infantry:

The death of this brilliant officer was occasioned by one of the most curious of wounds. He was inspecting a new battery in an earthwork, and was lying at full length in one of the embrasures with a telescope in his hands when he turned his face and said with a smile, "they are just going to fire." And sure enough , they did. The shot took away the whole of the back of his head, leaving his face like a mask still on his neck. His was the most important loss we had sustained after that of our chief commander, Sir Henry Lawrence.

This detailed account of the desperate nature of the fighting was given by the Residency surgeon, Dr. Joseph Fayrer, who defended his own house with fifty-four other men, of whom fourteen were killed and forty wounded:

Mine was a much-exposed post. The enemy swarmed in all round us. They occupied the buildings near to and overlooking us, some of them only a few yards distant. They loopholed walls and commenced a heavy fire upon us, and it seemed as if they must rush in at any moment and overwhelm us. We did all we could to make arrangements to fight it out to the last if there was such a rush. Every window and door in the house was barricaded with boxes of earth; and the eleven women and seven children under our care were sent into the cellars as the rooms upstairs were not safe against shot and shell, which frequently penetrated the brick walls.

On the 1st of July, for instance, the eighteen-year-old daughter of Colonel Palmer of the 48th Native Infantry, who was in a room of the Residency above the cellar, had one of her legs nearly carried off by a nine-pound shot which passed through the wall. I went immediate-ly—150 yards under a shower of bullets, which were cutting up the ground all about me—and amputated the poor girl's leg above the knee. She did not survive very long, as the shock was too great.

Many others were hit in this manner, including our leader, Sir Henry Lawrence. During the night of July the 1st, a roundshot had passed through the wall of his room in the Residency, where he was sitting; but he was not hurt, though covered with plaster. He was entreated to move, but laughingly remarked that as lightning does not strike twice in the same place, so it was with enemy shot. The next morning, an 8-inch howitzer shell came in through the window and exploded, the fragments of which lacerated and fractured his left hip and thigh. The Residency was already much battered by shot and shell; the room he was in was knocked almost to pieces; so I had him carried to my house, on which the fire was not yet so heavy. The enemy must have found out; for he was scarcely there when a most fiendish fire was rained upon the place, and both roundshot and mus-ketry shot came fast and furiously. I did all I could for him under the circumstances, but he died on the morning of July the 4th.

From that day on the fire upon us rapidly increased in force and frequency, coming from all directions day and night. Shot and shell came crashing in, with a perfect hail of musketry. The bullets found their way everywhere, and people were hit in places that seemed safe. Nails, bolts, ramrods, bayonets, spears, stones, bricks, pieces of tele-graph wire, printer's type, logs of wood bound with iron, grenades, fireballs or red-hot shot, fire bombs, even stink bombs, and God knows what else were fired at us.

My journal entry for July the 3rd was typical of subsequent ones: "A perfect storm of fire upon the house; some were wounded. The ladies are doing all they can for them. My 9-pounder and 18-pounder were kept hard at work—Dr. Partridge (assistant surgeon of the 2nd Oudh Cavalry) and I helping to load and fire. We made some effective shots and silenced one of the enemy's batteries more than once."

I also had constant practice with my rifle and shotguns, either from the sandbagged veranda or from the parapeted roof, and had a heavy cavalry saber ready if the enemy got in. I was quite determined that they should not take me alive and that I would kill as many of them as I could before they killed me.

Constant threats of attack kept us on duty for eighteen or twenty hours at a time, so a little rest and food and a bath and change of clothes were luxuries; and when not actually fighting, we were repairing damages and strengthening defenses.

By the 15th of July, Captain Anderson's house (in a most exposed position) was almost entirely destroyed by roundshot; and on two occasions, some of the defenders had to be dug out when part of it fell. On one occasion, a roundshot carried away almost the greater part of the parapet round the roof and went clean through the body of a Sikh who was in the act of firing. The poor fellow never moved; the shot had made a hole of four inches in diameter in his chest and had passed through his back.

On the 20th of July, at 10:15 A.M., a tremendous explosion in the direction of the Redan Battery took place; and a column of smoke and earth ascended high in the air. The enemy had sprung a mine about twenty-five yards from our inner defenses. It had evidently been intended to blow up the Redan Battery, but had taken a wrong direction and exploded on one side of it. This was the signal for a general attack.

Immediately the smoke and dust subsided, a terrific fire was opened on us from all sides; every gun that could be brought to bear on us was at work at once; and at the same time, a hail of musketry was poured in. The enemy attempted to storm the Redan, Lieutenant Innes's house, the Post Office, and my house. Every one of us was at his post and poured shot, shell, and musketry into them as hard and fast as possible . The noise was frightful, the enemy shouting and urging each other on and blowing bugles and beating drums. It certainly seemed to me as if our time had come.

Our two guns were fired as rapidly as possible as hundreds of the enemy came swarming over the wall and into the garden. Mr. Partridge and I, with the other officers, kept our rifles and shotguns going as fast as we could load and shoot, until our shoulders were black and blue ; whilst the 9- and 18-pounders poured grapeshot and bags of bullets into the attackers until at length they fell back and were hustled out with hand grenades as they ran across the garden, leaving scores of dead and wounded, who were dragged away after dark.

Notwithstanding the fierceness of the attack, we managed to shelter ourselves so well that our own loss was comparatively small—only four killed and twelve wounded in the entire garrison—though our house was frightfully damaged. Lieutenant Macfarlane, who had done splendid service with his artillery, had a portion of his skull shot away; and Mr. Bailey, a Eurasian volunteer, suffered a singular wound from which (contrary to expectation) he recovered. A musket ball had smashed his chin and exited through his neck.

The attack lasted till about one P.M., but was repulsed on every side. This was the enemy's first great attempt to take us by storm, and they paid dearly for it. But we knew they would try and try again; and so we lived in a constant state of tension and anxiety, which was aggravated by the extreme heat and wet, and the sickening stench, the millions of flies and mosquitoes, the painful boils and contusions, the fever and scurvy, the dysentery and cholera, and not least of all by the new threat—that of mining.

Day and night we had to listen for the sound of subterranean workers; and this more than any other danger terrified the poor women and children, who expected any moment to be blown out of their damp, rat-infested holes. Then the heavy rains flooded our trenches, causing the occupants to crowd into the other shelters.

On the 10th of August, at ten A.M., another mine was sprung, which blew up a great part of the post occupied by fifty armed boys of the Martinière College, destroying palisades and other defenses for sixty feet and sending the timber and other debris flying far and wide. Fortunately, none of the boys were killed though some were injured. Immediately after this the enemy came on under a heavy fire and surrounded the nearby Cawnpore Battery, which they tried to take by assault. Some thirty of them lodged themselves in the ditch of this battery, close under the mouths of our guns; but some hand grenades eJected them, and they bolted.

An assault was also made on Mr. Sago's house, where the enemy again exploded a mine, which destroyed some outhouses and blew two soldiers into the air—who, strange to say, were unhurt and got back safely to their posts. The enemy then came on to the attack, but were driven back with severe loss. After this, they kept up a heavy fire for about two hours.

At five P.M., they attacked Captain Saunders's post, but were driven back. One of them actually got hold of the bayonet of an 84th Queen's man, who immediately shot him dead. The fire then slackened. At nine P.M., however, they made another attack but were again repulsed everywhere after hard fighting.

My post, as usual, came in for much of the heavy cannonade and fusillade. But we threw back no less than 150 8-inch howitzer shells, besides great quantities of 9- and 18-pound roundshot and grape, and destroyed a large number of attackers. Their leader and his standard-bearer were both hit in the face by two discharges of buckshot and went off howling with pain.

After ten P.M., the enemy quieted down, having lost nearly five hundred men killed, and having failed in their second great attempt to annihilate us. We lost only five killed and about a dozen wounded.

What little peace we had between attacks was broken by the usual flies and stinkbugs and other torments; but I suffered most from seeing my wife and little boy wasting away with cholera in that verminous hole which could at any moment be blown apart. They tried to sleep in the dining room, which was in the center of the house, but were driven out of it by roundshot. There was little use in barricading the windows and doorways with boxes of earth when shot and shell came right through the brick walls!

On the 18th of August, at daylight, a mine exploded in the outer Sikh Square: a post held by our loyal Punjabees. Three officers and two sentries on the top of the house were blown into the air, and eleven Sikh sepoys were buried in the ruins and killed. The three officers and one of the sentries fell on the ruins inside, and though much bruised and shaken, escaped with their lives. Another sentry fell outside and was killed—beheaded, in fact—by the enemy. A breach of about thirty feet was made in our defenses, whereon the enemy made a rush; but their leader being shot through the head and the next man in front (his standard-bearer) sharing his fate—pierced by seven bullets, in fact—they all retreated. The breach was then barricaded; and a sortie was immediately made, in which we blew up several houses in the neighborhood, bayoneted eleven of the enemy who were in them, and destroyed two of the enemy's mines.

This success was followed up on August the 21st by another sortie, in which we lost three killed and two wounded but succeeded in blowing up an enemy house and spiking two guns.

The 26th of August was rather an eventful day for me, as I had a narrow escape of my life. Early in the morning, there was a sudden alarm: bugling, shouting, with heavy fire of musketry and big guns. I was lying down in the inner room; and hearing the "turn out," I jumped up and went out into the veranda. I had hardly got there when I was struck to the ground by a violent blow between the shoulders, which half stunned and paralyzed me for a moment. I at the same time heard the rush and shrieking of grape as it passed in a shower, raking my front garden and the veranda. A 32nd Queen's man close to me fell with a groan, a grapeshot having passed through his left thigh.

My companions rushed out and picked me up; and Dr. Partridge found a large contusion upon my back discolored and swollen already. They took me inside and made me lie down. The pain was severe and the shock considerable, but I was soon about and at work again. The poor soldier died. I was saved by my particular pellet of grape having passed through a wooden screen and the back of a chair standing in the veranda before it hit me. It was not the first time I was contused by a spent shot, but it was the only occasion worth mentioning. We thought little now of the rain of shot, as we lived in constant apprehension of being blown into the air.

A remarkable incident occurred in the Post Office garrison on September 1st. Lieutenant Hall of the 2nd Bengal Fusiliers was lying on a cot with his head resting upon a pillow which projected. A round-shot passed through the room, tore away the pillow and scattered its contents. Hall was untouched, though rather startled.

The outer walls of most of our buildings had by now been crumbled by the constant impact of the enemy's shot, which increased the difficulty of sheltering our already crowded garrison; but many clung to the ruined rooms, though much exposed to the destructive fire, rather than go into the fetid and stifling atmosphere of a crowded building. The women and children also now preferred to risk their lives in the open air, foul though it was, than to suffer below ground; and on one occasion, a nine-pound shrapnel shell entered my house and exploded in the small room where my wife was lying ill. Bullets and fragments flew all about, but left the occupants untouched, although my wife's bedclothes caught fire and almost every article in the room was destroyed.

On the 5th of September, soon after daylight, the enemy commenced the heaviest cannonade we had endured since the siege began. Masses of infantry and cavalry were seen at sunrise moving round our position, evidently preparing for an attack; and at ten A.M., the enemy exploded two mines—one at Mr. Gubbins's house, the other near the Brigade messhouse—but the explosions occurred short of the defenses and did us no harm. Then, under a tremendous fire, the enemy assaulted Gubbins's post, placing ladders against the bastion; but they were not able to get in, being received with musketry and hand grenades. After many had been killed, they fell back into their houses, where they kept up a heavy fire. At all points they were beaten back with great loss, and later they were seen carrying off their killed and wounded in carts.

On our side, three sepoys of the 13th Native Infantry were killed, a soldier of the 32nd Queen's had one of his hands carried off by a roundshot, and a European volunteer lost one of his legs. We were very fortunate, considering the nature of the attack, to have suffered so little. But as our work ever increased, so our working power decreased; and we were now reduced by death and disability to nearly half of our original effective strength, so that even the sick and wounded had to drag themselves to the defenses in an emergency though some died from the effort.

On September 17th, the sentry of the 32nd Queen's at the churchyard had his head carried off by a roundshot. It seemed only too probable that our remaining chaplain, the Reverend Mr. Harris, would be knocked over some night into the common grave with those he was burying there; but he was spared that trick of fate. Not so a poor Indian water bearer of ours who was shot dead on September the 21st while drawing water and fell into the well. The body was got out with great difficulty—under fire. On another occasion, a stray bullock fell into the well, the top masonry of which had been shot away, and was got out with even greater difficulty—under fire.

An idea may be had of the fire we underwent when I tell you that 280 roundshot, varying in size from three to twenty-four pounds, were gathered from the top of the Brigade messhouse alone in one day (September 7th) and fired back at the enemy.

2

TAKE THOSE DAMNED GUNS!

The political and strategic importance of Lucknow necessitated its immediate recapture, and this necessity was made all the more urgent because of the three thousand Europeans and Eurasians and loyal Indians who were besieged there by an ever-increasing enemy. So relief troops had to be rushed from such outposts as Madras and Ceylon and Bombay; and in early July of 1857, a scratch force of less than two thousand Europeans and Indians, with only eight light fieldpieces, advanced from the base of operations at Allahabad under Brigadier General Henry Havelock. This small army forced-marched a hundred and twenty miles northward through sweltering heat and torrential rain, and thrice routed an enemy force of thirty-five hundred men and fifteen heavy guns before encountering one of twice that size outside Cawnpore.

At this point, Havelock would have to cross the Ganges River in order to march on Lucknow, which was fifty miles to the northeast. His passage was blocked by Maharaja Dhoondoo Punth, better known by his nickname of Nana Sahib or "Little Master." He had recently annihilated the small garrison at Cawnpore after a harrowing three-week siege that ended in surrender and betrayal, and he now defied Havelock by outmanning and out-gunning him in a formidable position. How Havelock met this challenge was described by his son and aide-de-camp, Lieutenant Harry Havelock:

After a sixteen-mile forced march of five and a half hours, most of which was made in the blazing sunlight, we of the Allahabad Movable Column arrived at a village about six miles south of Cawnpore at 10:30 A.M. on July 16th. Here we rested in the shade of a mango grove and had a breakfast of hard biscuits and rum grog, all our meat having been spoiled overnight by the heat and insects. Here, also, we learned that the rebels were three miles ahead—strongly entrenched in several villages at the fork of the Grand Trunk and Cawnpore roads—their position forming a crescent of about a mile and a quarter in length, with artillery emplaced to command the fork and sweep the approach with a flanking fire. Their right flank rested on the railway embankment; while their left, which was their most exposed but by no means their weakest point, was defended by four 24-pounders in earthworks outside a walled and fortified hamlet near the river. It was General Havelock's decision to turn this flank. "An attack in front," he said to his staff officers, "would expose us to a murderous fire. I resolve, therefore to turn their left by making a flank movement to the right."

The estimated strength of the enemy was between ten and twelve thousand, with thirteen or fourteen guns, although only between five and seven thousand of these, with eight guns, were then in position outside the city. The rest were being held in reserve.

We advanced at half past one P.M., when the sun was at its worst; but to have delayed the action would have allowed the enemy time to strengthen their position to an even more formidable extent, thus making it unlikely that we could take it without considerable reinforcements. As it was, we were running a fearful risk by attempting it with the small and battle-weary force we had.

"I am trying you sorely, men," the General addressed the troops before departure, but I know the stuff you are made of. Think of the poor women and children at Lucknow. With God's help we shall save them, or every man of us die in the attempt."

There were no cheers—only a low growl—but the General remarked to his staff officers "They'll cheer when I show them the enemy and the bugles sound the 'charge.'"

It was a short but severe march. Every soldier had to carry sixty rounds of ball cartridge in his ammunition pouch and his haversack, and had to march on all but an empty stomach. The heat was scorching, and the glare was blinding and seemed to burn into our brains. And it was annoying to hear the carrion birds squawking overhead as they followed us in anticipation of the feast. At almost every step, a man fell out of the ranks and threw himself down at the side of the road; and the calls for water were constant all along the way. So many fell out that I dare say there could not have been more than one thousand men in action on our side opposed to at least five thousand of the enemy. There were the usual number of slackers and stragglers, of course, but several of the "fall-outs" died from sunstroke; and others, who were unable to stagger back to the hospital wagons, were cut to pieces by a party of the enemy's cavalry which suddenly came down between the main column and the rearguard when we were making our flank movement. Fortunately, they were driven off before they could do any more damage.

When we arrived about half to three-quarters of a mile from the fork, the General ordered our infantry and artillery to turn off to the right and our cavalry to proceed on down the road as a diversion to draw the enemy fire till our flank attack was launched, then to turn back and rejoin the main force. The enemy, however, were not deceived. They had had their vedettes out all morning; and even though our flank movement was made along a line of mango groves, they could perceive our advance through an occasional break in the trees; and they let us know it, when we had gone but half a mile, by opening fire with their heavy guns, which sent roundshot and canister crashing through the trees, scattering a horde of screeching monkeys and flocks of birds. Fortunately, at first, their range was too high, or we must have suffered a heavy loss in that fifteen-minute march. As it was, we lost some of our best men.

One of the very first shots, from a 24-pounder, carried away the lower part of Captain Currie's seat and smashed his horse's back. I never saw such a ghastly sight before. The horse died almost at once, but poor Currie lingered in agony for nearly three days. He had commanded the detachment of Her Majesty's 84th Regiment.

The same shot, which was deflected by Currie's sword scabbard, also struck one of his men in the chest. Another ghastly sight! Other poor fellows had their heads and legs and arms taken off by round-shot, and the exploding canister shells sent shrapnel tearing into a number of others.

A private of Her Majesty's 64th, whose left thigh was shattered by a roundshot, was amongst those who lay disabled on the ground with no one at hand to assist or remove him; for strict orders had been given not to break ranks to help anyone, but to let the medical staff take care of the casualties. Well, there he was when the rebel cavalry came sweeping round to our rear to cut him up with the other wounded. They fancied he was as helpless as they were; but while lying on his back he coolly shot the first horseman who approached him. When this man fell from his saddle the others drew back, allowing him to reload and shoot down another of them. They all then came on with a yell; but when a third trooper fell from his horse, thanks to our fellow's unerring aim, the rest of them reeled round and left him to be removed to safety by our native litter bearers. His leg was amputated the next morning, but he died of complications.

At the same time the enemy were cannonading us, they seemed to taunt us with a sepoy band playing a medley of our national songs, including "Rule, Britannia," "The British Grenadiers," "Britons, Strike Home," and even "God Save the Queen."

Worst of all, that one-mile march was through swampy fields, which prevented our advancing as rapidly as possible and bogged down our guns, which in some places were up to their axles in mud and the poor gun bullocks knee-deep in it, with their native drivers twisting their tails and thrashing and yelling at them in an attempt to get them on.

At last, however, we reached the turning point of our flank march at the end of the grove, where the ground then sloped down to the Ganges; and to our left, around the fringe of the trees and about nine hundred to a thousand yards away, was that exposed but nonetheless formidable left flank of the enemy; thus we were, so to speak, between the Devil and the deep. We must either take that position or be driven into the river, for already the enemy cavalry were advancing to outflank us in turn; but fortunately for us, the heavy ground held them off until a wing of our 1st Madras Fusiliers could extend into skirmishing order to keep them in check.

Directly our front ranks were clear of the trees, the General gave the command: "Upon debouching, each battalion will wheel left about into line of double ranks in open order and in direct echelon from the left."

I conveyed this to each of the commanding officers; and as each battalion come up in quarter-distance column of fours, the words of command rang out: "Sections, by twos to the left! About wheel into line!" "Right shoulders forward. By the left, about wheel!" "Fours left—about wheel!" And so forth, until the entire column was deployed into battle lines in battalion echelon.

When this maneuver had been accomplished, our infantry were ordered to lie down while our artillery attempted to silence the enemy's four 24-pounders, which were now turned and opened upon us with a vengeance. At the same time, our Fusilier skirmishers held back the enemy cavalry beyond a thousand yards with their new Enfield rifles, which were effective up to that distance. Would that our artillery was as effective! But the guns were too light—only 9-pounders—and the range too far to disable such heavy and well-entrenched pieces; so there was nothing for it but to take the enemy battery by storm. The 78th Highlanders were positioned directly in front of it and so had the honor of leading the attack, though they numbered only about two hundred and eighty of the headquarters wing.

The General rode up to their colonel, "Old Wattie" Hamilton, and said, "The 78th will advance and take that battery, Colonel."

Hamilton nodded and saluted, and swung his horse around and shouted, "Stand up, 78th, and fix bayonets!"

The Highlanders rose with a wild cheer. Then there was the familiar clatter of "cold steel" as bayonets were fixed. The General then addressed them; "Men of the 78th! Hold your fire till I give the word, then deliver a volley and charge bayonets, and the guns will be yours. Now, Highlanders—let yonder fellows see what you are made of. The line will advance, Colonel—quick march."

"The 78th will slope arms and advance at a quick march," said the Colonel, and his subordinates shouted, "78th, slope arms! Forward—quick march!"

The Colonel then said, "Pipe Major, sound the pibroch." And with a salute, the head piper piped up "The Pibroch of Donuil Dhu," the war tune of the 78th, followed by his pipe-and-drum band.

The Highlanders advanced with a shout of defiance, with bagpipes skirling, drums beating and colors flying. They were a dreadful sight—rough-bearded, shaggy-haired, without jackets, their shirts stained and torn (with the sleeves rolled up), their kilts and trews tattered and dirty, their stockings and shoes full of holes, and with turbans wrapped around their forage caps—but they marched steady and straight, as if on parade, in a battle line of two ranks in extended order. I dare say the dressing and cadence were perfect, though it was over soggy ground they went—through a hail of roundshot and grape, which fortunately was fired too high or was too spent to do much damage as it flew overhead or dropped at their feet or bounded through their open ranks.

Occasionally, however, a man was hit and fell out of line; and then you heard the sharp words of command: "Steady, lads! Close up! Mind your step and dressing!" And on they went, closing up the gaps made by their fallen comrades.

Nothing could faze that silent array of grimly determined men—not even when a roundshot smashed one poor fellow's head, scattering the bones like shrapnel and splattering his comrades with blood and brains and bits of flesh and hair. They simply wiped the mess out of their eyes and kept on going without missing a step.

Colonel Hamilton's big white charger staggered and sank beneath him, struck in the front right pastern by a musket ball, but the white-haired warrior sprang clear and continued on foot. "Nothing can stop these dour Scots," the General remarked with a smile to his staff officers as they rode with him on the right flank.

When we were within a hundred yards and effective musket range of the enemy, the General said, "Now, Colonel Hamilton. Go and take that battery."

Hamilton drew his claymore or broadsword and turned and shouted, "The 78th will prepare to charge! Take close order in single rank on the center, fire a volley, then charge bayonets!"

"Close up on the center!" his subordinates shouted. "Single rank! Close up! A volley, then charge!"

Without halting, the men closed ranks and presented their rifles and delivered a rolling volley, then leveled their bayonets "at the charge" and let out a howl and broke into a run like a pack of foxhounds racing in for the kill, with the officers waving their swords and hurrahing, and the Pipe Major and his five pipers playing them on like mad; and in an instant they were over the earthworks and into the battery, driving the gunners and sepoys before them, and bayoneting dozens of the fugitives as they ran into the fortified hamlet.

We were met with musketry from the outer walls, but not for long. The enemy fought fiercely and well; but the Highlanders were even more furious, and the slaughter was proportionate. As the Nana Sahib himself said of them, "They seem to draw fresh life from every blast of their unearthly pipes, and they fight like devils."

Many of the mutineers ran up the narrow winding staircase in the gatehouse and out onto the ramparts with those who were already there; and they held their own for a while, owing to the difficulty of getting at them. Only one man at a time was able to get up that staircase; but at last a way was forced, and all the fugitives and others were bayoneted and pitched over the parapets—some of them by that thrust known as "the haymaker's lift," in which the bayonet is wielded like a pitchfork.

Those of the enemy who took shelter in the houses commenced firing at us from the windows; but our men burst open the doors by blowing off the locks and hinges with their rifles, then rushed in and made short work of those inside. The narrow staircases leading to the flat roofs echoed with the crash of musketry and the yells and curses as the rebels were driven step by step to the housetops, where they were bayoneted and then hurled over the parapets to the ground.

Some of the sepoys fought so desperately that they were more dangerous when wounded. One, for instance, had received seven bayonet wounds before he was finally dispatched by an officer thrusting his sword through him to the hilt; and still the man had strength enough to call his killer a "petticoated devil" as he fell. (Our Highlanders were also called "red-bearded cannibals" and "sons of Satan"; and since no rebel ever got ahold of a Highlander long enough to find out otherwise, it was commonly thought that they wore "petticoats" because they were the Queen of England's regiment of eunuchs.)

A color sergeant of the 78th told me that as soon as he kicked open the door of a shed, a fellow behind it made a chop at him with his razor-edged "tulwar" or curved sword. The sergeant jumped back just in time, firing at him without raising his rifle to his shoulder, and put a Minié ball clean through him. Now this hollow-based bullet expands when fired, making an ugly wound, and yet that rebel came rushing right out onto all twenty-two-and-three-quarters inches of the sergeant's sword bayonet. He had to force the fellow back and pin him to the doorpost with it; and even then the fellow tried to cut at him, gasping out every word of abuse he could think of till another of the 78th came up and blew the fellow's brains out.

Perhaps the poor devil was maddened by bhang, as many of them were, but I dare say they crossed bayonets and swords with ours and sold their lives dearly because they knew that no mercy would be shown if they surrendered. What was left of the besieged garrison at Cawnpore had surrendered on condition that they be given quarter; but the enemy gave no quarter and massacred the lot of them, including women and children, so they could expect no consideration. That's not to say that some of them didn't beg for mercy—especially from our Sikhs of the Ferozepore Regiment, who also fought like devils, or rather like lions; for so they call themselves: the Singh Lôg or "Lion Folk." But it was a civil war we were fighting, and the fact that a number of Sikh women and children and helpless old men had been tortured and murdered by the rebels made the Sikhs even more savage than the Highlanders. I saw one mutineer who had had both of his hands cut off by a Sikh's tulwar, was then shot several times in the body and bayoneted twice in the chest by some other Sikhs; and still he lived, till another Sikh cut off his head. Even then, the eyes rolled and the lips moved. And the Sikhs were as ruthless with the bayonet as our Highlanders. One Sikh pinned two rebels at once against a wall, sending a foot of his rifle barrel into the first man and bending his bayonet like a corkscrew.

As soon as the General rode into the hamlet, he took off his forage cap and waved it and shouted, "Well done, 78th! Another charge like that wins the day!" The regiment lost only three killed and fifteen wounded in that assault, besides two or three killed by the sun, while the enemy lost at least ten times that number.

The few remaining rebels on the left fell back on their center: another fortified village, with an entrenched 24-pounder howitzer and a 9-pounder field gun. Breathless though they were, the 78th quickly re-formed, eager to have the honor of taking another position before their supports could come up.

The General pointed his sword at the objective and said, "Now, Highlanders—one more charge, before they turn their guns on you." And so, with another mad rush, the center battery was taken by the 78th before the guns could be swung round on them; the village was soon cleared of the enemy.

"Well done again, 78th!" the General said, waving his cap. "Never have I witnessed conduct more admirable."

At the same time, the 64th and Sikhs had stormed and cleared out another fortified hamlet, capturing two 9-pounders, on the enemy right. The rebels then rallied in a fortified village about half a mile back from the center. To give our infantry a rest, the General hoped to shell them out of this position; but our poor gun bullocks were too exhausted to go on through the deep mud, and the gunners and drivers were a long time in dragging the guns themselves.

This was no time for delay. The momentum of victory demanded instant action, before the enemy could reinforce their center. Our brigade had now re-formed: Fusiliers on the right, 78th in the center, 64th on the left, and 84th and Sikhs in the rear. The General waved his cap. "Come! Who will take that village—the Highlanders or the 64th?" He clearly favored the Highlanders; and they knew it and responded accordingly, outrunning the 64th and taking the village. The General rode with them this time; and although his horse was shot dead under him, he was on his feet at once and astride a pony ridden by one of his orderlies.

When we emerged from the village, we were confronted by a reserve howitzer (about three-quarters of a mile ahead on the Cawnpore Road) defended by a mass of sepoys in line to the left and right of the gun, which immediately opened on us with 24-pound shot. Volleys from the sepoys were then followed by a continuous file (or independent) firing; but they were out of range with their old smoothbores, and it was merely a demonstration of defiance. I was about eighty yards behind the 64th at the time, in company with Lieutenant Moorsom, an additional aide. Our line was immediately ordered to take ground to the right and to halt behind the slope of the Cawnpore Plateau, to enable our guns to come up. They were more than a mile in the rear.

Eager to get ahead of the Highlanders, the 64th had got a little in advance of the front lines when all at once a shrapnel shell from the 24-pounder in their front struck their No. 5 Company, burst, and knocked over six men, one of whom was killed and the other five awfully mutilated. At this, someone shouted out that they were to lie down. They got into confusion. Many broke their ranks and ran back into the village for shelter, and it looked as if they were going to break into a general rout.

Moorsom shouted out, "Shame, men, shame!" And I rode up, dismounted, and got the men out of the village by abuse and entreaties. (I'll bet the survivors will never print what I said to them!) I then got them to lie down in the front line. There the wounded men were left groaning a few paces in advance of the line; and Major Stirling, the commander, instead of sending a few men to remove them, kept beckoning and calling out to me, in the presence of his regiment, "For God's sake, get some help for these poor fellows," and lamenting what had happened in a way that was in itself enough to cause discouragement.

I at last went over and quietly spoke to him about it, and he left off his whining and the men were removed as I suggested. I had noticed earlier in the day that his nerves were badly shaken, and now the thing was critical enough in itself without his making it worse. And I confess that I thought it was all up with us.

We were completely surrounded by the enemy, who were only kept off by our meager artillery and skirmishers and cavalry. And what a time they had of it! About a dozen Fusilier skirmishers were themselves cut off and charged by a large body of rebel cavalry; but they formed square and received the troopers with a volley, every bullet of which brought down a man, and they drove them off and rejoined their regiment unhurt. Our European volunteer cavalry, only eighteen in number, were also cut off and had to charge hundreds of rebel horsemen; but they cut a path through them and lost only three men wounded and one killed, though he was found lying hacked all over. And our artillery were set upon on all sides and had to shoot their way out.

Our men had been marching fifteen hours and fighting for three under a blazing July sun. Many of them were so done up that they sank down on the ground, even under fire, and went off to sleep. There were scarcely eight or nine hundred of them in line, lying down behind that slope; none of our cavalry in sight; our guns a mile or two in the rear and apparently inextricably stuck; while the enemy, about twelve hundred yards off and therefore secure out of effective Enfield range, were pounding us desperately with their reserve 24-pounder and now a 6-pounder beside it. Their five thousand infantry swarmed in our front; and their five hundred cavalry hovered on both flanks, waving their swords and shouting defiantly, with their band playing "Hail to the Chief" and "See, the Conquering Hero Comes," while some of them were hacking to pieces the sick and wounded in our rear. Some "swell" on an elephant—they said it was the Nana himself, but no one knows for sure—was riding about amongst the infantry, trying to spirit them up to come on; their drums and cymbals and trumpets were making a fearful row with the same idea; and our men were dispirited by being compelled to lie still for about three quarters of an hour under a tremendous fire, for the 24-pounder had just the right range. It was the turning point of the day, and of our campaign. If we had receded one inch, not a hundred of us would ever have got back to the shelter of the walls of Allahabad. I must confess that I felt absolutely sick with apprehension; and if I looked calm, I never was before and hope never to be again in such a funk in my life. The enemy thought we were lying down from fears!

Just then, the General rode bareheaded to the front. He was the only man who dared raise his head, so close and thick was the fire that rained upon us; but he had a charmed life, and had come out of some thirty actions without a scratch, though he had lost many a mount. He pulled up with his back to the fire; and smiling, he said clearly and calmly, "The longer you look at it, men, the less you will like it. We must silence those noisy guns. Rise up! The brigade will extend into skirmishing order to the left, in battalion echelon from the left."

I think I was the first on my feet, shouting, "Get up, men, and take those damned guns!"

Up sprang the line with a roar, and would have rushed on like a disorderly mob; but the General spurred forward and stopped them, ordering the 78th and Fusiliers back in echelon behind the 64th, and then saying: "Attention, 64th! You will advance in an orderly fashion with arms at the slope. Don't fire a shot till I tell you, then rush in and take those guns at the point of the bayonet. Now, the brigade will advance—left battalion leading at a quick march." He then turned and at a walk march rode at the head of the 78th, with the 64th leading in quick time on the left.

I rode on the right flank of the 64th. When we topped the plateau, the familiar sounds of shellbursts and of cannonshot as it flew past us were even more unpleasant than before; and I could see and feel that the soldiers wanted to break loose and make short work of it before any more of them were knocked over. But with the Nana or some other swell looking on, the General would have none of that. He wanted a demonstration of British sang-froid, cost what it may. So the commissioned officers of the 64th kept shouting, "Steady, men! Keep steady! Hold your line and your fire! Keep open order, but mind your dressing!"

However, contrary to the General's wishes and the rules of the Service, these same officers had dismounted and were advancing on foot so as to be less exposed. They were hardly visible to their men and consequently lost in the ranks as far as example or leadership was concerned.

Major Stirling later claimed that he was on foot because his pony was rendered unrideable by a shell bursting close by. If this was the same animal he was riding the day before, I can understand its excitability; for I saw it on the loose and advancing on its hind legs, determined to bite some other horse if possible, and I had to draw my sword to defend my own mount if necessary. But it doesn't explain the Major's allowing his subordinates to dismount. And worst of all, he was merely grazed on the left shoulder and immediately went to the rear. I then asked each of the three other senior officers of the regiment to take his place; but they all declined, saying it was not their duty to do so. This was poppycock, of course, and they knew it; but there was no time to argue the matter; so I rode forward at once and led the regiment myself, shaming and ridiculing them into steadiness over those twelve hundred yards of level ground, with the enemy blazing shot and shell into us the whole way. (As the General wrote in his dispatch, "The enemy sent roundshot into our ranks until we were within three hundred yards, and then poured in grape with such precision and determination as I have seldom witnessed.")

To say nothing of the other officers, this action of mine was in itself highly irregular; and I got criticized for it afterwards, especially as I did it without orders; but I had no regrets, considering the irregular conduct of the other officers, and the General thought it was an action worthy of the Victoria Cross; for if it didn't save India, at least it saved the day.

In any case, something had to be done; for after about one hundred yards—or at eleven hundred yards from the guns—the 64th again began to charge, which would have blown and disorganized them before they had covered half the distance. I stopped that with some rather strong language and gestured and persuaded them to continue advancing steadily at a quick march. Then, lo and behold! When they got to within four hundred yards of the guns—the enemy fire getting awfully galling—they stopped dead short and began firing. Now this might have settled the whole business unfavorably for us, as the enemy immediately began howling and shouting and redoubling their fire, thinking we could no longer face them; and there is no knowing what the result might have been. But I rode along the front, swearing like a trooper, and knocking up the rifles with my sword, stopped the fire, and got the men on again in good order; and from that moment it was all right.

When we were about eighty yards from the enemy, who had not depressed their guns and were now firing too high to do us any damage, I called a halt and said, "Close on the center! Close up and take order! Prepare to fire! Ready! Present! Fire! Prepare to charge! Now, at 'em with the bayonet! Charge!"

Little more than a third of the original four hundred and thirty-five of that detachment of the 64th were in line to deliver that volley and lead the charge; but the guns were taken by them, the enemy driven off the field at bayonet point by the entire brigade, and the battle won after nearly five hours of hard fighting. The Nana abandoned Cawnpore that night, and the way was now clear for us to cross the Ganges into Oudh for the fifty-mile march on Lucknow.

The General and I shared a biscuit and a flask half full of port in celebration. It was all we had, with our cloaks for beds and our saddlebags for pillows. In fact, the entire brigade bivouacked on the battlefield, without food or baggage of any sort until morning, when the supply train finally came up. Many of the soldiers had nothing but dirty ditchwater to drink, but it tasted like nectar to those who had been biting cartridges all afternoon.

We buried our dead by moonlight, the soldiers digging their graves with bayonets, while the pipers played "The Flowers of the Forest." Our total casualties were a hundred and fifty. There were six killed, eighty-six wounded, forty-eight disabled or dead from exposure, and ten missing. In the 64th alone, one officer and six men were killed and five officers and thirty men wounded—mostly in that last action.

The rebels lost about two hundred and fifty killed and countless others wounded. They weren't able to take away their casualties; so all night long we heard the squabbling and snarling of the carrion birds and beasts, to say nothing of the cries and groans of the wounded. But few of us could sleep much anyway, because of our nervous excitement. In eight days, we had marched a hundred and twenty-six miles, fought four actions, and taken twenty-four guns.

3

HOT WORK, THIS

For two months, it was feared that the fate of the Lucknow garrison would be that of Cawnpore. But having routed Nana Sahib's army, General Havelock lost no time in attempting to dispel that fear. Leaving a detachment of three hundred men and four guns to hold Cawnpore, the new base of operations, he advanced into Oudh on July 25, 1857 with only fifteen hundred men and ten light guns. (The heavy ones that had been captured would have impeded his rapid advance and were short on ammunition.) Opposed to him, in fortified towns and villages en route, were at least thirty thousand men and fifty guns of various calibers.

It was a "forlorn hope," and Havelock had to fall back several times because of casualties—mostly from disease, exposure, and fatigue. But he managed to drive the rebels before him and inflict heavy losses each time he advanced. And he sent this advice to Brigadier General John Inglis, who commanded the Lucknow garrisons in answer to his appeals for help: "I can only say, hold on and do not negotiate or capitulate, but rather perish sword in hand." It was no more than what Inglis's predecessor, Brigadier Sir Henry Lawrence, had advised on his deathbed: "Remember Cawnpore, and never surrender. Let every man die at his post, but never make terms. God help the poor women and children."

"My force is reduced to seven hundred effectives," Havelock informed the Commander in Chief on August 20. "I am willing to fight against all odds; but unless I am reinforced, I see little or no chance of relieving the garrison at Lucknow. With one or two thousand more soldiers, nothing shall stand in my way. Without them, I risk annihilation."

With the requested reinforcements, Havelock made his final advance on September 21. Still, despite his optimism, it was another gamble; for he had little more than three thousand troops and eighteen guns, and awaiting him at Lucknow were from fifty to sixty thousand rebels with from fifty to sixty guns. "But I shall make the attempt at every risk," he assured the Commander in Chief; and he said to his staff, "If the worst comes to the worst, we can but die with our swords in our hands." And they nearly did so.

In the usual torrential rain and sweltering heat, they drove the enemy off their route as before and broke through the enemy lines at Lucknow on September 25; but they had to run gauntlets of heavy fire almost all the way from their encampment, nearly two miles south of the city, to the residency compound, several miles further on. The swampy country around the city, then impassable for artillery, prevented them from approaching the besieged position except by a perilous route through the heart of the fortified city. A longer but safer route around the outskirts to a point close to the besieged position could have been taken without the artillery, and yet every moment was precious. The besieged were in desperation; at any moment they could be overwhelmed; and whatever the cost, as Havelock said, a desperate effort had to be made to save them. But it was the kind of calculated risk that had established and maintained British India, as Sir John Lawrence (brother of Sir Henry) reminded the "croakers": "Where have we failed when we acted vigorously? Where have we succeeded when guided by timid counsels?"

There was nerve-racking combat after Havelock left the suburbs and entered the city. The rebels remained behind their fortifications and the attackers were too weak and too determined upon reaching the besieged garrison to attempt to storm all the defenses. Besides, seeing how strongly fortified the city was, they had no hope of recapturing it or even of evacuating the garrison—only of reinforcing the 980 defenders. But, as Havelock wrote, "the column rushed on with a desperate gallantry through a perpetual fire."

The ordeal was described by Henry Willock, a political officer on the staff of Major General Sir James Outram, the new Chief Commissioner and commander of the Military Division of Oudh, who accompanied Havelock's Column:

The Goomtee Canal forms the southern boundary of Lucknow; and the suburbs on the south side of the canal are made up of thickly wooded gardens with high walls and long narrow lanes with straggling lines of masonry houses and mud huts, forming excellent covers for the enemy. And indeed, there were thousands of them in every house and garden and behind every wall and tree. Beyond this is the open country, with a scattering of villages surrounded by fields of tall corn, sugar cane, and other grasses, in which thousands more of the enemy were lurking.

Well, we had to go through at least three quarters of a mile of this open country; and our first big obstacle was a two-gun battery situated about a thousand yards up the road, at the commencement of the suburbs. It was close to the right side of the road, and could sweep the approach; and a little further on, there was another battery on the right and one on the left; while those several thousands of the rebels who were lurking in the huts and the high, thick crops on both sides were only from fifty to a hundred yards away.

We had not gone two hundred yards when they opened a heavy crossfire; and the road was soon strewn with dead and wounded men and horses and gun bullocks and damaged gun carriages, obliging the gunners and drivers to drag the guns themselves. And there was such a crush and confusion caused by the falling and fallen men and animals, and all the branches of trees which were struck down by the storm of roundshot and grape and canister and musketry, that we had to keep halting in order to clear the way by filling the ditches at the roadside with the obstructions. Worst of all, we could hardly return a shot—seeing no one to shoot at. Nonetheless our soldiers were wonderfully steady—advancing as if on parade. The shot and shell passed over and about us in a perpetual humming and screaming; and luckily, they were mostly high, or none of us could have advanced as far as we did and lived to tell about it.

We had proceeded about four or five hundred yards when we had to stop and open up with our guns in an attempt to silence those of the enemy, which had finally got our range and were pitching every shot right into our ranks. Our troops, meanwhile, had to lie down on and alongside the road, where they remained for about twenty minutes under "a most murderous fire," as General Outram styled it in his dispatch next day. It was indeed most fearful. The roundshot and grape and shrapnel literally tore the road up, cutting our brave fellows to pieces, while the bullets fell among them like a shower of hail. The thick lines of trees which overhung both sides of the road were all literally torn to pieces and how any of us survived that terrible storm I don't know. But this much I can say: that as I lay on my face among the soldiers, I never for a moment expected to see night—the fire was so dreadful.

Captain Francis Maude commanded the light field battery of the Royal Artillery that advanced in front of the 1st Brigade of the Oudh Field Force, and he described what happened next:

I had room to deploy only two of my 9-pounders on the road, and they were too light to have any immediate effect at such range; but I suppose it was assumed that if our heavy battery had taken the lead, it would have delayed our advance. But it was delayed anyway!

General Outram was by my side on his big strawberry-roan "Waler" when the enemy let us have it hot and heavy; and almost at once the upper part of his right arm was shot through by a musket ball. It luckily missed the bone and artery, although the wound bled profusely; but he only smiled and asked Lieutenant Chamier, his additional aide-de-camp, to tie his handkerchief tightly above the wound. When entreated to dismount and have the wound properly dressed, he replied, "Not till we reach the Residency." And he puffed at his cigar with no more concern than if he were sitting in a club. But this was the man who had hunted and killed on foot, and armed only with a hogspear, a hundred and ninety-one tigers and fifteen leopards. And when one of them nearly got him, he said, "What do I care for the clawing of a cat?" Then his aide-de-camp, Lieutenant Sitwell, received a similar wound; and I was struck by a spent bullet in the right hand, which raised an awful welt and paralyzed my hand for a time.

Almost at the same moment, the finest soldier in my battery and the best artilleryman I have ever known—Sergeant Major Alexander Lamont—had the whole of his stomach and entrails carried away by a roundshot. My natural impulse was to dismount, but the code of military conduct forbade it. He looked up at me with a piteous expression, but only had strength to utter two words—"Oh, God!"—when he sank dead on the road.

Just then, another roundshot took off the right leg (high up the thigh) of the next senior sergeant, John Kiernan. The bone being shattered, the limb hung by shreds, which were severed with his sword by one of his men, who there bound up the stump with the turban that was wrapped round his forage cap. He was immediately carried back to our camp, but soon died from the shock.

Another tragic sight on that road was the death of a fine young gunner: the only one, I believe, who wore an artillery jacket that day—it was so hot and humid. A roundshot took his head clean off; and for about a second the body stood straight up, spouting blood like a fountain, and then fell flat on the road.

But as fast as the men of my leading gun detachments were swept away by the enemy's fire, I replaced them with men from the other guns and finally with volunteers from the infantry. Several times, I turned to General Outram and asked him to allow us to advance, as our fire was having little or no effect. He agreed with me, but did not like to take the responsibility of ordering us to go on. "General Havelock commands today!" he said, alluding to his noble gesture of letting Havelock lead the column.

At last, General Havelock (who led the column at the head of the 2nd Brigade, in deference to Outram) got the message and sent the welcome order to advance. Had he been at the front, instead of sending his aides and orderlies to report on the situations we should not have had the destructive delay; but so much for military courtesy! Fortunately, however, our advance caused the enemy to withdraw their two nearest guns down a lane to the right of the road, which there took a bend to the left about a hundred yards from the canal. Our infantry were able to take these guns before they could fire at us; but as soon as we turned the corner, we got it again—from a battery on the other side of the canal—only this time we were close enough to do some damage ourselves. Meanwhile, our infantry stormed and cleared the garden enclosures on both sides of the road and took the other two batteries.

Some of this action was described by Lieutenant Henry Delafosse, who was orderly-officer to Major James Simmons of Her Majesty's 5th Fusiliers:

When we started the advance, two companies of the 5th were in front of our leading guns and two were behind. Major Simmons and I were mounted at the head of the first two companies, but the fire was so hot from the right and in front that Simmons's horse reared and plunged in such a manner as to oblige him to dismount. Our position then was frightful.

The enemy in front were enfilading the road with grape, canister, and roundshot, which came plowing up the ground, tearing down branches of trees over our heads, smashing through artillery wagons and causing some of them to explode, knocking down poor fellows right and left; while the men were frequently wounded by the unseen enemy sharpshooters on our right, who were firing at them from behind the huts and long grass, besides another gun, which they had in position in a small village on our far right. This went on for some time, when finally General Outram (who was close by) gave the order: "5th, charge the guns!"

Major Simmons immediately ordered the men to advance up the road at the double, which they did—God knows how—through a deadly hail. About a hundred yards ahead was a loopholed house inside a walled garden—the wall also loopholed—from which the enemy kept up a sharp fire of musketry. When we were approaching this, volley after volley were poured out; but before we could storm the place, the enemy deserted it and moved on to meet us at some other defense. It was a marvel to me how I escaped, exposed as I was on horseback.

A little higher up the road, another road crossed it diagonally. We turned down it to the right and were opposed by a tremendous fire of musketry from its further end, where the enemy were swarming. The Major gave the order: "Fire two volleys by sections into the middle of them!" This had the desired effect of driving back the enemy still further. We were then ordered to clear out a garden on our left.

I was a little behind the Major, and had just turned my horse's head towards the gardens when a roundshot came and knocked the poor brute over and killed three men close by me. So now I too was dismounted!

As we entered the garden, the enemy's artillery opened upon us from the left side of the crossroads with grape and shell; and so well did they pitch their shells that they burst immediately over the gate we entered by, killing and wounding many of us. But we rushed on through the garden, clearing it of rebels as we went, and then skirmished along that side of it facing the canal, until we came out a little to the left of the canal bridge, where the enemy had some heavy guns in position. Meanwhile, a company of the Madras Fusiliers charged and captured the two guns on the left side of the crossroads. (For our part, we had not yet taken a gun, as the enemy had made off with those we were ordered to take before we could get at them.) Captain Grant, who was a crack shot, picked off the gunners as fast as rifles were handed to him by his men; whereupon they all rushed in and took and spiked the guns. At the same time, the enclosures and guns on the right were captured and cleared by the rest of our brigade, but with considerable loss on our side.

A slightly different story was told by Captain Frederick Willis, who commanded the detachment of Her Majesty's 84th Regiment of Foot:

The 5th Fusiliers were ordered to advance and take the house on the right at the crossroads, which they did—and bayoneted a lot of the enemy. But they got very much scattered, and so the 84th were then ordered to the front to take and clear the houses on each side of the road leading to the canal bridge.

I had just time to address a few words to my men, telling them I expected great deeds from them: that a company of some fifty of their comrades were in front, forming a part of the besieged garrison, anxiously expecting us to relieve them. So we all set up a cheer; and with my friend Captain Pakenham by my side, gallantly leading on his grenadiers, we charged up the side streets, driving the rebels out of the houses.

We had not advanced a hundred yards when my poor friend was shot down, the ball passing through his right side from front to rear. He never spoke again. But if anyone was prepared to die, it was he: waving his sword and cheering on the men to the last gasp. He was only twenty-four years of age, and I took off his watch to send to his family.

As the enemy ran before us, loading as they did so—often by shoving the cartridges into the muzzles with their fingers and then banging their musket butts on the ground to send the charges home—and without stopping, they turned from time to time to fire. But it was a fire which was not returned, so eager were we to get at them with the bayonet.

We advanced until where the main road turned to the left, and I had to send a company here and another there into the gardens behind the houses to enable Captain Maude's battery to come up and prevent the houses being reoccupied, so that I found myself in the road with but a handful of men until the rest or the brigade came up.

After turning down this road to the left, about a hundred yards from the corners you came to the bridge over the canal, which was the only means of direct access to the city from the south. A trench had been dug across the road on our side of the bridges which we would have to fill in and which incurred additional delay; and directly on the other side, completely blocking that end of the bridge, was a ten-foot-high stockade with loopholes and embrasures and with two heavy guns and a lot of men posted behind it; and on either side of it were strong breastworks, in which were four more guns of lighter caliber. All this we had to force our way through!

It was at this time that my poor mare had a musket ball through her left shoulder, and I was reduced to my legs. The opposite side of the canal was lined with musketry, and so I sent two companies to the left to occupy the houses overlooking the canal and to try and enfilade the battery and pick off the gunners with their Enfields, which were deadly accurate at that range. During this operation, a young subaltern named Bateman was shot dead through the head.

I never saw, before or since, such a frightful fire of grape and roundshot as this bridge battery poured down the road. Maude's guns came up, and two were brought into action, and for about ten minutes it was a case of give-and-take. At one of our guns, five men were knocked over in as many seconds. I am happy to say, however, that one of my old company (Private Jack Holmes) was first to volunteer as a "number" at the gun in place of a poor fellow who had been killed; and he remained working at it until it limbered up, for which I recommended him for distinguished conduct. With his and the help of others of my regiment, Maude worked his guns very bravely and steadily.

Indeed, owing to that formidable battery at the city end of the canal bridge, the game was still in Captain Maude's hands. "But for his nerve and coolness," General Outram declared, "the column could not have advanced." The struggle cost him one third of his men, however. Captain Willis added:

I shall never forget seeing those two leading guns of Maude's battery unlimber and come into action on the road at very close range—only one hundred and fifty yards—under that murderous fire from the enemy's guns in position on the further side of the canal bridge. The first discharge from one of the enemy's 24-pounders disabled one of Maude's 9-pounders, killing or wounding the greater portion of the detachment serving it. It was then I offered to assist him by calling for volunteers from my regiment, many of whom had been instructed in gun drill for just such an emergency. So the gun was again served.

Lieutenant George Blake, who took command of the Grenadier Company of the 84th after Captain Pakenham's death, stated that he saw Captain Maude "standing by his guns, calmly smoking a cheroot, with sixteen dead gunners lying around him. He said to me, as I was passing by with my company, 'Lend me some of your men, old fellow, until some more of mine can come up.' A number of the infantry had to do double duty on that day!"

Maude himself wrote:

With the enemy having six guns—two being 24-pounders—behind a strong barricade and some strongly constructed earthworks, while we had only two 9-pounders in the open, it's no wonder my men were fatigued and disheartened by a severe action in which we had lost twenty-one of our finest. Yet we held our own for half an hour against those tremendous odds; and although the range was only a hundred and fifty yards, which is considered point-blank for artillery, we really lost comparatively few men keeping the enemy's fire down—if we did not exactly silence all their guns—while our infantry were clearing the suburbs and preparing to storm the bridge. Bear in mind: our guns were of the old pattern, dating probably from the days of Clive; and the only means provided for priming the vents was a large leather pouch full of loose powder, carried on the right side. The "gun number" whose duty it was to prime simply took a handful out of his pouch and poured it in the vent. As the road was very narrow, the two leading guns were exceedingly close to one another; and when they recoiled past each other, amid a shower of sparks and smoke, they frequently set fire to the loose powder in the priming pouches and blew the poor gunners up, if not burning them very severely. In this way, four or five men were injured that morning, besides others at other times.

Believe me, there's nothing worse than the sight of a man who has been blown up. If he isn't in pieces, his charred flesh is hanging in shreds from his broken bones; and the smell of burnt hair and flesh is perfectly sickening. Even worse, though the poor fellows begged to be put out of their misery by a bullet in the brain, we couldn't do this, but had to let them suffer to death.

It was also sad to see our hardworking cattle knocked over by shot or blown up by exploding tumbrels, but we only once had serious trouble with a wounded gun bullock. The poor creature had lost both its forefeet from a roundshot and was careering wildly about on the stumps, perfectly mad with pain, until one of our gunners brought it down with a shot from his carbine. (Incidentally, another of the Bengal Horse Artillery told me that he emptied all five chambers of his Adams revolver into the head of a badly wounded horse; and yet the animal somehow got up again and was later seen eating grass as if nothing were the matter! "We were afraid to touch him after that," the officer added, "so we just left him there; and he may still be alive!")

Notwithstanding all the hazards, every man behaved well; and Lieutenant Eardley Maitland, my second in command and only remaining officer, set an example by his cool and steady bearing under fire. He himself served one of the guns, exchanging round for round of case and solid shot until the enemy's fire was almost silenced. He had his nerves so well under control that he could let a shot pass close to him without even blinking. I confess I never arrived at that point, though I do not believe more than two or three men in our battery ever even bobbed their heads when shot came at them. That was considered "bad form" among the Royal gunners. One might move one's head slightly from side to side, but never actually bob; for it was considered better to lose one's head than one's nerve. But most soldiers eventually become too indifferent to any sort of fire to take much notice of it, and a kind of fatalism sets in. "If I am to be shot, I shall be shot," they say, "no matter what I do." And they're right. Death often comes to men in the safest corners and avoids those in the open. As the natives of India say, "No one dies before his time; and when that time comes, nothing can save him." Or as we say, "If you're born to hang, you'll never drown."

One of the most conspicuous of fatalists, whose daredevilry earned him the nicknames of "Hellfire Bill" and "Mad Billy," was Captain Olpherts, who commanded a heavy field battery of the Bengal Horse Artillery, which was positioned between the 1st and 2nd Brigades. My own battery had cleared out the first village on our right and silenced the gun that was emplaced in front of it; but it would have taken too much of our ammunition to flush out the hundreds of snipers who were still in the fields and picking off our gunners and drivers and draft animals, who were unable to lie down or take cover with the infantry. So Olpherts rushed back to General Havelock and said, "If we don't clean out those snipers, sir, I'll need more men; but I'd rather take them into those fields, by God, than have them knocked over on the road!" So Havelock turned to Colonel Campbell, who commanded the 90th Light Infantry (the headquarters wing of which headed the 2nd Brigade), and ordered him to clear the fields. Campbell then told his men to stand and take skirmishing order, but the dread of going into that sea of tall grass after unseen marksmen made them flinch— until Olpherts shouted, "Listen, men—we've got to make a move one way or another! Either we allow ourselves to be potted by those rascals yonder, or we go in and clean them out! I say 'Come on—let's clean them out!'"

Suddenly, a bullet struck him in the left shoulder; and he swayed for a second in the saddle; but instantly regaining his grip, he waved his sword and shouted "Come on! Follow me!" and dashed off into the fields. As one section of men followed him with a shout, so did another and then another, until at last all of them had rushed into the fields and flushed out the snipers like hunters driving bevies of quail from cover, downing many of them as they bolted.

Undeterred by his wound, Olpherts remained with his battery for the rest of the day, seated on a limber and rightly pleased with himself for having helped to clear the way. "I'd have welcomed a slug in the other shoulder as well, by God," he remarked, "if that's what it would have taken to get those damned footdraggers to move!"

The story is now continued by Lieutenant Harry Havelock, adjutant to Brigadier General Henry Havelock:

While Captain Maude was attempting to beat down the enemy's artillery fire, General Outram went off to the right with some of the 5th Fusiliers in an effort to bring a flanking fire to bear on the enemy battery across the bridge. At the same time, a skirmishing party of the Madras Fusiliers under Lieutenant Arnold was thrown forward along the bank to the left of the bridge in an attempt to beat down the musketry fire from the tall houses on the other side of the canal.

The rest of the Madras Fusiliers were lying down under cover of

one of the garden walls at the corner of the road, close behind
Maude's battery. Brigadier Neill, the commander of the 1st Brigade,
was standing in a bay of that wall, waiting for Outram's and Arnold's
flank movements to take effect; and I was mounted on the other side
of the road, somewhat in advance, behind another wall. I had just
been sent up to the front by General Havelock to see how things were
progressing. You may ask why he himself wasn't up as usual in the
thick of things. Well, he was gallantly deferring to Outram, who out-
ranked him. That was a big part of our problem that day; a divided
command and haphazard leadership. Anyway, although the enemy fire
had slackened, matters were still at a deadlock; and Outram and
Arnold showed no sign of progress, as the enemy gunners and musketeers were all behind loopholes and barricades. So Maude called out
to me: "I can't fight these guns much longer! For God's sake, do something!"

I then rode across to Neill through the enemy fire, and in my new
capacity as adjutant or senior staff officer, urged on him the need for
an immediate assault. It was like preaching to the wise. The old
fire-eater saw the necessity; but he, like General Havelock, had to keep
his place in the presence of General Outram.

"I am not in command," he said gruffly. "I cannot take the responsibility. And Outram must turn up soon."

I then turned and rode off along the road towards the rear—osten-
sibly to where General Havelock was, at the head of the 2nd Brigade.
But after a short disappearance around the bend, I came back at a gallop, reined up in front of Neill, and saluted him with my sword and
said, "General Havelock's compliments. You are to carry the bridge at
once, sir."

Neill frowned at me, but replied, "Get the leading regiment together, then, and see it formed up." (The leading regiment was, of course,
Neill's own—the Madras Fusiliers—which now headed the 1st
Brigade in the absence of the 5th Fusiliers, who were with Outram and
also helping to clear the last garden enclosures.)

At the word from me, and without waiting for the rest of his regiment to rise and form, Lieutenant Arnold sprang up with a shout from
his advanced position and dashed onto the bridge, followed by his
skirmishers—only twenty-eight men in all.

Colonel Tytler, who was our chief quartermaster, had just been sent
forward by General Havelock to find out what had happened to me;

and I said to him, "The fire is destroying Maude's guns. There's nothing for it but a rush."

Tytler agreed; and so he and I, as eager as Arnold, put spurs to our horses and were alongside of him in a moment. Then the iron storm blew. Two 24-pounders swept the bridge with grapeshot. Arnold and ten of his men dropped at once, mortally wounded—Arnold shot through both thighs, which were broken. Tytler and his horse went down with a crash—the horse killed, but Tytler miraculously spared, only to be later shot in the groin: a wound commonly fatal, but which he survived, thanks to the constant care of his native servant.

The bridge was swept clear except for me—still unwounded in the saddle, waving my sword and shouting to the rest of the Fusiliers to come on—and except for a corporal named Jakes (or Jacques, to be precise), who coolly remarked to me as he rammed a bullet into his Enfield, "Never fear, sir! We'll damn soon have the beggars out of there!" And he was as good as his word.

Before the enemy guns could be loaded again, the men of Madras were on the bridge in a headlong mass. Seconds later, they were across it. Oblivious to the musketry fire in front of them, they stormed the barricades, cleared the battery, and bayoneted the rebel gunners and sepoys where they stood.

It was at this moment that a rebel sepoy jumped onto the parapet of one of the earthworks, within ten or fifteen yards of me, and took deliberate aim and fired. But my name wasn't on the bullet, which passed through the center of the top of my forage cap, singeing my hair as it went. (Only seconds before, another bullet had grazed my forehead and cut off a lock of my hair.) Instantly sheathing my sword, I drew my revolver and shot the sepoy dead as he was attempting to reload his musket. Corporal Jakes survived the storm also, only to be shot dead by a stray bullet later in the day.

Captain Maude then came galloping up to shake my hand. "Thank God, sir!" he said. "You've relieved me from a most unequal contest." To which I replied, smiling, "The sound of your guns is like music to the ladies in the Lucknow garrison."

So the first round was won, but at a heavy cost. Of the original 900 men of the Madras Fusiliers, only about 150 survived the campaign—nearly a hundred having been shot down on this day. About 140 were all that were left of the original 455 of the 64th Foot, and the other regiments suffered as well. The 78th Highlanders lost 139

out of 550, and theirs was the heaviest loss in proportion to their original numbers. It's only wonderful how so many escaped.

I should add that as Colonel Tytler regained his feet, he noticed
that two uncaptured guns were opening upon the bridge from our far
left; so he ran back to General Havelock, who directed him to take the
nearest regiment and capture the guns at all hazards. That regiment
happened to be the 90th Light Infantry, commanded by Colonel
Campbell; so Tytler, holding onto the mane of Campbell's horse, conducted the regiment to the enemy's guns. They were taken in a rush,
with a trifling loss on our side. (Colonel Campbell, incidentally, was
struck later in the day by a musket ball below his left knee; and he died
on November 12th from the aftereffects of amputation of his leg.
Ironically, during the attack on the guns, he had been saved from
death by the failure of a bullet to force its way through a small prayer
book which he carried in the breast pocket of his jacket, just over his
heart. He showed me this after he was struck in the leg, saying he had
been saved by obeying his wife's wish that he always carry this little
present of hers with him. Poor man, he thought he would survive the
leg wound! In his regiment alone, fifteen other officers were killed or
wounded, as were thirteen of the Madras Fusiliers and seven of the 5th
Fusiliers. The 78th lost nine and the 84th seven.)

With the route leading into the city finally open, the rest of our column promptly crossed over the canal and then turned sharp to the
right and advanced in ankle-deep mud for nearly two miles along the
winding lane that skirts the left bank, past suburbs teeming with
rebels, and then (by a sharp turn to the left) through the two-mile
maze of fortified palaces and bazaars east of the Residency. The 78th
Highlanders, about 350 strong, were detached with orders to relieve
the Fusilier skirmishers in holding the bridgehead and covering the
crossing by keeping down the enemy fire until the entire column had
passed over, and then to follow it as rearguard. This "holding" and
"covering" they effectually did, but the "following" is another story.

*Before that story is told, here is a continuation of Captain Willis's
account of his doings with the Queen's 84th:*

I was in a front house at the crossroads when a gallant young lance
corporal named Boulger came running up and said, "Oh, sir! The
Madras Fusiliers are ordered up to take the battery. We can't let them

go in front of the 84th!"

"Certainly not," I said, although the Madras men had not yet had their turn in front. "If you will collect eight or ten men, I will go over the bridge with you."

He got some men; and as the Fusiliers came up, we all charged together. As we rushed into the road, we received a shower of grape, which took five men on my right and cut their legs right from under them. The leading officer of the Fusiliers (Lieutenant Bailey, who was at my side) had his left foot shot off at the ankle.

I was struck above the left knee and came down, but picked myself up, and finding no bones broken, rushed on for my bare life; and we were all cheering like madmen, and that one round was the last the enemy fired from those guns. The battery was ours in an instant; and Corporal Boulger, always in front, shot down a gunner just as he was going to fire another round. (I recommended him for the V.C., and he got it.)

We drove the enemy on down the main street for some distance. I stopped to tie my pocket handkerchief round my knee and look at my small wound. It was a deep cut, but not long—I think done by a piece of telegraph wire, which the rebels used mixed with the grape. I then brought up my stragglers, who were joining me from their different skirmishing points.

At a crossroad, one of the enemy fired at me from the street on my right and hit me just behind the right thigh. The ball went through trouser leg and shirttail and cut the flesh; but how it came not to make a more severe wound, God alone can tell. It felt at first like a blow from a racket ball, which I had often experienced. I put my left forefinger through the hole in the trousers and shirt and found there was blood; but again, no bones broken, thank God!

The "recall" sounded, for it was found we had gone the wrong road. My old company (the Light Company, which had gone off to try and intercept the enemy with their guns on the right) took a 9-pounder; and just as they came up to it, Lieutenant Woolhouse had his right elbow smashed by a shot. The arm was later amputated.

We came back to where the bridge battery was and destroyed the guns and ammunition and went on again, having lost a few men who were careless in disposing of the explosives, and from this point up to the Residency was a regular fight into Lucknow: guns in position at every crossroad, storming and taking them and running the gauntlet of fire through narrow and crooked streets, the houses of which were all loopholed and full of armed men—and women!

The enemy appeared from behind every bush and wall of the suburbs north of the canal, but their fire was irregular until we began to enter the city itself; and as soon as we got opposite the main palace of the former King of Oudh, which is in the center of Lucknow, a most terrible fire was opened upon us from artillery and musketry. It was then that a bullet hit the scabbard of my sword and bent it, nearly knocking me down. It was now a mad rush to get into the enclosed gardens of the Palace, where we could gain cover; but we got into a long narrow road instead, with a heavy gun facing us at the other end, and had to turn back and take another route to find shelter. Every house and wall seemed alive with the enemy, and their guns commanded every street.

When one thinks of it now, it seems terrific; but at the time, one was worked up to such a state of frenzy and excitement that nothing was thought of but our poor comrades and other countrymen in the besieged garrison; and, as to protecting our rear, that was soon seen to be impossible; and we at once knew that when we did get to the Residency, there was no getting out again without help from Cawnpore.

We were eleven hours street fighting; and at seven o'clock P.M., just as it was getting dark, we heard the cheers of our besieged garrison. What a shout we sent up in reply! But it was then that poor General Neill (our brigade commander) was shot dead in the midst of my regiment, whilst we were passing under a large archway. The top of the arch was occupied by enemy sharpshooters; and as we were rushing under it, the General stood by quite coolly, seeing that we all got through when a black eunuch in a yellow robe leaned forward from a window above the arch, with his hunting rifle held out at arm's length and almost touching Neill's head, which was turned aside. The troops were past, and Neill was then watching a gun going through the archway, when the eunuch fired. His bullet struck the side of Neill's head behind and a little above the left ear, killing him instantly. He fell from his horse, which bolted in fright, but his body was saved and put on the gun limber and buried the following evening in the Residency churchyard. The fellow who shot him was probably the very one known as "Bob the Nailer," because he had accounted for quite a number of our men until he himself was finally nailed in one of our sorties; and I should add that all of these guardians of the harems, be they eunuchs or matrons, were armed and dangerous.

Neill was the biggest and best-looking man I ever saw, and he feared nothing and nobody. With two hundred men he had defeated two thousand mutineers at Benares, with three hundred he had routed three thousand at Allahabad, and with the same number he had held off six thousand at Cawnpore. As he said, "I will hold my own against any odds." He was the sternest but kindest and best-hearted of men, and was unquestionably our greatest loss that day. As one of our Highlanders said, he was "the idol of the British Army." I remember him saying to me with a smile as I passed him under the archway, "Hot work, this." They were the last words he ever spoke.

We lost forty-eight officers that day and nearly a third of our men. A more desperate thing was never done, and the Commander in Chief called it a "feat of arms."

I had another miraculous escape during the day. In my haversack I had three hard-ration biscuits. A musket ball struck the biscuits, smashing them to pieces and tearing a tremendous hole in the haversack, yet doing no further damage. But for the biscuits, I should have been terribly wounded in the thigh—and perhaps lost my leg. As long as I kept moving, my wounds did not hurt me; but they got very stiff towards night.

I had three officers killed and four wounded, including myself. Besides those already mentioned, Lieutenant Barry got a severe contusion in the stomach; and Lieutenant Oakley got a severe wound in the head—the ball tearing the flesh from his right temple and just behind the ear, the top of which it carried away. They all did well, however.

Lieutenant John Gordon was aide-de-camp to Brigadier General James Neill, and he related his experiences with the 1st Brigade of the Oudh Field Force:

Soon after we had got onto the road which leads along the south bank of the Goomtee and straight towards the Residency, and little dreaming of the opposition which we had yet to meet, the General said, "How very thankful we should feel for having been preserved through the dangers of the day"—it was now between two and three in the afternoon—"and I for having escaped when my horse was killed under me!" (This had happened when we were on the road to the bridge, but the General had a spare horse in rear of the brigade.)

Well, we were riding quietly along the road at the head of the column, admiring the beauty of some of the buildings on our left and the country on the other side of the river, when some guns from that very side suddenly opened on us; and at the same time, a sharp fire of muskets came from the former messhouse of the Queen's 32nd Regiment and from the walls of the Kaiser Bagh or "Caesar's Garden" (the main palace of the former King of Oudh) on our left. And two or three guns also kept firing at us from one of the gates of the Kaiser Bagh.

The messhouse was within one hundred yards of us. It was a two-storied building with a turret at each corner, and shots poured out at every window and loophole, and our own musketry fire could not keep down the enemy's, and we had not time to wait and storm the place; for it was most essential that relief should reach the garrison that very night, so we were just obliged to push on.

The General had two or three rounds fired into the house from one of our guns, which caused the musketry fire to cease for a short time. We then got into a walled enclosure and rested for a little and allowed the troops to close up. The General dismounted and sat down on a stone bench and had a cigar and some tea.

We then started again, and had to go along a lane and then through what had been the compound of an officer's bungalow. All this time, we were concealed from the enemy's view; but at the end of the compound we had to come out onto one of the main roads, fully exposed to the Kaiser Bagh and several large mosques and other buildings; and for about two hundred yards we had to go through an incessant storm of bullets, grape, and other missiles, to which what we had been exposed to in the morning was not to be compared in fierceness. Men were cut down on all sides, and how any single one escaped was perfectly miraculous. I was in such a state of excitement with the yelling and cheering of the men, who were running as hard as they could, that I scarcely knew what happened; but it was worth living any length of time to have such an experience.

At the end of the two hundred yards, we got behind the shelter of a large house, which was immediately occupied by the Madras Fusiliers, who (by the General's order) tried hard to keep down the musketry fire from the mosque behind; but it wasn't until after repeated discharges from our guns that it was even partially silenced.

We then moved into a lane with a brick wall on either side and intersected in one or two places by cross streets, up which the enemy poured a most destructive fire as we crossed the openings. We were delayed for some time in this lane, not knowing which was the best route to take to the Residency, from which we were still about three quarters of a mile distant. All the streets were full of sepoys; and it was evident that, whichever way we went, we should meet with dreadful opposition.

It was now sunset, and it was necessary to make a move; and the route fixed on was one which required those regiments that had gone farthest up the lane to face about and come back again, so the order of march became somewhat changed; and the 78th Highlanders and the Ferozepore Sikh Regiment, which had been behind us and consequently not so far up the lane, turned down at once into the opening through which we were to advance to the Residency and thus got in front of the 1st Brigade. When they had forced their entrance into the main street, General Havelock sent back for the assistance of the Madras Fusiliers, which accordingly became separated for the time from the 1st Brigade; and General Neill regretted much that he could not accompany them, but must remain with the other regiments of his brigade. Also, a number of guns had to move between the brigades, so that we were some distance apart.

When we got out of the lane and into the courtyard through which we had to go, we found a great crush of guns and bullocks. It was now getting dusk; and our infantry were marching through the courtyard, which had flat-roofed houses on either side and at the far end, with an archway in the middle of the far end, under which we had to go. A heavy musketry fire was opened on us from the tops of the houses on either side and through loopholes in the parapet that ran along the top of the archway and houses at the far end. This fire knocked down numbers of our poor soldiers; and the fire that we gave in return was useless, as the sepoys were protected by the parapet that ran along the whole front of the flat-roofed houses; and the houses themselves had all the doorways on the other side, so could not be entered from where we were.

The General was sitting on his horse quite coolly, giving his orders and trying to prevent too hasty a rush through the archway, as one of our guns had not yet been got out of the lane where we had been halting. He sent me back to see what was the delay in getting the gun on; and these were the last words I heard him utter, as I rode off immediately to the lane, and in about three minutes returned with the gun—when, to my great grief and horror, I was told that he was no more.

His death was so unexpected by everyone. He seemed to move about with a charmed life, and he had been so long looked on as the master spirit of our force by those around him that his being suddenly cut off came upon us with a terrible shock. The best I can say of him was what Lord Canning said: "There was no leader more reliable, no soldier more forward, than Neill."

Here is the conclusion of the narrative of Lieutenant Delafosse, the orderly-officer of the Queen's 5th Fusiliers:

We were at the head of the column, with the Sikhs close behind us. We skirted the suburbs north of the canal, then pressed on into the city, shooting great numbers of the enemy and losing men ourselves. On every side of me, men were falling. In fact, we were shot down like so many sheep. But at least we could force our way through, as our route was quite different from what the enemy expected. They thought we would take the direct route to the Residency, which was the bridge road, and so those two miles were cut up with entrenchments and defended by heavy guns.

To our right, when we came in sight of the main palace, there was a large house which was occupied by the enemy. We were ordered to take it and hold it. To get to it, we had to cross a small open space. This we did one by one at the double—every man as he doubled feeling the danger to which he was exposed. The bullets from houses on both sides whizzed over and about us by hundreds, and it was regularly running the gauntlet through a hailstorm of bullets. Several men and horses were killed and wounded here; but there was no hesitation on our side, and our brave fellows filed through this as willingly as if they had been in their then-hungry state going to a sumptuous banquet.

We took the house as ordered, breaking and blowing open the doors with our rifles and forcing all the unfriendly occupants out by the windows at sword and bayonet point; and here we halted till the other regiments came up, when the houses right and left were broken into and many more rebels shot and bayoneted. We all felt at every step we took as if we could not take another to save our lives; but we went stumbling on with our mouths open, as dry as bones. This was a cloudless day in the hottest month of the year; and after the last several days of incessant rain, the evaporation from the ground was very thick and made it doubly oppressive.

About three o'clock, we pushed on under an immensely heavy crossfire over a small bridge, where again we sustained a considerable loss in charging and taking a gun on the other side, and then found ourselves between rows of houses with loopholed walls, being coolly picked off by unseen hands.

This street and house fighting went on till dusk, and it was cruel work. At one place in particular, just as we turned a corner into an open square surrounded by high walls, the 84th Foot was in the act of passing through an archway, and we were close behind them, when a murderous fire was opened from these loopholed walls; and poor Brigadier General Neill was shot dead off his horse. The men seemed seized with a fit of fury for the time. They left their ranks and fired a volley against those walls with the forlorn hope that some stray bullets might enter the loopholes and kill the men sheltered behind.

When order was restored, we commenced passing through. It was a horrid business; and it was getting dark, which made it worse. You could see the flashes from the loopholes just over your head as you moved on and felt powerless, for we were unable to stop their firing or drive them from their stronghold.

It was quite dark before our work was over; and we slept that night without food or drink except a ration of grog—or covering of any kind, since we were in light marching order—in the muddy road leading into the garrison, about one hundred yards from the gate. We gave and received three cheers from the people inside, and that was the only proof that night we had of the other's existence. It was a terrible day altogether, and one I shall not easily forget. But we slept well after our labor.

And here is the conclusion of the narrative of Mr. Willock, the political officer:

About five P.M., we found ourselves opposite the main palace, from the gates of which a very heavy artillery fire was opened; and the musketry fire poured like rain from the loopholes. We had to run double-quick in front of it as hard as we could, and a scene of great confusion ensued when we took shelter and halted in some garden enclosures: guns and infantry all mixed up, soldiers wandering in search of their companies, and the wounded carried here and there without any orders.

After about half an hour, order was re-established and we started again and ran the gauntlet regularly through the street—our men being knocked down like sheep without being able to return the fire with any effect.

After we passed the Palace, we came to a sudden turning to the left with a huge gateway in front; and through this we had to pass under a shower of musket balls from the houses on each side. The Sikhs and 5th Fusiliers were in front and kept up a steady fire at the houses for some time, but it was of no use. Excited men can seldom fire into loopholes with any certainty; and so we had to make the best of our way up the street, turning sharp round to the right, when we found ourselves in a long wide street, with sheets of fire shooting out from the houses.

But on we went about a quarter of a mile, being peppered from all sides, when suddenly we found ourselves opposite to a large gateway with folding doors completely riddled by roundshot and musket balls: the entrance to a large enclosure. At the right side of this was a small doorway, half blocked up by a low mud wall, and the Europeans and Sikhs were struggling to get through while the bullets were whistling about them.

I could not think why we should be going in there; but after forcing my way up to the door and getting my head and shoulders over the wall, I found myself being pulled all the way over by a great unwashed hairy creature who set me on my feet and patted me on the back; and to my astonishment, I found myself in the long-looked-for Bailey Guard or gatehouse of the Residency compound.

What an entry, compared with what I had promised myself! I had expected us to march in with bands playing and colors flying; but instead of this, we entered as a disorderly crowd, or like so many lost sheep.

4

WE EXPECTED TO FIND ONLY YOUR BONES!

The head of Havelock's column fought through the narrow streets of Lucknow toward the Residency; but now to the story of the rearguard, beginning with the actions of Her Majesty's 78th Highlanders, as told by Ensign William Tweedie:

For a short while, we were relatively undisturbed at the bridgehead; and we employed the interval of leisure in hurling the captured bridge battery and its ammunition into the deep waters of the canal. Just then, however, a rebel horde came pouring down the main road upon us with demoniacal yells; and for three hours, alone and unsupported, we maintained a fierce fight against overwhelming numbers.

About a hundred yards up the road, there was a small temple which the enemy occupied; and from it, as well as from right and left, they plied us with a galling musketry fire, which filled the air like a swarm of bees. Having had enough of this, Captain Hastings sprang to the front, calling for volunteers. In an instant, Lieutenant and Adjutant Macpherson was on one side of him and Lieutenant Webster on the other, with half the regiment at their backs. There was a rush up to the temple, and a desperate hand-to-hand fight raged around it and inside it. The garrison held it stoutly, but it was eventually taken by storm. Some of its defenders were slain where they stood; the rest were pitched out of windows or over parapets.

After an hour's hard fighting, the enemy (failing to drive us from the temple) brought up three brass guns and swept the road with their fire to prevent us "petticoated devils" from leaving and reinforcements from arriving. Worst of all, for a time, our fellows had to keep in shelter and let the enemy blaze away, as the long-continued wet weather had so swelled our reserve cartridges that they would not go into the barrels of our rifles. But Lieutenant Havelock, who was the staff officer superintending at the bridge, opportunely sent up a fresh supply; and the time had come again for active measures.

The stalwart Mr. Webster stepped forward and thundered: "Who's for those infernal guns?"

From a hundred throats came the answering shout: "I'm for the guns!"

Far in advance of the rush of howling "devils" went Webster, vociferating violently as he ran—the very incarnation of "Old Clootie," the Prince of Devils. Armed with a heavy cavalry saber—he despised the lighter and straight regulation sword—he made the weapon whistle round his head as he reached the guns and then brought it down hard on the head of a rebel gunner just as his portfire was at the touchhole. When the combat was finished, the gunner's corpse was examined. Webster's saber had cut him down almost to the collarbone. The strong arm was soon to be powerless, however; for before nightfall, Webster was lying on his face near the guardhouse gate of the Residency compound with a bullet through his brain. But at least he had seen the object of our endeavor before he died.

With the remaining enemy in flight up the road, with Mr. Macpherson on their heels and the guns taken, a formal procession was formed with Piper Campbell at its head. The guns were dragged in triumph to the canal and hurled into its waters.

By this time, the last supply wagon was across the bridge; and young Havelock declared that we were now free to bring up the rear. As he spoke, he fell with a bullet through his left elbow, which smashed the bones. The enemy had again come down, and had to be beaten back yet again before the position could be abandoned. Meanwhile, Mr. Havelock was borne away to safety in a litter.

By the time we were finally able to start, we had lost all contact with the main body and were, in effect, an independent force for the time being. We had lost several officers and men; and it was with great difficulty that we carried our wounded, as all of the native litter bearers had gone on with the rest of the column. The dead we had to abandon without burial, as the rest of our force were obliged to do, and deliberately stripped them so that they would not be identified as Highlanders by the enemy and because their clothes were invaluable items to those of us who needed or would need them.

We followed for some distance the narrow canal-side road, along which the last wagon had moved out of sight; but when we left the canal at a point where we heard some musketry fire, the trail was lost. There were two roads. We took the one known to be the more direct, chancing whether or not it might be the more arduous.

We turned off to the left along the narrow street of a bazaar or market quarter, from the tall houses lining which a steady fire rained down upon us and inflicted heavy loss. The enemy now knew that we were alone in rear, and so began to surround us on all sides in numbers twenty or thirty times greater than ours; but at every available place, we made a stand and drove them back for a short time.

As we struggled along this deadly route, Ensign Kerbey (who was carrying the Queen's colors) was shot down. As he fell, the flag was grabbed by a bandsman named Glen, who also fell and from whom it was wrenched by Sergeant Reid. A few paces further, and Sergeant Reid was struck down. Then the colors passed to Assistant Surgeon McMaster, who continued to carry them until we halted and they could be handed over to Color Sergeant McPherson.

A wounded piper and three privates who had fired their last rounds of ammunition were charged by half a dozen rebel troopers from a side street. The three privates prepared to defend themselves with the bayonet; but as soon as the troopers were within about twenty paces of the stragglers, the piper pointed the drones of his bagpipes straight at them and blew such a wild blast that they turned tail and fled, mistaking the "doodlesack" for some infernal machine.

While we were undergoing this crossfire ordeal, we heard a continuous and louder sound of firing on our right and right front. It was not the rattle of musketry alone—that noise was so constant on our own route that a distant fusillade might have gone unheeded— but there was the deep roar of big guns to tell us that our comrades-at-arms, if they were succeeding at all, were not achieving an uncontested victory.

Soon enough, we gained on and to some extent overlapped the locality where the boom of the guns was loudest. Steadily advancing, firing right and left as we did so, we suddenly emerged into a large open area, where we found ourselves on the flank of an entrenched four-gun battery in action in front of an immense and ornate building. That structure was none other than the Kaiser Bagh or "Caesar's Garden," the main palace of the former King of Oudh; and the battery, manned by professional gunners, was firing across the open at the men of our main column as they emerged from the narrow passage between the Motee Mahul or "Pearl Palace" and the former messhouse of Her Majesty's 32nd Light Infantry.

Without waiting to look closely into the situation, we dashed into the battery, killed most of the gunners and drove off the rest, and were able to spike the guns with some musket ramrods. Then we had time to look about us. To our amazement, we found that because of the shorter route we had taken through the bazaar, we were actually now at the head of the main column instead of being in the rear.

Pressing on through a dropping fire and a small herd of maddened cavalry horses which had somehow got loose from the Palace stables, we debouched into the courtyard of the Chutter Munzil or "Umbrella Mansion"—so called from the shape of its main door—which was considerably sheltered from the enemy fire that raged everywhere else. Here were assembled the chiefs of the Oudh Field Force.

On his big mottled "Waler" sat General Outram, short and thick and dark-bearded, with a splash of blood across his smoke-grimed face and one bloody arm in a sling from a flesh wound he received on the bridge road, and with a stout gold-handled Malacca cane in his grip—he never carried a sword, but wielded the cane like a club—and with a fresh cheroot between his teeth. (Although an asthmatic, he never stopped smoking except to eat and sleep, and stuffed his saddle holsters with cigars instead of pistols.) General Havelock, short and thin and white-bearded, was on foot—his horse had just been shot under him, and he had lost so many that it was said to be a waste of horseflesh to keep him mounted—and he was pacing nervously back and forth at Outram's side, halting now and then to emphasize his rapid words; for the debate between the two Generals was heated. All around them, at a short distance, were staff and field officers; and outside of this large circle were soldiers, native servants, guns, litters, gun bullocks, commissariat camels, and all the rest of the disorganized mass that was pouring and crowding into the courtyard.

Now that their goal was almost reached, Havelock no longer deferred to Outram. He was determined to push on at once up the main street leading to the Bailey-Guard Gate of the Residency compound and to relieve the garrison before nightfall, which was fast approaching. Outram, however, wanted to halt where they were—if not for the night, then at least for a couple of hours—to enable all the troops and guns and supplies to come up and the troops to rest and re-form. But Havelock would not yield. "There is the last street," said he, pointing ahead. "We have seen the worst. We shall be slated no matter what we do; but we can push through and get it over with before nightfall and before the enemy can surround us and cut us off."

Most of the other officers agreed. It was the cutting-off that they feared. Lieutenant Charles Havelock, the General's nephew and aide, blurted out at Outram: "For God's sake, let us go on, sir!"

Outram's usually even temper then got the better of him; and snatching the cigar from his mouth, he exclaimed, "Let us go on, then, in God's name!"

That settled it. Havelock's staff officers took their orders and rode away with them, and soon a semblance of order was made of the disorderly mass of troops who were still surging and cramming into the courtyard.

The honor of leading the advance was given to the 78th Highlanders, with Captain Brasyer's Ferozepore Regiment of Sikhs in immediate support. Generals Havelock and Outram, with their staff officers, rode up to the head of the Highlanders—Havelock on a borrowed nag. The word was then given by Havelock, the advance began at a quick march, and presently the foremost soldiers entered the street which led with several curves up to the Bailey-Guard Gate of the Residency compound, only half a mile ahead.

Then, from side streets, from the front, from every window and loophole, and from every balcony and the top of every house, there poured a constant stream of bullets upon the men who were doggedly pushing forward, savage at their inability to return fire with equal effect. For except where now and then a section of troops (facing momentarily outward) got a chance to send a volley into the mass of rebels holding the head of a crossroad, there was little opportunity for retaliation. All of the doors and lower windows were heavily barricaded, so that the houses could not be taken by storm. The rebels ensconced on the flat parapeted and loopholed roofs and balconies, and lurking behind the shuttered upper windows were seen only fleetingly (if at all) as they fired down into the street and then drew back hurriedly to reload. Some of their women also wielded muskets; a few even moved along the housetops with their skirts stretched out, so as to cover the men as they crept about from point to point; while others hurled down bricks and stones and pieces of furniture and other missiles, and even spat on the passing soldiery, who shook their fists and shouted up in vain at them.

One poor madwoman stood on a parapet with an infant in her arms, hissing and yelling curses until (unable to control her fury) she hurled the babe down upon the bayonet points of the "petticoated devils." They spared her, but the Sikhs behind them had no compunction; and the wretched woman, riddled with bullets, fell to the ground with a wild shriek.

A downward shot then crashed through Private McGrath's back, and he fell; but unflinching, undeterred even by trenches cut in the road, he crawled forward on his hands and knees for over a hundred yards before another bullet struck him dead.

In the foremost company were two staunch comrades named Glandell and McDonough. Private McDonough's right leg was shattered by a bullet, and he fell; but he was not left to die. His stalwart chum lifted him onto his back and trudged on with him. Nor did Private Glandell permit himself to be made a noncombatant by this heavy burden. Whenever he had a chance to fire a shot, Glandell propped McDonough up against a wall and made use of his rifle, then picked McDonough up again and staggered cheerily onward.

The ordeal of fire had been endured for a distance of over fifteen hundred paces when, from the leaders and staff officers in front, there ran down the column an electrifying shout. For through the fast-gathering gloom of night had been discerned the battered archway of the Bailey-Guard Gate, from atop which came an answering shout of glad welcome and a waving of caps.

The mounted officers gave spur; the men on foot lost their weariness and kept pace with them; and with a final rush, the head of the column was at the gate. But earth had been piled up against it from the insides and there was no immediate entrance. However, in the low wall to the right of the gate was a wicket doorway, out of which protruded the muzzle of the big gun from which Lieutenant Aitken (the commander of the native guard) had steadily hurled death on his assailants. Aitken and his loyal sepoys hauled back the big piece.

General Outram rode at the doorway; but his ungainly Waler balked at leaping through it, as it was partially blocked by a parapet of sandbags. So there was a scramble and a shout among the foremost of the Highlanders; and rider and horse were suddenly inside, hoisted bodily through the embrasure by strong arms.

General Havelock and his staff followed, and then over the wall and through the opening rushed the eager soldiers—powder-grimed, muddy, and bloody—a moment before, raging with the passion of battle; now, melting in tears of joy. The otherwise stony hearts of the big, rough-bearded warriors softened as they frantically clasped the outstretched hands, exclaiming, "Thank God, this is better than Cawnpore!" and "God bless you! Why, we expected to find only your bones!" They snatched the little children out of their elders' arms, or up from the ground, kissing them with tears rolling down their dingy cheeks and thanking God that they had come in time to save them from the fate of those at Cawnpore.

With the sudden and unexpected appearance of these saviors, the garrison's long-pent-up feelings of anxiety and suspense burst forth in a succession of deafening cheers of relief from every rifle pit, trench, and battery; from behind every barricade and the sandbags piled on shattered houses; from every post and outpost rose cheer upon cheer. Even from the hospital, many of the sick and wounded crawled forth to join in that glad shout of welcome. It was a moment never to be forgotten.

But the cheering was over when we counted the cost: 196 killed and 535 wounded, or nearly a third of the force—to which 522 more casualties would be added before the garrison was finally relieved. The 78th Highlanders lost the most of any regiment: over one third of about four hundred. Two officers and thirty-seven men were killed, six officers and seventy-five men were wounded, and six men were missing. Those soldiers who brought up the rear suffered the next-highest casualties: sixty-one killed and seventy-seven wounded and missing. At least forty of the wounded were killed in their abandoned litters, by being shot or stabbed or burned to death. Those dead and wounded who were not picked up were beheaded in the streets. Lieutenant Harry Havelock, with his left arm shattered at the elbow, and a wounded Highlander lying beside him, was in the leading litter and would have suffered the same fate had it not been for Private Ward of the 78th, who forced the bearers to go on at bayonet point. For that he was awarded the Victoria Cross.

When Mr. Gubbins, the Financial Commissioner of Oudh, asked General Outram how his arm was, the new Chief Commissioner replied, "Oh, damn the arm! I have lost nearly a third of my force. I'm afraid, Mr. Gubbins, we must all remain here until a larger force can come to our relief."

The original garrison of 1,720 had been reduced by casualties to 980. They were now reinforced to about 3,100, but were still outnumbered by at least ten to one.

Captain Frank Maude, R.A., commented:

It is difficult to resist the conclusion that the whole affair was a muddle, however gloriously conducted, from beginning to end. Most of our wounded were left behind with our dead, and many of them were horribly burnt to death as they lay in their abandoned litters. We lost the whole of our baggage, most of our supplies, and all the ammunition of our heavy guns. The officers led their men right well; but of generalship that day there was little if any at all, owing to the divided command and difference of opinion between Outram and Havelock, neither of whom (in deference to the other) dared to take a decisive stand until it was too late to matter.

The tragic story of the sick and wounded is also part of the story of the reargurd; and it was told by Dr. Anthony Home, the surgeon of Her Majesty's 90th Light Infantry, which had to bring up the rear when the 78th Highlanders failed to show:

Our sick and wounded were very numerous and were brought on with great difficulty. Litter bearers fell or deserted in large numbers, and eventually it was necessary to place the invalids on the limbers of the guns. At this critical time, our advance was also sorely impeded by most of the guns having to be dragged by hand, as large numbers of the horses and oxen and elephants who were pulling them and the ammunition wagons were deliberately killed by the enemy. And to add to this, the 90th Regiment was ordered back in support of the 78th, which was under heavy attack and in a perilous position at the bridgehead. But the 78th having extricated themselves and gone off in another direction, the 90th in turn became the rearguard, which was now much delayed in protecting the slowly moving hospital transport, which seemed to be the target of the severest fire.

It was two o'clock, and we had arrived at about a mile from the Residency. Now commenced the hardest part. The enemy had possession of a bridge which we had to cross. On the far side of this bridge was a battery of three guns; and there were at different points three other batteries, all bearing on us. The houses and gardens all about us were full of the enemy, and we were in such a fire! To use the phrase "storm of musketry" is no metaphorical exaggeration.

I was with the wounded, about three hundred yards from this bridge battery. The enemy fired a round of grape at us from one gun and killed eight of my litter bearers. Altogether, I lost eighty-four litter bearers that day killed and wounded; this out of three hundred and ninety-four. Of course, many invalids were killed in the litters as we went along; and whenever the bearers of a particular litter were shot down or deserted and there was no room in another litter, as only two men could fit in each, the poor occupants had to be abandoned. It was heartbreaking. All the more so because the officers took precedence over the men, who cheerfully gave place and were left with rifles and pistols in their hands to defend themselves as best they could. And you can bet they sold their lives dearly!

Men were falling all round me; and the shot was tearing huge branches off trees, which fell on our heads, and throwing up mud in our faces. We had to halt through all this whilst the advance guard deployed to clear the way. After a while, we had the order to advance. The old thing did it. The bayonet and a cheer sent the enemy helter-skelter, and the guns were ours and the bridge clear.

About four in the afternoon, we got into comparative safety with the rest of the column in a palace having a large oblong square, where we were all very much crammed together; a veritable pandemonium of men and animals. A council of war voted to press on at once to the Residency, and the headquarters wing of the 90th Regiment was ordered to remain behind with the invalids and two of the heavy guns and some ammunition wagons and all the other impediments. So there we passed the night; and a night of great horror it was, what with the unceasing cries and groans of men and animals and the almost incessant fire of the enemy, which rattled on the outer walls of the palace.

As long as daylight lasted, we medical officers could attend to our patients; but, as much of the medical equipment and stores had been abandoned or captured during the day, the work was carried on under the greatest difficulties. Lanterns and candles were few, and most of our matches had been ruined by the wet weather, so the necessary surgical operations could not be undertaken before daybreak. Besides, lights only served to guide the enemy's fire. It was a sad night indeed, and few if any of us slept through it.

Daylight came at last, and with it the power to serve. But it was then that the enemy got our range with their heavy guns and kept pouring their shot and shell into us, killing numbers. We were like rats in a trap, and there was nowhere to hide for shelter.

One poor fellow, an assistant surgeon in the Bengal Artillery, was anxious for me to assist him in an operation. I was on my way with him to do it; the shots were whistling all about us; and I said, "Well, Bartrum, I wish I could see my way out of this."

"Oh," he said, "there's no danger whatever." Next minute, he was shot dead beside me with a bullet through his brain.

Two minutes before, he spoke of the pleasure he expected in rejoining his wife and child in the Residency, where they had taken refuge whilst he remained with his regiment at an outstation. He considered our day's achievement the most wonderful in history, whilst I considered it the rashest: less than three thousand men being shot down by unseen enemies in the streets of a very large city. At least forty thousand of them were behind loopholed walls, with great numbers of guns. To my mind, the only wonderful thing about it is that any of us lived through it.

Our situation was now more critical than ever. The enemy were pressing very close all round us and kept up a storm of shot, shell, and musketry on us. We were cut off from the main body of our force by nearly a mile; and they could not help us, as they themselves were fighting hard to hold the Residency, which was now under the severest fire ever.

At last, Colonel Campbell came to me and told me that a native courier had come in with orders for him to abandon his position and fight his way into the Residency—communication with which could be had through an apparently deserted bazaar quarter—and that a guide would be sent to bring in the invalids, and he could then force his way in with the rearguard. The Colonel then said he would give me an escort of a hundred and fifty men, and with them I was to get the invalids into the Residency as best I could. How wonderful!

In a very short time, Bensley Thornhill (a political officer and a nephew-in-law of General Havelock) arrived from the Residency as a guide. I got the invalids together and ready in a long column of litters; and after taking a deep breath, I left the palace square with them and Mr. Thornhill and our escort.

Thornhill advised me that the great point was surprise: to hurry on the proceeding so that it might in great measure be accomplished before the enemy were aware. "But then what?" I asked.

"Then," he said rather grimly, "it's happen what may."

We filed out of the square into a deserted lane that led to the apparently deserted bazaar; and for about two hundred yards the enemy did us no harm, as their shots flew overhead even if they saw us. But then we had to cross a broad drainage ditch full of water from the late rains. It took me nearly up to my chest, and such a fire we got into here! Numbers of litter bearers were hit or abandoned their burdens, and some of the invalids were drowned—some killed—but most got across; and on we went between the walls of a lane to the bazaar, where we were promised comparative safety.

Our escort preceded us, firing all the way, but they had really no chance. They were shot down right and left by unseen assailants behind the loopholed walls. When I got to the entrance of the main street of the bazaar, I found a number of them lying wounded or dead; and most of the others had rushed on for their lives. On looking round, I found that the litter bearers were being shot at from the buildings in the street as well as the walls of the lane; and those not hit flung down their burdens, thinking it was the invalids that the enemy were shooting at, and no threat or entreaty could prevail on them to lift them again.

The bazaar, which twenty minutes before seemed deserted, was now occupied in force by the enemy, who poured out a heavy fire from the roofs and windows, killing both invalids and bearers alike. Mr. Thornhill was amongst those severely wounded. He was hit under the left eye by a musket ball, whilst another bullet smashed his right arm. The arm was later amputated but his skull was hopelessly injured, and he died of blood poisoning on October 12th.

The gateway at the far end of the main street was now blocked by the heavy fire from that direction. There was no other accessible outlet besides the one we had entered, and so there was no hope but to turn back as many of the litters as possible which happened to be near that entrance and bypass the loopholed walls through a small gate on the left.

Under the able conduct of Assistant Surgeon Bradshaw of my regiment, and of Mr. Hurst of the Subordinate Medical Staff, some litters were saved and finally reached the Residency by a path along the river. (One of them contained Lieutenant Havelock, the General's son and adjutant, his left arm badly broken by a musket ball.) For most of the litters in the street, however, the case was hopeless. The bearers were either shot down or had saved themselves by running. I tried to get a few of the ambulatory patients together, but by this time the enemy had gathered round us in almost every house and had nothing to do but to bring us down at their leisure. And when some of us tried to sleek shelter in the verandas or porticoes, they were fired upon within a few paces, so that the bullets tore through several men at the same time.

All hope seemed gone; but as a last resource, I ran back with four others into the small empty gatehouse at the entrance through which we had come. Other fugitives then joined us: some stragglers from the main column and some soldiers from the escort who had escaped, and two badly wounded officers.

The enemy now commenced yelling fearfully. I calculated their numbers at from five hundred to a thousand. Their leaders tried to get them to charge down on us, but as often as they came on in swarms of fifty or so, we gave them a volley from the windows and doorway; and off they went, leaving many dead and wounded behind—some of them nearly at our feet. Then they began their yelling again, and reviled us in their own language as well as in English, telling us that in a few minutes we should all be massacred. Many of them were not more than five yards off, but sheltered from our fire in other houses.

At this time, we expected instant death. It seemed incredible that ten effective men could resist one thousand, who were firing a fearful hail of shot through the open windows and doorway. Three of our number were struck down wounded, and this diminished our fire. Worse, the enemy all this time were massacring the invalids in the litters. They killed perhaps forty of them by firing volleys at the litters. A little later on, they set fire to some of them—a further attempt to terrorize us—and all who were not already dead perished. But we managed to rescue two more wounded officers and five more wounded men.

Private Ryan, a straggler from the Madras Fusiliers, could not be prevented from attempting to save his officer, Lieutenant Arnold, who was lying wounded in a litter at some distance. (He had both legs fractured by grapeshot whilst leading the charge on the canal bridge.) Private McManus, a straggler from the 5th Fusiliers, though hurt in the left foot, joined Ryan in dashing into the street under a heavy musketry fire, dragging Arnold out of his litter, and carrying him into the gatehouse. They escaped unhurt, but Arnold was shot through the right thigh whilst in their arms. Another sortie was then made and a disabled soldier brought in. He also was mortally wounded—twice—whilst his rescuers remained uninjured. They didn't give up, however, until another officer and four more men were saved. (All of us who survived were awarded the V.C.)

Private Hollowell, a straggler from the 78th Highlanders, was the crack shot of our little band. Whenever the enemy came forward to storm the house, he repeatedly killed the foremost man; and the rest fell back. At last, he had an opportunity of taking a long shot at their chief leader—a vociferous old man with a red beard and turban, and armed with sword and shield—who died on the spot. After that, most of the enemy went away. And none too soon, as we had only seven rounds left to fire. But seeing the headless trunks of several of their comrades lying in the street, our men were determined to hold out to the last gasp.

Well, as I said, the remaining enemy now gave up the attempt to storm us; but they crept up to the windows and fired in on us so we had to lie down on the floor for a time and let them fire over us—which was no hardship, as we were dead beat.

Just as there were no shutters to the windows, there was no door to the doorway; so we made a barricade of sandbags by digging up the floor with swords and bayonets and using the dead rebels' clothes to hold the dirt. These we had to drag in off the portico at great risk, but their pouches replenished our supply of ammunition. We also piled up the dead so as to keep men from rushing in on us.

My duties, as the only unwounded officer, were to direct and encourage the men; as a surgeon, to attend the wounded; and as a man, to use a rifle belonging to a wounded soldier when he fell. (I should add that my rank as senior medical officer of the Oudh Field Force originally made me the leader of this forlorn hope.)

After a while, we saw that most of the remaining enemy were tired of rushing on us. We had killed over twenty of them, and must have wounded many more. This put a damper on them. But a few were still game, and we had to be ready for them; so we now told off one man to fire from each window and three from the doorway. My post was at a window. I had only one revolver, with only five shots left.

Sure enough, one of the game rebels came creeping up to fire as usual through my window—quite unconscious that at this time an equally game opponent had him covered with a revolver. When he got about three yards from me, I shot him dead; and another, who was coming up, was shot down by one of the men.

For nearly an hour now, the enemy were very cautious—only firing at a distance. Then all at once we heard in the street a dull rumbling noise, which froze me to the very heart. I jumped up and said, "Now, men! Now or never! Let us rush out and die in the open air, and not be killed like rats in a hole! They are bringing a gun on us!"

The men were quite ready; but we now saw that it was not a gun but a mantlet or movable bulletproof screen on wheels, commonly used to cover the approach of men who are storming a fort, with a heavy planking in front—too thick for our bullets to penetrate. The rebels brought it to the very window I was firing at. I could touch it, but my shots were useless. So I had to lie flat on the floor again and let them fire away through a couple of loopholes in the planks, just big enough to allow a slight turning of their musket barrels.

After half an hour of this amusement, seeing that it did not demoralize us, they set the thatch roof of the house on fire. But we were able to escape by a back window—there was no back door—and rushed into a shed behind the house and outside the walls of the quarter, carrying our wounded with us. Three of them were mortally wounded whilst we were carrying them; and strange to say, we sound men did not get a scratch.

It was now three in the afternoon, and our position seemed hopeless. Surely the enemy would set the shed on fire as well. But just as they had not fired the house immediately, they played cat-and-mouse with us here as well.

Imagine our horror when we found that the shed was loopholed all round. It had been used the day before as a place to fire on our troops from; and the enemy now came creeping up to the loopholes, firing in suddenly, and then off they went again. We now put a man at every loophole as far as they would go. Even wounded were put to watch, and this soon checked the second assault. We then had a worse alarm.

The enemy brought some ladders and got onto the roof, bored holes through it, and fired down on us. The first two shots were fired at me—the muzzles of the muskets being, perhaps, four feet from me—but neither shot hurt me beyond a lot of stuff from the roof being sent with force into my face and a trifling nick in my right hand.

Nothing more wonderful in the way of narrow escapes was ever seen, I dare say!

This game could not last, so two of us went cautiously out into the courtyard behind the shed to reconnoiter. For some time, the enemy did not see us, as it was getting dark. About fifty yards off was a mosque with no one in it, as I found by creeping on all fours into it; but before we could got the wounded out of the shed and into the mosque, we were discovered. We now ran back to the shed.

However, we had secured along the way an earthen pitcher full of excellent well water belonging to the enemy; and what a prize it was! The wounded were dying with thirst, and we who had been biting cartridges all day were just as bad. It gave us one good drink all round; and after it, we felt twice the men we did before.

The shed being a very long one, we had a great deal to defend; but luckily the enemy found out that if they could fire through the roof, so could we—with the advantage of knowing exactly where they were by the noise of their feet—so they kept off the roof.

We now organized our defense: told off each man to his alarm post, and told off the sentries and reliefs. Including wounded, there were nine men fit for sentry and seven men fit to fight; and of these seven, six were unhurt, including myself. It was agreed that if the enemy forced the shed, we should rush out and die outside.

By this time, all our abandoned wounded were in their possession; and they were put to death with horrible tortures right before our faces. As I said, some were burnt alive in the litters; and the shrieks of these men chilled one's blood. To be sure, the terrors of that awful night were almost maddening: raging thirst; anger and resentment against those who, as we thought, had left us to perish without any attempt at rescue; uncertainty as to where and how the enemy would next attack us; and added to this, the exhaustion produced by want of food and rest, and the heat and anxiety.

I now proposed to our men either to fight our way back to the rearguard or forward to the Residency. But there were only two who would go; and so I refused to go, as we could not for shame desert eight wounded men. Still, I tried to persuade all to make the attempt. Someone might escape. As it was, no one could. But I tried in vain.

Day broke soon after, and we had all fallen into perfect apathy. Our nerves, so highly strung for twenty hours, seemed now to have gone quite the other way. Suddenly, a few shots were fired outside—then more. Then we heard the sharp crack of Enfield rifles. Private Ryan, who was standing sentry, now shouted, "Oh, boys! Them's our own chaps!"

Still we were uncertain, till presently we heard a regular rattling volley and a cheer such as no sepoy would give. Oh, how our hearts jumped into our mouths then! Up we got; and now I said, "Men, cheer together!"

Our people outside heard us and sent another cheer back. We replied like madmen and shouted to them to keep off our side. We then fired through all the loopholes at the enemy, to keep them from firing at our men advancing. It not only silenced them; it put them to flight. In five minutes we were all rescued and in the midst of our own people. Half an hour after, we were settled down like conquerors in one of the former King of Oudh's palaces—just captured by our rescuers.

On that same morning, under the guidance of Lieutenant Moorsom of the General Staff, the rearguard fought its way into the Residency compound. My first sensation on getting within those defenses was one of unbounded wonder how anyone there had managed to survive the rain of musket balls and artillery missiles of all kinds that poured in nearly incessantly during eighty-seven days of siege. Every building was bespattered with the marks of bullets and honeycombed and shattered by cannonshot, and to an incredible extent.

How the rearguard fought its way into the Residency defenses was described by Major Edward Lowe, commander of Her Majesty's 32nd Light Infantry:

On the morning of September 26th, a detachment of 250 of the 5th Fusiliers under Major Simmons and a party of Sikhs under Captain Brasyer were sent to reinforce and rescue Colonel Campbell and the majority of sick and wounded, two of the heavy guns, and a number of ammunition wagons, with about one hundred men of the 90th Light Infantry, in a walled passage in front of the Motee Mahul or "Pearl Palace," where they were invested by the enemy. But Simmons and Brasyer got no farther than a large house and walled garden between Campbell's position and the palace, which they were forced to occupy.

As they gradually emerged from the cover of the Furhut-Buksh Mahul or "Pleasure-Giving Palace," they had to cross a ditch waist-deep in water under a very heavy fire which killed and wounded some of them before they reached the house and garden, just on the other side, where they were also invested. Two poor Sikhs had their legs bowled off by roundshot as they were entering the premises.

When this situation became known at the Residency, Colonel Napier (our Chief Engineer) received orders to proceed to their assistance with one hundred of the 78th Highlanders under Colonel Stisted and Captain Hardinge's native troopers of the 3rd Oudh Cavalry. they reached Simmons's and Brasyer's position under a smart fire, but were unable to extricate them; so an additional reinforcement of a company of the 32nd Light Infantry under myself, another detachment of Sikhs, and fifty more of the 78th was sent out, but got no farther than the others.

All in all, we had an uncommonly unpleasant day of it. Our rearguard had got jammed up in a lane between two walls and were exposed to a murderous fire whenever anyone showed himself, and 18- and 24-pound roundshot were being sent into the house our men were put into for the day. What rendered it more mortifying was that the enemy fired at us out of our old messhouse and my former quarters. Owing to the strong musketry and artillery fire, it was impossible to move our heavy guns during the day. All that afternoon and night, the roundshot and musket balls were flying about like hail from all directions; while from a 32-pounder on the other side of the river, shots were coming in with frightful precision, smashing through the masonry walls and striking the wooden rafters of the house and sending pieces of stonework and splinters of wood here and there, frightfully wounding our brave but (for the time) helpless men.

At three A.M., however, the whole force proceeded undiscovered through the enemy posts until they reached the Chutter Munzil or "Umbrella Mansion," when a body of sepoys was discovered in a walled garden there by our advance guard (consisting of men of the 5th, 32nd, and 90th), who gallantly charged in, led by Colonel Purnell of the 90th and Captain McCabe of the 32nd, and almost annihilated them, securing the garden as the rear of our position. Then, while the rest of the force went on to extricate Campbell, 150 of the 32nd under myself were sent to clear the Soobahdar or "Captain's" Bazaar and adjoining posts occupied by the enemy, who were taken by surprise and fled to the river, where nearly all of them were shot or drowned. Two guns were captured, two others spiked, and a large powder magazine blown up.

5

UNDER FIRE NIGHT
AND DAY

Rather than relieved by a raising of the three-month siege, the Lucknow garrison was merely reinforced. It would have been risking disaster to attempt to evacuate the large numbers of women and children and sick and wounded through fortified streets and a countryside teeming with marksmen, who could only have been cleared out and off by a larger force with ample artillery. So the siege continued for two more months, but with the odds less unfavorable to the besieged. Their position could now be extended and strengthened by the taking of more buildings along the Goomtee River and in the center of the city; and yet, ironically, that extension also had its inherent weaknesses, as General Outram wrote in one of his dispatches:

Our position is more untenable than that of the previous garrison because we are obliged to occupy the neighboring palaces outside the entrenchment, which positions the enemy are able to mine from cover of neighboring buildings. I am aware of no parallel to our series of mines in modern war. Twenty-one shafts, aggregating two hundred feet in depth, and 3,291 feet of gallery have been executed. The enemy have advanced twenty mines against the palaces and outposts; of these, they have exploded three which caused us loss of life and two which did no injury; seven have been blown in; and out of seven others the enemy have been driven and their galleries taken possession of by our miners.

A line of gardens, courts, and dwellings without fortified enclosures or flanking defenses, covering an area of some sixty acres and closely connected with the buildings of the city, has been maintained for eight weeks in a certain degree of security, notwithstanding the close and constant musketry fire from loopholed walls and windows (often within thirty yards) and from the top of every lofty building within rifle range, and notwithstanding a frequent though desultory fire of roundshot and grape from guns posted at various distances from seventy to five hundred yards. This result has been obtained by the same cool determination that our soldiers had previously exhibited when forcing their way into Lucknow at the point of the bayonet and amid a most murderous fire.

Lieutenant George Parker of Her Majesty's 78th Highlanders gave this account of his experiences:

On the morning of September 26th, the day after we entered Lucknow, I was sent out of the Residency compound with fifty men to take and hold a house nearby. The taking was easy enough, as the enemy bolted directly they saw us coming; but we had hot work all day holding it, what with four big guns playing on it, knocking down the walls and the supporting pillars, and musket shot flying in at every window.

The picket duty was very heavy, as we were so reduced in numbers and the positions to be defended so many that we were continually on duty and under fire night and day.

On the 28th and 29th, all the available fighting men were ordered to sally out and take those guns which were greatly annoying us and had been hammering away at the garrison for nearly three months. We of the 78th charged one of them and killed all the gunners, blew up the house they were in, and brought the gun in. We lost one killed and seven wounded, but the total loss was upwards of sixty—the other parties getting hotter work than we in taking the guns assigned to them. Owing to some mismanagement on the first day, after having spiked three of the guns, one of our parties was obliged to retreat under heavy fire from the enemy, who then swarmed out of their houses and from behind their walls and retook them. But on the next day, we succeeded in blowing up these same guns: one a particularly troublesome 32-pounder. We soon found it was no good spiking a gun and leaving it behind, for the enemy only returned and either worked out the spike or turned the gun over and made a vent on the other side. The only effectual action was to burst the barrel.

On October 1st, the rebels having undermined and blown up part of our outer wall, an attack was made on the breach, but was soon repulsed. Repairs were immediately made, while nearly all the available infantry were sent out to destroy some more guns and houses. It was the kind of work they were getting good at, and so they did it in style. They pushed on from house to house, rushing down streets under a terrible fire, blowing up several houses and guns which had long annoyed the garrison, and tearing back again—my regiment alone remaining to hold a sort of square, which was the key of our position, against some thousands of rebels, who were now mining and dodging all round us.

About twice in those twenty-four hours, they made a show of attacking us; and when they actually did so, they invariably got the worst of it. Still, every day we had some of our own men killed or wounded; and the only wonder is that so many of us escaped. Night and day, the air was filled with shot and shell and whizzing with bullets; and though we relieved the garrison by destroying numerous guns and houses, killing vast numbers of the enemy, and occupying a long row of palaces along the bank of the river on one side of them, still we were half in a state of siege ourselves and on half rations with nothing to drink but water drawn from wells at great risk, as wells were prime targets of enemy fire. So we each lived on water, coarse flour, and three quarters of a pound of gun-bullock beef per day. But most of us seemed to thrive very well on this scanty and monotonous fare; and it was astonishing how we kept our health, what with heat and wet and hard work and the constant anxiety.

We loopholed and barricaded our houses so well that the rebels found they could not drive us out and took to mining in hopes of driving us up instead. It was rather unpleasant to try and sleep in a place which you knew was being undermined and where you heard the dull sounds of the pickaxe and spade going tap-tap day and night. But we set all our men who knew anything of mining to work at countermining the rebels. It was very tiring and perilous work for them, but they were well paid, and we generally managed to blow in the enemy mines. But in one place they were ahead of us and blew ours up, killing one of our men. It then became a contest as to who could blow the other up first.

On October 5th, the enemy sprang a mine in one of our picket gardens and charged the breach made in the wall; but our men soon drove them back, without even using the bayonet. A few shots seemed to have the desired effect; and when several of the attackers fell, the rest thought it prudent to retreat. After that, despite constant alarms and threats of attack, they kept their distance and concentrated on merely harassing us.

In mid-October, the rebels had a 9-pounder and a 24-pounder in position about four hundred yards from us and pounded our houses most unmercifully. Luckily, they did little mischief beyond smashing the outer walls; but their big cannonballs were objectionable things to be flying about one's head all day. I had gone into an upper room of the house I occupied (the walls of which were riddled with 24-pound shot) for the purpose of looking through the loophole of one of the barricaded windows, to endeavor to get a sight of the parties who were sapping under our walls when a man fired at me from a loop-holed house about thirty yards off. He most fortunately aimed an inch too high, or I should not be here to tell the tale.

The bullet must have struck a loose brick close to my forehead and sent it with great force onto the upper part of my face, blinding me for a few hours and cutting my nose in a beastly manner. For a few moments, I thought I was done for; but after feeling about to find whether the ball had entered my eye or head or wherever, to my great relief I found there was no hole. Still, I was on the sick list for a couple of days with a bulldog sort of countenance and two ferocious-looking black eyes.

I had many narrow escapes, but this was the narrowest. At least I did not have to stay in the hospital, which was a chamber of horrors and in a very exposed place. One of our poor fellows, who had nearly recovered from his wounds, was struck at the doorway by a round-shot and had both legs carried off. He died the next day. One of the apothecaries was killed the same day inside the hospital. Another roundshot took off his head. The enemy always had several guns playing upon all our positions, for we no sooner silenced one than they brought out another. They seemed to have an inexhaustible supply.

This account of one of the sorties was given by Lieutenant John Edmondstoune of Her Majesty's 32nd Light Infantry:

On the 29th September, three sorties wore made in several directions—in each case led by parties of the Queen's 32nd, which was the main European force of the original garrison. I, with twelve men (the only effective ones remaining in my company), was ordered to lead a sortie towards the Iron Bridge, which spans the Goomtee on the north side of Lucknow. The rest of the attacking force consisted of one hundred men of the Queen's 64th and thirty of the 84th, all under command of Captain Shute of the 64th. Captain Graydon, of the 44th Native Infantry, was sent as guide.

Shute, as commanding, in my opinion, ought to have been in front alongside me. But he thought the rear was the best place; and there he stuck, and there Graydon and I had to go for him whenever he was wanted. Graydon, a very fine fellow, stuck alongside throughout the morning.

We started before daybreak and got within one hundred yards of the bridge without being noticed. Directly ahead of us were two guns: the main object of our attack. One of my men then said, "I can see the guns now, about a hundred yards off."

I said, "Men, there are your guns! Take them!"

My men then went down the road with a cheer, Graydon and I leading them. The enemy let us come within twenty yards, when they fired grape into us from both guns and then ran for it. A little musketry was opened on us from the local houses, but did no harm. Nor did the grape, which we avoided by advancing in open order.

We spiked the two guns and then turned down a lane to look for more, and here our misfortunes commenced. A cry arose amongst the 64th and 84th: "We are being taken in the rear!"

I went back and saw it was false, so returned to the front and went on down the lane, when a musketry fire was opened on us and which we returned.

I proposed charging on down the lane, which the strange men of the 64th and 84th did not like at all. My own poor fellows were awfully disgusted at this, saying to one another, "Did you ever see such a cowardly set?"

I then said to Graydon, "I will go on with our own men." I called, "32nd!" They gathered round me at once and sprang forward directly I gave the word—the others bringing up the rear.

We took three more guns, which fired grape into us; also two mortars. Graydon, Private Webster, and myself were the first at every gun; but oddly enough, none of us were hit. At the last gun, we had one man hit in four or five places. He was the first that got it. We then took a 24-pounder and made preparations to burst it, at the same time occupying the houses round it. (An order had been given to occupy the houses at the entrance of the lane so as to secure our retreat, which Graydon and I thought had been done. The subaltern who got the order confessed to having received it, but only said, "I did not do it.")

The big gun was burst, the small guns and mortars spiked, and we commenced our retreat, when a heavy fire was opened upon us from the houses that were ordered to be occupied. We doubled back up the lane, intending to charge the houses and nail the sepoys; but about halfway up, I got a bullet in the head, which floored me; and I fell half senseless amongst the 64th men, who ran over me, never offering to lift me up.

I said, "Lift me up, men," but got no help; and so I again said, "Lift me up, for I think I can walk." No attention was paid. I, however, contrived to get my hands onto a doorstep and stagger to my feet and walk forward a little, where I got hold of a man of my own, who took charge of me.

We got on till we caught up the leading lot, who were standing under a wall, keeping up a fire into the houses. I then saw Graydon. He was bleeding fearfully; and I thought he was badly hurt, but found it was only a scratch on his left ear. He got a few men together and charged across the lane and took possession of the lower stories of the nearest houses, the two men who had me between them carrying me over close after him. There we stood for some time. I was begging the 64th men to take possession of the upper stories; but no, they had no appetite for that sort of work.

I had two men wounded, and two men were employed looking after each wounded man, so I could not send the remaining force by themselves up to the tops of the houses. Graydon begged the other men, of the 84th, to follow him up; but no, they wouldn't do it either. Their own officer then ordered them to go up, but did not offer to lead them, so they would not stir.

I then left them and made the best of my way home, my wound quite unfitting me for any more work. I met Brigadier Inglis on my return and told him plainly that the other regiments had not backed me up. My wound kept me a month in hospital; but I was made a captain for my pains so "all's well that ends well." Except for poor Graydon, who was mortally wounded on October 27th: shot through the heart while on outlying-picket duty. The 32nd Regiment (or as the Commander in Chief called us, "the gallant remnant") was eventually reduced by casualties from 950 to 250.

Brigadier Jack Inglis, who was colonel of the regiment, wrote after the "relief": "The losses sustained by H.M.'s 32nd, which is now barely 300 strong, show at least that they knew how to die in the cause of their countrymen."

Julia Inglis, the Brigadier's wife, wrote of the action on September 29:

This affair of spiking the enemy's guns was far from being successful. Only seven guns were spiked, and our loss was most severe. Poor Captain McCabe of the 32nd was carried past our door, shot through the lungs. Mr. Edmondstoune, also of the 32nd, was slightly wounded in the head. He behaved most bravely, though—having with three of the 32nd rushed forward to spike a gun when a good many of the others fell back. He and two of the men were hit, the remaining one spiking the gun—an act worthy of the V.C. Privates Cluney and Smith of the 32nd were both killed. Two braver men never lived. Cluney had no right to be out, as he was on the sick list; but he could not resist accompanying the party, as his comrade Smith and he had been together all through the siege.

Lieutenant Fred Birch, the Brigadier's aide-de-camp also wrote:

As an example of brilliant courage, which to my mind made him one of the heroes of the siege, I must mention Private Cluney of Her Majesty's 32nd. His exploits were marvelous. He was backed by a loyal sepoy named Kundial, who simply adored him. Single-handed, and without any orders, Cluney would go outside our position; and he knew more of the enemy's movements than anyone else. It was impossible to be really angry with him. Over and over again he was put into the guardroom for disobedience of orders, and as often let out when there was fighting to be done. On one occasion, he surprised one of the enemy's batteries, into which he crawled, followed by his faithful sepoy, bayoneting four men and spiking the guns. He was often wounded, and several times left his bed to volunteer for a sortie.

Private Henry Metcalfe of the 32nd mentioned such a man: "I asked a comrade of mine one day how he was getting on. He said, 'All right.' 'Why,' said I, 'I heard you were very sick, Jim.' 'Sick be hanged, man!' said he. 'A fellow hasn't time to get sick nowadays.'"

Nothing deterred Cluney—not even this warning in the Divisional Order of 10 October 1857, forbidding anyone from going outside the pickets on any pretext: "The bodies of five men belonging to the Bengal Artillery, who had gone out (it is supposed) in search of liquor two days ago, were found without their heads."

An account of one of the sorties on September 29 was also given by Lieutenant George Blake of Her Majesty's 84th Regiment of Foot:

My company (the Grenadiers) was part of the force of 350 men under Major Simmons of the 5th Fusiliers, which was sent out about 150 yards from the Residency to capture two 18-pounders and a battery of four 9-pounders and to blow up two tall houses full of musketeers.

Just before daylight on 29th September, we left silently through a hole that was knocked in the compound wall nearest to the first battery. We were guided by Captain McCabe of the 32nd Regiment, the firing of whose pistol was to be the signal for the attack to begin.

After we had crept forward about 100 yards, bang! went the pistol. We rushed at the two guns; and in a moment they were ours, though not before the enemy had fired a round each of grape and canister from them. Luckily, we were too near and only lost three or four men.

The gunners had run to a house a little way off. Major Simmons led us to attack it, and we rushed at the door and kicked it open. Next moment, he fell back nearly onto me, shot through the left eye and quite dead. We charged on into the house and shot or bayoneted every man in it, but not before Captain McCabe had received his death wound too—one bullet shattering his right hand and another going into his heart.

The other battery was close by and was soon taken also, without losses on our side. The enemy fled into one of the houses which we were ordered to blow up. We got into it as easily as the other, looked into every hole and corner, and went to a dark narrow room where we knew most of them were hiding. We could not see them; but by throwing a grenade, we discovered by its light about twenty or thirty of them—some of whom were blown apart on the spot. They saw that they were up against it and endeavored to get away by knocking a hole with their musket butts in the wall at the end furthest from us, where a window had recently been blocked up. This settled them; as the moment the daylight was let in, our men went at them and cut them up.

I searched one of the other small rooms, accompanied by two men of the 5th Fusiliers. On our kicking open the door, bang! went a musket inside, filling all the room with smoke, so that nothing could be seen. We stayed quiet for a few seconds, not knowing how many rebels were there. When the smoke began to clear away a bit, the first thing I saw was an Oudh irregular standing in one corner, armed with a "tulwar" or curved sword and a round brass-mounted leather shield. I immediately rushed at him and made a cut at his head. He put up his tulwar to repel the blow; but my sword, being the heavier, bent it almost double and slightly wounded him on the right cheek. I then drew my blade back and gave him the point, which entered his mouth and came out at the back of his neck. The two men of the 5th soon polished off the other two rebels who were in the room.

On coming out of the house, I found another armed man hidden in the shrubbery and just cut off his head before he could make a move against me. He was so surprised that his eyes blinked and his lips quivered for a few seconds in his severed head.

We now placed two barrels of powder in the lower front room, laid and fired a train, and left the house; but on going out, we found the tops of all the surrounding houses swarming with mutineers, who also brought a 6-pounder to bear on us. Our men suffered severely, but at last the powder exploded and the house went up in the air. It took us two hours more to get back to the Residency, pinned down as we were by the enemy fire, having lost rather more than half our strength killed and wounded, but having accomplished a good deal.

Another account of the action on September 28–29, with other incidents of the siege, was given by Private Harry Metcalfe of Her Majesty's 32nd Light Infantry:

On or about the 28th or 29th September, I was one of some volunteers who were called on to storm a two-story house called Johannes's House. This was on the very border of our position, and which we stormed once before and beat the enemy out of it; but owing to our paucity of numbers, we were not able to occupy it; and the Brigadier thought that after being thrashed out of it once, the enemy would not have the cheek to occupy it again; but he was deceived. They occupied it again the same night. Those fellows who did so proved very troublesome to us; and so the Brigadier determined to make another attempt, and after taking it, to blow the place up with gunpowder.

Well, anyway, there happened to be a great tall soldier of our Grenadier Company with the storming party. There were two bamboo ladders placed by our laddermen against the two upper windows where the enemy sharpshooters were posted, and the word "Forward!" was then given. We all rushed off together; and whether me being light or small, or what, I reached one of the ladders just as the tall grenadier reached the other; and it was a race between him and me; and although I reached every rung of my ladder as soon as he reached his, still he seemed to be higher than I was; and so he was, and I never allowed for his height. However, I believe he got in at his window before I got in at mine; but when I got in, I could not see anyone in my room. Consequently, I concluded that the enemy did not wait for us, but took to their heels as soon as we rushed forward. (Those of us who broke in on the first floor didn't see anyone either, nor did those who came behind me on the ladder and then went on into the other upper rooms.)

Well, anyway, I looked round the room to see if there was anything worth laying hands on in the shape of provisions, etc.; and there was a very large box: something about or nearly resembling a large flour bin. The lid was partly up, so I threw it entirely up; and what was my astonishment to see three of our Oudhian antagonists sitting on their haunches in this big box!

Well, anyway, I shot one and bayoneted another; but the third was on me like mad; and before I knew it, he had hold of my musket by the muzzle, so that I could not use the bayonet at him. So there I was: he chopping away at me with his "tulwar" or native sword, and me defending myself the best way I could by throwing up the butt of my musket to protect my head and trying to close with him, which I knew was my only chance. In doing this, I received a chop from his sword on the left hand, which divided the knuckle and nearly cut off my thumb. Well, anyway, he had his sword raised to give me (I suppose) the final stroke, when in rushed the tall grenadier.

Tom Carroll—such was his name—took in the situation at a glance and soon put an end to my "friend" by burying the hammer of his musket in the fellow's skull; and when he saw me all covered with blood, he shouted out a great horselaugh and said, "You little swab, you were very near being done for!" And indeed so I was! I then showed him the box and its contents, and I can tell you it rather astonished him. I was laid up with my hand for a few days. Mine was one of many miraculous escapes during the siege, a few of which I will relate.

About ten o'clock one night, I was on sentry duty. It was a beautiful night, as calm as possible, with very little firing for a wonder. Just then, I saw a mortar shell being thrown from the enemy's position and going in the direction of the post of Jem, a comrade of mine; and sure enough, it did. It landed at the exact spot, exploded, and pitched him into the trench, smashed the small bottle of rum which was under his pillow (for he was lying down at the time), also tore the pillow (which was under his head) into fragments, wounded Major Lowe and one or two others, but strange to say, never hurt the chap who it pitched into the trench, except stoning him for the time being; and when he came to himself, his first inquiry was: "Is my dram of grog all right?"; and one of the officers who heard this laughed and said, "I'm afraid not, my man; but never mind—I will give you one, since that's all you care about."

You will wonder, perhaps, about me seeing the flight of a shell; but it was quite easy; for a spherical shell fired from a mortar does not attain the same velocity as the regular elongated shell; and besides, the fuse which is attached to the shell to explode it on its arrival at its destination emits sparks all the way in its flight, so that you may easily trace its direction.

Well, anyway, I paid my friend Jem a visit the following morning, when the above tale was told to me—he remarking at the time that he would never be killed after that. It would have been just as well if he had been, for the poor fellow was reserved for a more painful and lingering death. That night, as he was on sentry close to the same spot, he was hit with a roundshot which completely shattered one of his legs. Of course, the leg had to be amputated; and there being no chloroform, the poor fellow could not bear up against his sufferings and expired in great agony.

Another narrow escape from a shell—this to myself. I was one day at an outpost, accompanied by my dog (a beautiful white terrier) as usual, and also a sergeant by the name of Varney. We were looking from loopholes and taking an occasional potshot at some fellows who were employed in digging trenches at some distance from our position. Sometimes, we could only see their spades when they threw up the earth; but when a head appeared, we took a snap shot at it—usually only putting a ball through the turban, which didn't faze the wearer one bit. Well, anyway, I was just returning my musket from a loop-hole, but never shifted my position, when in came a shell, right through the loophole, and struck the wall in rear of me and exploded, knocking bricks and mortar all about the place. You may be sure I was startled, and the dog barking like mad! At last, after a lot of scratch-ing about, he found me, covered all over with bricks and mortar. I looked more like a miller than a soldier.

The officer commanding my company shouted, "Is there anyone hurt?"; and the sergeant shouted, "Yes, I think young Metcalfe is killed!"; for he thought it was impossible to escape that explosion. However, I shouted that I was all right; and when I presented myself, I looked such a picture that I was jolly well laughed at. I thought this was rather queer sympathy, but my faithful quadruped showed me plenty as far as licking and pawing went. How I escaped on that occa-sion I cannot tell. I only had a few scratches from fragments of broken bricks. I suppose the Almighty thought proper to spare me for more hardships.

I will now mention an instance of the foolhardiness of some sol-diers, and I may say, flying in the face of God. We were one day rest-ing after a very heavy night engaged in burying dead battery horses for fear of sickness arising from the stench caused by them. Well, as I was saying, we were resting, when the cry of "Turn out!" made us all start—sick, lame, and lazy—just as we were, and none too soon; for the enemy were making for our battery. We had two guns in this bat-tery, and one of these was very soon disabled by the enemy's fire. The other got knocked off the platform by a couple of well-placed shells, and we had hard work to get it right again. We had only one artillery-man with us; for I may say that the greater part of our artillerymen were either killed or wounded, so that we infantrymen had to learn to aim and load and fire the guns ourselves.

Well, anyway, the bullets were whizzing both thick and fast; and the men were ducking from them; and indeed, he must be a very self-possessed individual (or a damned fool) who will not duck his head occasionally! However, this old artilleryman—his name was Barry—rebuked the lads for ducking so to musket shots. He said you should never duck to anything under a nine-pound shot. While he was going on at this rate, a fine young grenadier was shot through the head with a musket ball.

This hardened old gunner then made remark: "Ha! that fellow has ducked to musket balls, at all events"; and he added, "If ever I am to be killed in action, I hope it will be from a cannonball—and right in the head, so that my death may be soon and sudden." And indeed, his wish was complied with—perhaps sooner than he anticipated; for the next day, and at the same hour and the same place, he was accommodated with a roundshot right in the head. I need not say his death was soon and sudden.

I may say that soldiers are callous to danger, but good-natured and generous when out of it, perhaps sometimes to a fault. We had a man by the name of Tomlinson who, when he had his allowance of grog, no one could stop his tongue from wagging—so much so that he got the sobriquet of "Chatterbox." Well, one day, after he had his allowance, he must have a look over the parapet of our earthwork to see how his friends the rebels were getting on; and to show your head was the signal to get a bullet through it. Well, anyway, this poor individual showed himself and of course received the usual "pill" in the head, which naturally put an end to his career. Upon this, his comrade remarked, "It serves you jolly well right, you confounded ass. I often told you you would be served like that before you were done, and my words have come true."

However after considering a while and contemplating the corpse of his comrade, he burst out crying and said, "Well, I am sorry, poor Jack. You were as good a comrade as ever a soldier had"; and it was hard to see this generous-hearted soldier shed tears. But so it was: from recklessness to tears and from tears back to recklessness again, and so on.

Another example of callousness in danger: I was stationed at an outpost called Sago's House, which was very near the enemy's position—so much so, indeed, that we could hear them giving and receiving orders. One day—the 10th of August, I believe—there was a severe attack commenced by their blowing up a mine under our outworks. Two of our men were blown out into the road, but were miraculously unhurt; and in the smoke and dust they escaped back into our position again.

Well, anyway, on the enemy came—very determinedly; and we had very hard work to keep them out of our defenses—so much so, that I was dispatched to Captain "Bernie" McCabe for help. I went; and he said, "Well, Metcalfe, what's the matter at Sago's?"

I said, "We are attacked, and I am afraid greatly outnumbered, and am sent to you for help."

"Well, Metcalfe," said he, "I can't afford you any help from my post. We are as bad off as yourselves. Go back and tell your officer that he must keep the post at every risk"—at the same time asking me who the officer was and, when I told him, said, "Well, I think I will go with you myself"; and indeed, that was something; for he was really a host in himself—was one of the most indefatigable officers in the garrison, and one in whom the Brigadier placed great confidence—and the men thought so much of him that they thought he was as good as twenty men. Anyway, back we ran as fast as we could.

In the meantime, our poor fellows were very hard-pressed; and on our way, we encountered one of the half-caste young men who were serving as civilian volunteers, on his knees, praying away for himself. As soon as Captain McCabe saw this, and knowing that the fellow should be helping our men, he gave the poor chap a cuff on the ear and knocked him off his knees and said, "What do you mean, you damned swab? Now is no time for praying, when the position is nearly in the hands of the rebels!"

We did not wait to see how the poor fellow took it, but scampered on and only just arrived in time. I need not say that the gallant McCabe was equal to the occasion. He had recourse to a ruse which succeeded admirably. We made such a hubbub in running to the help of our comrades, McCabe shouting as if he had a whole regiment with him, that the enemy attack stopped almost at once. He shouted "No. 1 will advance, No. 2 support, No. 3 reserve! Charge!" as loud as he could, which had the desired effect. I need not say that the enemy did not wait for the sham charge, but took to their heels.

One of the enemy's mass attacks, and other action, was described by Lieutenant Harry Delafosse, a regimental staff officer of Her Majesty's 5th Fusiliers:

On the 6th of October, there was a mine sprung by the enemy at a mosque near our quarters; and a simultaneous and persevering attack was made upon us from every direction. They swarmed everywhere, and you heard them yelling out defiance and abuse.

I was the only staff officer at the time at regimental headquarters, and so I accompanied a detail of twenty men ordered out to assist in repelling the attack. I had a house to keep, or rather the ground floor of a house, on a level with the garden where the attackers were swarming and yelling horribly. I stationed men at the iron-barred windows, concealing them as much as possible, and kept others right and left of some small doors through which I expected the enemy would try to effect an entrance.

We shot several men as they came rushing into the garden with drawn swords, muskets, and matchlocks, hallooing out, "Maro! maro! Chelo! chelo!" (Kill! kill! Come on! come on!) They gave me very much the idea of men intoxicated with bhang; for they seemed to come on without any definite design and rushed madly about, apparently unconscious where they were going to. They came within a few yards of us, and so excited were my men that they missed many even at that distance. Some Sikhs who were in the house with me were much cooler and more collected and did not throw away their fire near so much.

After some time, the enemy managed to get into the rooms above us by means of ladders; and before our men in another part of the garden (and in an exposed position) were aware of it, they opened a fire upon them, wounding many men.

Captain Scott, who was our new commanding officer after Major Simmons was shot through the head and killed during a sortie on the 29th of September, and who had joined another party of his men, was among the wounded and had gone to the hospital. So I now withdrew my men, having first seen that my part of the garden was cleared, and assisted in driving the enemy from the upper rooms. They fought us from room to room and from one corridor to another, and we made our way over the corpses of the killed. It was wretched fighting. In one small room, we shot and bayoneted no less than eight.

This kind of fighting went on till dark; and we then found our outlying picket near the mosque (from which they had been driven in the morning by the mine) leaving the enemy, I am sorry to say, in possession. From this place they kept up a fire upon our picket; and any man exposing himself at the windows, even though behind the wooden blinds, was nearly sure to be shot. Two men in the 90th Regiment, who would foolishly expose themselves, were shot close by me. One died instantly.

We were very busy now in the trenches, countermining and mining the enemy, and the 5th provided their quota of working parties.

The enemy were capital miners, and if not carefully watched, could do us an immensity of harm. In that explosion on the 6th, they blew up two of our poor fellows and buried them in the ruins, besides wounding others.

On the 11th of October, we retook the mosque—seven men wounded in the affair. As I was walking with another officer to the picket garden, a shell burst over us, scattering its pieces close by, but providentially doing us no hurt. Such escapes were quite common in the garrison. The night before, an officer while asleep had his pillow cut in two by a roundshot which came in at his window without doing anybody any harm. We were frequently disturbed by shells bursting in and near our quarters; and roundshot came tearing through the upper lookout rooms morning, noon, and night. The bullets were like swarms of bees.

On the 17th of October, the enemy sprang a mine in our in-lying-picket garden and blew in our gate, and then a second at the mosque, blowing up two unfortunate sentries in the Madras Fusiliers and one Sikh, besides wounding three or four more Sikhs. One of the Sikhs had both his arms amputated immediately afterwards, but he died eventually. Seldom a day passed without some men being killed or wounded, to say nothing of sickness, and in two months we lost a fourth of our relief force and a sixth of the total garrison.

It was melancholy seeing men drop off one by one. Slowly but surely, bad food and want of hospital supplies did their work; and you watched men who were at first but slightly wounded waste away inch by inch under a diet hardly sufficient for a child. Major Stephenson of the Madras Fusiliers, for one, was struck by a musket ball which had previously gone through a door. The shot, though nearly spent, hit him high up in the pit of the stomachs but did not break the skin. Unfavorable symptoms speedily set in, however, and the wound—or rather contusion—sloughed away in a shocking manner until he died.

But as for the danger and discomfort, we got quite accustomed to this rough-and-ready kind of life; and were it not for the fear of our provisions falling short, we should not have vexed ourselves about the delay of the reinforcements that our native spies assured us were coming to our relief.

Had the siege lasted longer than it did, we must have devoured the hundreds of dead rebels, horses, camels, bullocks, and other animals that were lying about—to say nothing of rats and dogs—as well as our own live horses, which by the 1st of November were without grain and with little grass and were commencing to starve to death. As it was, we were already slaughtering and eating our artillery bullocks; and the commissariat camels would be next. We had enough coarse fare till the 1st of December; but the stench was so great and the flies so pestilent that we could scarcely sit and eat, and what we did eat was often purged out of us by diarrhea.

And our appearance suited our condition. We came in light marching order, with nothing but what we had on our backs; and we had to keep patching these rags with whatever other rags we could find, till they were no longer patchable, and then had to make use of the wall hangings and furniture and floor coverings of all kinds of colors and patterns—and even the baize billiard-table covers—that we found in the houses and palaces, without much attention to buttons or quality of stitching or fit, so that we looked like a lot of grotesque harlequins.

On the 2nd of November, I had a narrow escape of being shot which seemed more memorable than the others. I was behind a Venetian door in a turret of one of our buildings with Captain Grant of the Madras Fusiliers, shooting at the rebels on the top of a sand-bagged and loopholed house, from which they were keeping up a hot fire on our picket. While we were firing, they sent in several bullets, stinging us with the splinters from the door. Grant had only just picked out some of them from my neck, and was on the point of taking a shot, when he threw down his rifle and said, "I'm shot!" I took him downstairs and laid him down till the doctor came who extracted the bullet and dressed his wound, which was a serious one. But he survived it.

Captain Frank Maude, R.A., added:

On our entry into the Residency, Ned Grant and his company of the Madras Fusiliers were put in charge of one of the most important posts; and he held it with great gallantry, although it was once mined and blown up by the rebels. However, Grant came down on his feet none the worse for it; and after the engineers had put the post into some little repair, he returned to it.

Besides being blown up, he was seriously wounded. A musket ball passed clean through his body, grazing and slightly injuring his liver.

But that too he survived, though the doctors thought he was a "goner."

He used to go out every morning—"sniping," as he called it—carrying an Enfield rifle, with an ample supply of cartridges slung over his shoulder in a game net, in the most approved sportsmanlike style. He kept a regular "game book," in which he noted his daily "bag"; and believe me, it was quite full. He rarely missed bringing down his quarry.

I should add that Grant's recovery was all the more remarkable because the condition of the wounded was deplorable in the extreme. Hospital gangrene and blood poisoning were the rule, and an escape from one or the other of them was very rare. I believe that only one case of amputation resulted in a recovery. There were no medicines, no chloroform, no wine or spirits, no comforts of any kind, no clean rags even to dress wounds. The patients were crowded to suffocation—sick and wounded alike—like sardines in a tin, covered with blood and vomit and vermin, crying for water and groaning in agony, with blood and excreta all over the walls and floor, and amputated arms and legs lying about in heaps, covered with swarms of flies. It had to be seen to be believed.

Maude also added, in regard to the fortitude that kept the garrison defiant of all odds:

I never saw General Outram's equal for coolness. On one occasion, when the enemy had got our exact range, I saw him walk calmly up to one of our guns and say to the "number" in charge of the portfire, "Oblige me with a light for my cigar," taking no notice of the roundshot that were whizzing past. And when the gun was fired, while others turned away and held their ears, he didn't move a muscle, but calmly walked away covered with smoke and powder.

On another occasion, while he was sitting in a corner of his room, smoking and conversing with me, a 24-pound roundshot came flying in and struck the wall about two yards above his head, covering him with plaster and brick dust. But calmly brushing himself off, he continued the conversation as if nothing had occurred, refusing to move. And yet take the case of Lieutenant Dashwood of the 48th Native Infantry, who lost both his legs by a roundshot while sketching in the Residency compound. He had been warned by a first shot passing near him, but he would not stir.

Dr. Joseph Fayrer, the Residency surgeon, also observed that Outram was "utterly indifferent to fire. I was with him in many places where it was hot, but he took not the slightest notice of it. And yet others who were constantly under heavy fire, and were as brave as men need be, could not help ducking as the shot flew over them."

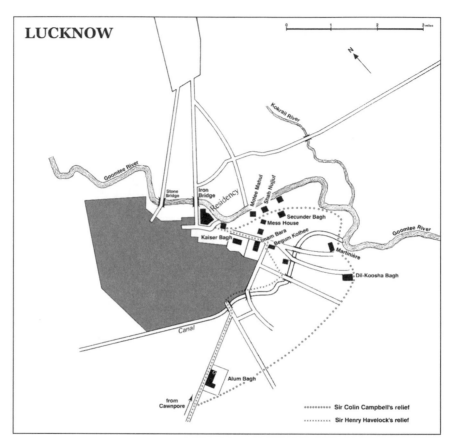

This map depicts the different routes taken by the Lucknow relief columns in the fall of 1857. On September 25, Henry Havelock's column suffered horrendous casualties and was forced to abandon many of its wounded after fighting through the built-up area of the city. On November 19, Colin Campbell, having been fore-warned, skirted the river and reached the Residency at less cost. Campbell dropped off troops to hold strongpoints along his route and was thus able to bring out the British women and children.

6

PLUCKY WEE BOBS IS DONE FOR!

At last, on November 16, the new Commander in Chief in British India—Lieutenant General Sir Colin Campbell—came to the rescue with little more than forty-five hundred men and thirty-five guns, including a detachment of the Royal Navy, enlisted from the troopships at Calcutta. But rescue was all it was.

"I am here with a very weak force," Campbell informed General Outram by an Indian messenger, "deficient in all essentials. I have not ammunition for more than three days' firing, but I have come to relieve the garrison. I have not means to attempt anything more, and I shall be thankful to effect this."

Knowing that Outram and Havelock had suffered severely in forcing their way through the closely fortified part of Lucknow, and also knowing that the enemy expected him to come the same way, Campbell took advantage of the favorable weather and dry terrain by making the detour or circuitous march that his predecessors could not and by approaching the city at its northeast corner, less than two miles from the Residency compound, then battering and storming the enemy's obstructive defenses between there and the besieged position with a hundred and sixty-three fewer casualties. And by establishing guard posts along the way, he made a cordon or corridor through which the garrison could be withdrawn to safety.

The garrison, of course, did its utmost to cooperate with Campbell's offensive. As soon as definite word of his advance was received and the sound of his heavy guns was heard south of the city, several days and nights were spent in placing batteries and mines for breaching the buildings intended to be stormed by the garrison.

At the time agreed upon—twelve noon on November 15—all the men that could be spared from the defenses were assembled and *formed into three columns of attack; and after two and a half hours of cannonading, the mines were exploded and the "advance" sounded. The three assault columns rushed out with a cheer to the several points of attack; the buildings were soon in their possession, which considerably shortened the route that Campbell had to take to reach them; and they shook hands with their rescuers in the afternoon of the seventeenth.*

The speed with which their objectives were taken was due more to the effectiveness of the bombardment than that of the undermining. Captain Maude and his men of the Royal Artillery, for instance, "worked a powerful battery of six 8-inch mortars"; and their shells "did fearful execution among the crowded masses of fleeing rebels in the courtyards of the royal palaces. On one occasion," Maude observed, "no less than thirteen of them were killed by the explosion of one of our mortar shells."

At least one of the mines exploded short of its target, and two others made insufficient breaches, so that scaling ladders and some fierce hand-to-hand combat were necessary to drive the enemy out of those positions that the artillery could not thoroughly clear. The struggle that took place in the Hurrin-Khanah Bagh or "Deer-Dwelling Garden," a large park enclosure directly across from the main palace and stronghold, was described by Lieutenant and Adjutant John Gordon (formerly General Neill's aide-de-camp) of the Ferozepore Regiment of Sikh Infantry:

Two breaches were to have been made in the walls; but one of the mines blew up about twenty yards short, so that the wing of our column destined for that point had to use their ladders; while we had only to scramble up the debris of the breach, encountering no opposition till we got inside. The other wing, meanwhile, had a rough go of it for a while, as their ladders were too short. (The walls were built higher than usual to keep in the deer that once roamed there.) By hugging the wall, however, they avoided much of the enemy fire, as the loopholes weren't large enough for the defenders to take aim at such an angle and the parapet was too high for them to fire over it; so they had to hold their muskets all the way out and fire down at random, which exposed them to having their hands and forearms wounded and soon put an end to their efforts on that side. And seeing them withdraw, our men joined us through the breach.

Immediately on jumping down into the enclosure, I had the satisfaction of seeing three men rushing at me with a yell. The first—a big and tall fellow, evidently excited almost to delirium by bhang—raised his sword and made a backhanded slash that must have sliced my head off had I not been able to parry the blow just in time. My heavy cavalry sword stood well, though a deep notch was made in the steel. However, my opponent being a bigger and stronger man than myself, my blade was beaten down before I could give point; and I got a slight cut in the lower part of my left cheek. But the force of the blow threw him off guard, and I now had my turn and immediately gave him a chop on the head that cracked his skull but did not split him down to the shoulders as I had expected—the skull being a very tough article, especially when protected by several thick folds of turban cloth. Anyway, at the same moment, one of our Sikhs bayoneted him in the back; and Captain Brasyer, our commander, ran him through the left side and finished him off.

I must say that Brasyer seemed to be everywhere at once, laying about him with his scimitar; and wherever there was action, his big red turban and flowing white beard and flashing sword were always conspicuous. At the same time he made a thrust at my opponent, a fallen rebel swordsman had enough strength to cut through his right boot and sock and make a mark on his instep before he was beheaded by Brasyer's Sikh orderly.

It was then that I got two more slight sword cuts—one just above the left wrist and the other across my left hip, just below the bone—made by a sword glancing off a Sikh's rifle barrel. The fellow who did it was immediately bayoneted in the throat; and a second later, another swordsman (a rather short little fellow) rushed at me and dealt a furious blow at my head. But being much taller, I easily parried it and gave him a gash across the neck and down the left shoulder; and he fell on his face to rise no more, for a dozen Sikh bayonets were stuck into him at once.

A number of Her Majesty's 84th then came in; and after a little more hand-to-hand fighting, the rebels were all shot down or bayoneted—except for about a dozen, who were hiding in one of the gardenhouses. Brasyer ordered several of our men to blow open the door and window shutters, which they did by firing at the hinges and latch. He then kicked the door down and attempted to enter, but got a clip on the head from the sword of a man who was concealed behind the doorway. Only the thick folds of his turban saved him from all but a momentarily stunning blow. He had made this sort of rash move before, and I suppose he thought he could do it again, only the first time he was armed with a hogspear.

It was after we had run the rebels out of Futtehpore, while on our march upcountry to Cawnpore. There was this shed that one of our native spies said was full of enemy fugitives. Brasyer ordered several of our men to blow the bolt and hinges off the door with their rifles. He then kicked it in and discovered a squad of eleven rebel swordsmen, who immediately attempted to attack him. But he stepped back a couple of paces; and as the first fellow appeared in the doorway, he met him with a fatal spear thrust, which forced him back into those behind him. And as each of these men tried to come through the doorway, which was so narrow that it impeded the immediate use of his sword, he was met with the same reception—until eleven dead and dying rebels were lying in a heap on the floor.

Anyway, Brasyer was lucky to get off with only a sore head this time; and as he stepped back from the doorway, I just as foolishly stepped forward and presented my double-barreled horse pistol at the rebel's breast when he half showed himself. But damn me if both barrels didn't misfire! So I got out of that doorway as fast as I could and then tried looking into the nearest window, and very nearly got a clip on the head myself. That was when Brasyer ordered a platoon of our men to rush inside, and such a clamor you never heard before. Those of the enemy who weren't taken at once came rushing madly out, swords in hand, and a furious melee ensued. They were fighting against overwhelming odds; but they were fighting for their lives, which they sold dearly.

One banged-up fellow, when his sword hand was lopped off by one of our "jemadars" or subalterns, lunged at him, snarling like a tiger, and actually sank his teeth into the jemadar's jaw. And when the jemadar dashed the hilt of his sword into the fellow's head, the fellow let loose all right, but then immediately sank his teeth in the jemadar's throat. Only several bayonet thrusts in the sides and back could get him loose; and an expanding or "man-stopping" Minié ball in the head ended the poor devil's suffering by shattering his skull and scattering his brains all over the place.

Another fellow came rushing right onto the point of my sword without even looking. A Sikh then got a chop at him from behind, laying his whole back open, and I then withdrew my blade and gave him such a swinging backhander that he fell dead with his head nearly severed from his body.

I then went at another fellow who was rushing by my left and thrust my sword through him nearly to the hilt and dropped him. I then looked round and saw a sword coming down on the left shoulder of one of our men, giving him a nasty cut right through his thick leather shoulder strap; and up went the sword again, and the next moment our follow might have been in eternity; but I ran forward and covered him with my sword and saved him by a cut and thrust.

The scuffle was now over, and we had polished off the last of the rebels—or so we thought. Two armed and dangerous women were still on one of the ramparts—firing pieces of telegraph wire at us, which inflicted nasty wounds, and defying us to come and get them. Well, none of us Europeans cared to take them on; but our Sikhs were game. They wanted satisfaction for the atrocities committed by such women against their own women, such as cutting off their noses and breasts: punishments commonly inflicted on adulteresses. But they had no intention of demeaning themselves by engaging in single combat with these "tiger-women." So first they shot them down, then they cut them up with their scimitars. Now you may think this rather savage; but such was the kind of war we were engaged in, and there was no help for it. And it was no worse than what these women had done to others who fell into their hands. Also, you must remember that the same kind of savagery was practiced during our own civil wars in Great Britain, when women and children were mutilated and massacred and traitors were tortured to death, drawn and quartered, and decapitated. So our Sikh friends were only a century behind us in their observance of the ancient law of retaliation.

But now to the movements of the Lucknow Relief force, as recounted first by Lieutenant and Adjutant Hugh Gough, who commanded a 180-man squadron of Hodson's Native Irregular Horse:

On November 12th, our whole force under Sir Colin Campbell marched from our base camp to the Alum Bagh or "Garden of Beauty" about six miles away. This high-walled estate was about a mile and three quarters south of Lucknow and was Havelock's base of operations. I, with my squadron, had the post of honor with the advance guard. It was not expected we should meet with opposition, as several hundred of Havelock's troops still held the Alum Bagh; but suddenly, as our column was advancing up the road, an attack developed itself on the right flank, where a body of the enemy (which we calculated at about two thousand strong, with two guns) had taken up a position. As these guns were troublesome, Brigadier Sir Hope Grant (who was commanding the advance) rode up to me and desired me to take my squadron and see if I could capture the guns.

With my small body of men, my only chance of success was by making a surprise flank attack; so I made a considerable detour under cover of some fields of tall corn and sugar cane and managed to arrive on the left flank of the enemy perfectly unseen. The guns were posted on a small mound; and a considerable body of the enemy had an admirable position in rear of this mound, in front of and amidst some trees and scrub. Between us and them lay a strip of marshland with long reedy grass: an unpleasant obstacle, but which served admirably to cover our movements.

I then advanced my men through this at a trot, and so concealed our movements till we got clear, when I gave the words "Form line!" and "Draw swords!" and then "Charge!" My men gave a ringing cheer, and we were into the masses of the enemy at once. The surprise was complete; and owing to its suddenness, they had no conception of our numbers; and so the shock to them and victory to us was as if we had been a whole brigade.

My charger, "Tearaway," carried me like a bird; and I soon found myself well ahead. I had to make a lane for myself as I rode along, and it seemed like cutting one's way through a field of corn as I swung my sword to right and left. The men followed me splendidly, wielding their blades with deadly effect; and in a very short time, the affair was over. The guns were captured, the enemy scattered, and the fight became a pursuit.

Our loss was very trifling, as is often the case in a sudden surprise; but we cut up numbers of the enemy, and should have accounted for more but for the nature of the ground. I came out of the fight untouched, and this I attribute to the pace I went; but my good horse suffered, having a saber slash over his left quarter and another saber wound on his right foreleg while my coatskirt was cut clean through and the turban which was wrapped round my forage cap was cut almost to the last fold, but by its thickness undoubtedly saved my head. Sir Colin Campbell, who witnessed the charge, got me a V.C. for it.

With regard to my horse's wounds, I should say that some of the enemy were as lithe and active as cats when pursued by our cavalry. They used to fling themselves flat on the ground; and then, as the horses jumped over or passed close to them, they would make an upward cut with their razor-edged "tulwars" or scimitars, which seldom failed to take effect, either upon the horses or their riders. Lieutenant Wilkin of the 7th Hussars, who had survived the charge of the Light Brigade at Balaclava, was lamed for life in this manner—the tulwar slicing clean through his boot and deep into the ball of his foot. Several others received similar wounds, including one of my own "sowars" or troopers. The rebel, lying on his back, had little or no room for his blow, yet he cut through four or five folds of thick leather and inflicted a wound that disabled the sowar for a month.

I mention these as instances of the extreme keenness of common India sword. But without a doubt, a horse is a great protection to the rider, especially from missiles coming from the the direct front; and life often depends on being well mounted, especially when you have to maneuver in a melee. But even the best of horses cannot always avoid every obstacle in a charge, and the worst of these for us were the numerous irrigation wells that were scattered over the fields. These unwalled or "blind" wells could not be seen until you were almost on top of them, and a number or horses and men went into them.

Lieutenant Younghusband, who commanded a squadron of the 5th Punjab Cavalry, was one of them; and he was quickly followed by two of his sowars. The well, though fifty feet deep, was almost dry; but the fall itself and the shock of the others falling on him must have been awful; yet, strange to say, he was taken out terribly bruised but alive: the sole survivor of the men and horses that went down. He had fallen to the bottom in a sitting position, with his back resting against the side of the well and his legs stretched out in front of him, while his horse fell standing and across him. He was thus protected from the weight of the other two horses and their riders. But fate can be fickle, and he was later shot through the lungs and killed by a rebel who was lying concealed in some tall grass.

Captain Hutchinson of the 9th Lancers, while charging at the head of his troop, also rode into one of these wells. A trooper followed; and then the horse of another trooper, after luckily throwing his rider in a vain attempt to avoid the obstacle, also descended. This well was between forty and fifty feet deep, but contained at least eight or ten feet of water; yet Hutchinson believed that he did not touch the bottom, which was a wonder in itself; for these unbricked wells are often shaped like the frustum of a cone—the diameter at the bottom being two or three tines as great as the diameter at the top—because the sides, trough perpendicular when the well is dug, are gradually eaten away below by the water. Although the three horses perished, Hutchinson and his trooper escaped almost without a bruise and were taken out with ropes. But fate treated Hutchinson the same as Younghusband, for he was later struck in the left eye and killed by an arrow that was shot by a female rebel who was concealed behind a mound but immediately lanced to death by several of the captain's men.

At another time, Lieutenant Evans of the Lancers went tumbling headlong—horse and all—into a well that was some fourteen or fifteen feet deep. Fortunately, the horse went down hindlegs foremost or else the rider must have been killed outright or suffocated to death. So there he was, sitting on his poor dead animal, when his comrades came with ropes and lifted him up. He was not hurt in the least, and fate favored him thereafter.

Camp was pitched outside the Alum Bagh in the evening of November 12; and two days later, after a running fight of about two hours, the rebels were driven from their outposts and across the canal. The way was now open for the final offensive. During this action on the fourteenth, according to Lieutenant Frederick Roberts (later Field Marshal Lord Roberts) of the General Staff, Lieutenant John Watson (commanding a squadron of the 1st Punjab Native Cavalry) greatly distinguished himself:

Entirely alone, while making a reconnaissance, he was challenged by the enemy's cavalry. Now Watson wasn't one to consider the odds when his honor was at stake, so he attacked the enemy's cavalry and was at once engaged with its leader and six of the front men. He fought gallantly; but the unequal contest could not have lasted much longer had not Lieutenant Probyn of the 2nd Punjab Cavalry, who was only about three hundred yards off, become aware of his comrade's critical position and dashed to his assistance with his own and

Watson's squadrons. Despite the odds, Watson merely received a cut on the face from a saber; but seeing it, one of the 2nd Punjab cavalrymen rushed to Probyn and said, "Watson Sahib has got a wound which is worth a lakh of rupees!"—that is, a hundred thousand. (That was a sight better than what was said of another poor officer: that he was "divided like a rupee"—that is, hacked into sixteen parts, there being that number of annas in a rupee.)

Watson, who was a master swordsman, managed to cut down the rebel leader and several others before he was assisted; but he had another narrow escape when the leader discharged his pistol at him within a few feet of his body, missing him by a hair. He was awarded the V.C. for his valor.

On the following afternoon, the enemy made a slight demonstration on the right, but were speedily driven back across the canal. They then opened fire with a 12-pounder howitzer, when a really most extraordinary incident happened. A shell—fortunately a "blind" one—came into Watson's squadron, which was drawn up behind an embankment. It struck a trooper's saddle in front, and must have lifted the man partly out of it; for it passed between one of his thighs and the horse, tearing the saddle to shreds and sending one piece of it high into the air. The horse was knocked down, but not hurt; the man's thigh was only badly bruised, and he was able to ride again in a few days.

When I told the story to Captain Sam Browne of the 2nd Punjab Cavalry, he said that something similar happened during the Sikh War in 1846. One of the men of a troop of horse artillery had his saddle completely carried away from under him by a small roundshot. The man, who happened at the moment to be standing up in his stirrups, escaped with only a bruise, as did the horse. But on the day of which I am speaking, Captain Wheatcroft and trooper Waite of the 9th Lancers were not so lucky. Wheatcroft's chest was torn open by a bombshell, and Waite's head was blown off by a roundshot. And another roundshot went through the chest and out the back of Lieutenant Mayne of the Bengal Artillery; but despite the impact and the fall from his horse, he was still wearing his monocle when found lying face up on the ground. He too had been reconnoitering: a deadly duty.

Corporal William Mitchell of Her Majesty's 93rd Highlanders described some of the infantry and artillery action that occurred on the fourteenth:

The only really complete regiment of the Lucknow Relief Force was my own, the 93rd Sutherland Highlanders, consisting of ten companies numbering a little over a thousand men, about seven hundred of whom were veterans of the Crimean War and had formed the famous "thin red line" at Balaclava, which repulsed a large force of elite Russian cavalry with only one volley. Together with the 53rd Light Infantry and the 4th Punjab Infantry, we were part of the 4th Infantry Brigade under Colonel the Honorable Adrian Hope of the 93rd as Brigadier.

Upon reviewing us, General Sir Colin Campbell (our old Crimean Highland Brigade chief) cautioned us that we had "harder work and greater dangers" before us than any we encountered in the Crimea—not only because we had to rescue women and children from certain death, but because we had to confront an enemy who was well armed and desperate. "So when we make an attack," he said, "you must come to close quarters as quickly as possible, keep well together, and use the bayonet. 93rd, you are my own lads! I rely on you to do the work!"

A voice from the ranks then called out: "Aye-aye, sir Colin! We'll bring the women and children out of Lucknow or die with you in the attempt!"

While we were halted outside the Alum Bagh, my company and No. 8 were in a field of beautiful carrots, which the men were pulling up and eating raw. I remember a young lad not turned twenty—Kenneth Mackenzie by name, of No. 8 Company—making a remark that these might be the last carrots most of us would get; and with that he asked the color sergeant of his company, who belonged to the same place as himself, to write to his mother should anything happen to him. The color sergeant of course promised to do so, telling young Mackenzie not to let such gloomy thoughts enter his mind. How prophetic they would soon be for him!

Leaving 350 men to guard our camp and communications, we commenced our advance from the Alum Bagh by daybreak on the 14th of November; and a young staff officer galloped to the front to reconnoiter. This was Lieutenant Fred Roberts of the Bengal Artillery and Deputy Assistant Quartermaster General, familiarly known among us as "Plucky Wee Bobs" because he was a regular "banty" or gamecock. About half of the regiment were forming into line right and left on the two center companies when we noticed him halt and wheel round to return, signaling to the horse artillery to advance; and immediately a masked battery of six 9-pounder guns opened fire on us, one by one, from a clump of trees ahead. The first roundshot passed harmlessly through our lines with that peculiar "whish" which, when once heard, was never forgotten; but the second shot struck Lieutenant Roberts's charger just behind the saddle, tearing the horse in two—both horse and rider falling in a confused heap amidst the dust where the shot struck ground after passing through the horse's loins.

Some of the men exclaimed, "Plucky wee Bobs is done for!"

The same shot ricocheted at almost a right angle and in its course struck poor young Private Kenneth Mackenzie on the right side of his head, taking the skull clean off just level with his ears. He fell right in front of me, and I had to step over his body before a single drop of blood had time to flow.

The color sergeant of his company turned to me and said, "Poor lad! How can I tell his poor mother? What would she think if she were to see him now? He was her favorite laddie!"

There was no leisure for moralizing, however. We were completely within the range of the enemy's guns; and the next shot cut down seven or eight of the Light Company, sending the severed left arm of one man smack into the face of the one behind him; and old Colonel Leith Hay was calling out: "Keep steady, men! Close up the ranks, and don't waver in face of a battery manned by cowardly traitors!"

The shots were now coming thick and fast, bounding along the hard ground; and Lieutenant and Adjutant "Willie" Macbean was behind the line, telling the men in an undertone, "Don't mind the Colonel. Open out and let them through"—meaning the shot. "Keep plenty of room and watch the shot."

By this time, Lieutenant Roberts—bruised and bloodied but still very much alive—had got clear of his dead horse; and the 93rd, seeing him on his feet again, gave him a rousing cheer. Captain Dalzell, with about half a dozen men of the Light Company, had rushed out of line to assist him; but he was too quick for them. I should add that only a minute or so before, the horse of a sowar of the 1st Punjab Cavalry who accompanied him as orderly was torn apart in almost the same way; whereupon Roberts coolly dismounted within close range of the

9-pounders and helped the sowar get out from under his dead horse. (About a month earlier, while Roberts was reconnoitering, this same orderly had another horse knocked over by a round of grapeshot; and Roberts himself was slightly wounded in the face, literally having a "close shave.")

Anyway, Roberts was soon in the saddle of a spare horse; and the horse artillery dashed to the front under his direction, taking the guns of the enemy in flank, and the rebel gunners bolted for shelter.

The 93rd had lost ten men killed and wounded by the time we had driven the enemy and their guns through the long grass by the canal, across the ford, and into their entrenchments on the other side. That cleared the way on our side of the canal. The next day was occupied in diversionary skirmishing on the left, to make our enemy think that we would be making our final move by the old route rather than by a wide sweep round to the right.

Some of this action was described by Ensign Charles Devereaux of the 5th Fusiliers:

We Fusiliers were ordered to make a diversionary movement to the left, to turn the enemy's attention from our real point of attack; and when we neared the canal, we came under fire of some of their heavy guns on the other side and had to hug the ground for a short time. This was my "baptism of fire"; but I soon got accustomed to the whistling of bullets and shells, which on first acquaintance was very disagreeable. One thing I never got accustomed to, though, was that so far as officers were concerned, it was considered ungentlemanly if not cowardly to duck or otherwise dodge an approaching round-shot—although it was perfectly proper to hit the ground when a shell exploded. Another thing, too, is that the mesmeric effect of an oncoming missile is fatally common. Many a man has watched one come at him until it is too late, not thinking that it will actually hit him, or has riveted his eyes on it with a fatal fascination.

Anyhow, one of the enemy's shots struck about three feet from the place where two other officers and I were lying. We just saw it in the air for a second; and seeing it was coming in our direction, by Jove how we burrowed down in the sand! I unwittingly shoved my head—nose, mouth, and all—into something very unpleasant that a cow had recently left behind, when all at once we heard a loud rushing and then felt the sand thrown all over us from where the shot had struck. We then knew it was past and jumped up. I looked at one of my fellow officers and he at me, and such objects we must have appeared that we both burst out laughing. But then watching the shot as it went ricocheting along, we saw it at the third bounce hit a poor unwary native forager of ours and break both his legs.

We were then thrown forward in skirmishing order; and as we advanced, our men loading and firing all the while, one of our gun elephants came charging through our line with the lower half of his trunk hanging by a strip of skin to the other half above it. This had been done by a roundshot, and the poor beast was trumpeting loudly from pain as he passed us and plunged headlong into the canal. Somehow he survived the crossfire, though, and we managed to recover him. He was given a heavy dose of morphia and the lower half of his trunk was surgically removed, and I'm glad to say he got on quite satisfactorily—his "mahout" or native keeper feeding him by hand and taking him daily into deep water to drink. He was the second of our elephants to lose his trunk by a roundshot; while others had their skulls smashed and were disemboweled, and one was drilled clean through from his chest to his hindquarters. (One of our staff officer's horses was hit in this manner—only from the rear—while taking his rider back from a reconnaissance at full gallop, which gave him a nasty tumble; and it was amazing how many chance shots like this hit with such deadly accuracy when you happened to be in the line of fire.)

We then moved on, after delivering a parting volley of Minié balls, and encountered some fierce opposition at a village that we had to clear before we could cross the canal. The men of my company rushed against the door of a house from which a sharp fire proceeded and found a whole lot of fellows in it. They defended themselves with their "tulwars" or native swords; but of little avail were they against an infuriated British soldier's bayonet, the blade of which measured between sixteen and twenty-six inches in length (depending on the make and model) and was of various widths and either straight or curved—the thin triangular blade or "poker" being the narrowest and the thick sword bayonet or "ripper" the widest. In whatever size and shape, they did their work; and fifteen of the rebels met their death in that one house.

By this time, other men of our force had spread through the rest of the village, lighting the thatching of the houses and so burning the rebels out. You would see the muzzle of a firearm shoved through a loophole, taking deliberate aim at you, and have just time to bob; and smack!—a bullet would go into the opposite wall. Our men performed wonders, climbing walls like cats and going in through the roofs, or watching a loophole for a long time till a head would show itself; and then bang! and you would hear a yell, telling how truly the bullet had carried out its owner's intention. But once a house was in flames, out came the occupants; and it was like shooting down game on the run. I'm sorry to say that some unarmed and perhaps innocent people were potted in this way, but there was no telling who was what in the heat of the moment when even women and children were shooting at us.

There was one house, surrounded by a high wall, that we Fusiliers knew was full of rebels by the fire they poured into us, and which we lit; but no rebel could we drive out. They all preferred to roast to death than face our bullets and bayonets, or perhaps they ended their own existence by shooting each other before the smoke and flames could finish them. One poor fellow, though, finally came running out with his head on fire and his flesh hanging like strips of charred meat from his bones; but a volley from some of us soon put him out of his misery.

In the courtyard was a large pile of loose straw, which I told a sergeant to light up. He had scarcely done so when up jumped a sepoy and tried to bolt past me, cutting at random with his tulwar. I had him, though, and sent my sword clean through him, pinning him to the wall. Thus was my maiden blade christened with sepoy blood, and I was so pleased at the time that I didn't bother to wipe it off and so spoil a good handkerchief. We found nine more in the straw, and such hacking and stabbing and clubbing you never saw before. It was like butcher's work, but it couldn't be helped. And we all looked like butchers when it was over—bloodied from head to foot—so it was well that we were wearing our red winter jackets and black trousers and shakos, as our summer whites would have looked even worse.

The village being in flames on all sides, most of the remaining rebels fled to the top floor of a small fort, where they intended to make a last stand. But a plucky Sikh of ours threw a firebrand on the roof and lit it and drove these fellows down into a dark room below, where they made a determined stand with their tulwars. I fired my revolver into the room; and then three other young officers and I rushed in, followed by the men. We never counted the dead bodies inside that dark room; but the bayonet and sword did their work, and no sepoy lived to tell the tale. Several tried to bolt from the village across the plain, but some of our 9th Lancers tore after them and cut—or rather skewered—them down.

The wells were choked with corpses—the Sikhs having pitched many of the slain on top of those who had jumped into them to escape their fury, thus burying them alive. It was extraordinary, the number of people on both sides who jumped, fell, or were thrown into wells during the Mutiny. Wells were convenient places of refuge, suicide, and mass burial; but they were also pitfalls, and some of our men stumbled into them while drunk or on night picket. That accounted for most of our missing, I suppose.

With the fight over, when I took the "pugree" or turban cover off my shako to wipe my face, I found a bullet had ripped clean through it and I never knew it.

I heard a lot said about the range and accuracy of the new Enfield rifle, but the old Minié was still a most wonderful weapon in the hands of a good shot. Though not as accurate as the Enfield, it was more effective at long range; and its higher caliber and "man-stopping" or expanding bullet made it a killing weapon, whereas the Enfield was more of a wounder. Anyhow, there was one cheeky "sowar" or rebel cavalryman who came prancing along at least eight hundred yards off, quite by himself. One of our men took a steady aim at him and fired; and a few seconds after, we saw him fall from his saddle and his horse gallop away, dragging him by a stirrup. Thus, while the Enfield was sighted for half a mile, it was fatal only at a quarter of a mile; whereas the Minié not only carried farther than the Enfield, but was fatal at almost twice the distance. The difference in caliber was .577-inch as compared with .702.

Various estimates were given of the effective range of the Enfield as compared with the Minié. The two models of Minié then in use were sighted up to 900 and 1,000 yards respectively, but were variously said to be "effective" up to 400, 600, and 1,000 yards, and "dangerous" up to 1,500 yards. The three models of Enfield were sighted up to 800, 900, and 1,000 yards, but were said to be "effective" up to 1,200 yards, "accurate" or "deadly" up to 800 yards or half a mile with a Minié ball, and "deadly" at 250 yards with an Enfield ball. Of course, many factors affected range and accur-

acy—weather conditions, the type and condition of cartridge, the condition of the rifle, the skill of the rifleman, etc.—but it was the "man-stopping" quality of the Minié that made it more desirable than the Enfield, even when a smaller-caliber Minié-type bullet was used. (Incidentally, it was Captain James Burton of the U.S. Arsenal at Harper's Ferry, Virginia, who redesigned and improved the original Enfield of 1853 and the Minié-type bullet for it; and he supervised the manufacturing of these at the Royal Arsenal in Enfield, England, with the help of American munitions artisans. The new cartridge, which was also manufactured in the East India Company's arsenal near Calcutta, was the principal cause of the Mutiny.)

The same was said of revolvers by Lieutenant Osborn Wilkinson of the General Staff:

An officer who especially prided himself on his pistol shooting was attacked by a stalwart mutineer armed with a heavy sword. The officer, unfortunately for himself, carried a Colt's Navy Revolver, which was of small caliber (.36-inch) and fired a sharp-pointed picket bullet of sixty to the pound and a heavy charge of powder—its range being at least 600 yards. This he proceeded to empty into the sepoy as he advanced; but having done so, he waited just one second too long to see the effect of his shooting and was cloven to the teeth by his antagonist, who then dropped down and died beside him. Five out of the six bullets had struck the sepoy close together in the chest and had all passed through him and out his back, so we all agreed that you were as good as dead if your life depended upon a .36-inch caliber single-action Colt six-shooter.

Another officer owed his life to a .44-inch caliber, double-action, five-shot Adams revolver when he was attacked by several men at once; for he said he could not have cocked the pistol fast enough before each shot to stop them all in their tracks. He was lucky, however, that it did not misfire! This was a problem with all percussion-lock weapons, due to defective caps and damp powder if not improper maintenance. In fact, the frequent misfiring of percussion-locked revolvers due to clogging and other problems rendered them virtually useless in the opinion of many officers. Still, the five-shot Adams was a superior weapon in design and construction than the Colt six-shooter. The Adams revolver also came in calibers .45-inch and .50-inch "Dragoon" models, but the .44 was the most popular.

General Outram's chief engineer, Captain George Hutchinson, told Major William Hodson (the commander of Hodson's Horse) how a revolver had twice failed him—once in a cavalry charge in Oudh and once in a mine in Lucknow—and asked him if he could trust the two Navy Colts that he carried in his saddle holsters. "No," Hodson replied. "The bullet does not always give sufficient shock to the system to stop a man." He mentioned one case in which he had shot an assailant through the throat and then had a stiff swordfight with him before he could kill him. It usually took at least two or three revolver shots in the head or heart to bring down the average mutineer, he added, and so he preferred a high-caliber carbine of not less than .56 or .58 caliber. With one shot from such a carbine he had killed a rebel leader, but it took two or three shots from a couple of Colt six-shooters in the region of the heart to kill three others.

But while some officers were condemning the Colt revolver for inefficiency, others were condemning the Minié and Enfield rifles for efficiency, saying that "they take the dash out of our men, make them prefer fighting at long range, and damp the characteristic eagerness to charge." Most agreed, however, that the Minié ball—which had a hollow base that expanded when fired—was the only effective "manstopper," which was why it was the standard rifle bullet of the U.S. Civil War and accounted for the enormous number of highly injurious and fatal wounds. It was the predecessor of the soft-nosed dumdum bullet, which expanded on impact and was introduced by the British arsenal at Dum-Dum (near Calcutta) "to stop a drug-crazed fanatic in his tracks." In this same arsenal originated the rumor of the "greased cartridge," which caused the Mutiny.

7

WILL WE GET MEDALS FOR THIS, SIR COLIN?

The Lucknow Relief Force had by now won its initial skirmishes and had closed up in preparation for breaking through to the Residency. Corporal William Mitchell of the 93rd Highlanders, who gave an account of the preliminary action on November 14, also described the main offensive of the 16th:

About two A.M. on the 16th of November, Captain William Peel's naval battery discharged several rockets as a signal to the Residency garrison that we were about to commence our final march on the city. We were then formed up and served with three days rations and double ammunition—sixty rounds in our cartridge pouches and sixty in our haversacks—and just before we started, Sir Colin Campbell reminded us that there was heavy work before us and that as soon as we stormed a position we must keep together as much as possible in threes and rely on nothing but the bayonet. The center man of each group of three was to lead the attack, and the other two were to assist him with their bayonets right and left. We were not to fire a single bullet after we got inside a position, unless we were certain of hitting our enemy, for fear of wounding our own men. In fact, he impressed upon us the necessity of using the bayonet as much as possible so as to conserve ammunition, of which we had a very limited supply, and of not halting to fire when we could avoid doing so, thereby maintaining the impetus of the attack. It was by strictly following this advice and keeping cool and mutually assisting each other that the bayonet was used with such terrible effect inside the Secunder Bagh, the first and strongest position stormed; and Sir Colin had assured us that by such action we should soon dispose of the enemy, although they might be ten to one against us.

For all that, the enemy fought like devils; and Sir Colin did warn us that they were desperate. In addition to their muskets, all the men in the Secunder Bagh were armed with swords; and the native tulwars were as sharp as razors. Moreover, when they had fired their muskets, they hurled them at us like javelins—bayonets first—and then drawing their tulwars, they rushed madly on to their destruction, slashing in blind fury and shouting "Deen! Deen!" (Faith! Faith!). Indeed, they actually threw themselves under our bayonets and slashed at our legs. It was owing to this fact that more than half of our wounded were injured by sword cuts.

Before daybreak, we of the Lucknow Relief Force slowly and silently commenced our advance across the canal at a dry ford that was out of range of the enemy's guns and where they could not see us because of the high grass—and which we were surprised to find undefended on the opposite side; and just as morning broke, by following the winding of the river for about two and a half miles, we had reached the outskirts of a village on the east side of the Secunder Bagh, which was about a mile and three quarters from the Residency. Here, a halt was made for the heavy guns to be brought to the front; while three companies of the 93rd, with some light artillery, were diverted to the left under command of Colonel Hay, to attack and clear out the old sepoy lines (a cluster of mud huts) and the old 32nd Light Infantry barracks: a large building in the form of a cross, strongly flanked with earthworks, also occupied by the enemy. The rest of the force then turned sharp to the left and advanced through the village by a long narrow street, coming immediately under a heavy musketry fire from the nearest houses on either side and from the southeast corner of the Secunder Bagh, directly ahead. The greatest confusion ensued, and for a time there was a complete blockage. The cavalry of the advance guard were checked by the fierce fire that was poured out from the front and flanks; and they had to force their way back through the advanced infantry and horse artillery, who were crammed in the lane and caught between the crossfire from the houses, making "confusion worse confounded."

"If the enemy allow one of us to get out of this cul-de-sac alive," one staff officer remarked to another, "they deserve to be hanged!"

As soon as the advanced cavalry had fallen back to the main column, Sir Colin (who was riding just behind the advance guard) shouted at the infantry and horse artillery, "Clear out those damned houses!"

The three advanced 18-pounders of Captain Blunt's troop of Bengal Horse Artillery were immediately unlimbered and loaded and blasted the houses on the right point-blank with shrapnel shells, which emptied them at once; while the advanced wing of the 53rd Light Infantry rushed into the houses on the left, quickly dislodging the snipers at bayonet point and driving them up the lane and into the Secunder Bagh. This momentarily ended the continual flight of bullets that were passing overhead from that direction.

About the center of the village, another short halt was made for the column to re-form and close up. Here we saw a stark-naked man of a strong, muscular build, with his head closely shaven except for the customary tuft on his crown and his face all streaked in the usual manner with white and red paint and his body smeared white with cow-dung ashes. He was sitting cross-legged on a leopard's skin, counting a string of prayer beads. A young staff officer was making his way to the front when a man of my company named James Wilson pointed to this apparent holyman, saying, "I would like to try my bayonet on the hide of that painted scoundrel, who looks a murderer."

The staff officer, overhearing him, replied: "Oh, don't touch him! These fellows are harmless jogees" (or ascetics) "and won't hurt us. It's the fanatical fakeers" (or mendicants) "that are to blame for this horrible Mutiny."

The words had scarcely been uttered when the so-called "jogee" stopped counting the beads, slipped a hand under the leopard skin, and as quick as lightning brought out a brass horse pistol and fired the contents of it into the officer's chest at a distance of only a few feet, killing him on the spot as he looked with compassion on the poor wretch. His action was as unexpected as it was quick, and the officer was as unable to avoid the shot as our men were to prevent it. Immediately, however, they were upon the assassin; there was no means of escape for him; and he was quickly bayoneted at least half a dozen times.

Upon examination, it was found by a tattoo on his right arm that he was a "half-caste" or Eurasian named Christie, whom some said was a deserter and others a cashiered soldier from the East India Company's army. He was locally feared and revered as an inspired madman and had called on the men of the village to defend it to the death. (I should add that a number of European, Eurasian, and American mercenaries were serving with the Lucknow rebels, chiefly as artillerists and engineers; but this poor lunatic was the only one we were able to nail.)

Just after this incident, we advanced through the rest of the village and came out in front of the Secunder Bagh—about 150 yards away—when a murderous fire was opened on us from the loopholed walls and turrets and from the windows and flat parapeted roof of a two-storied palace in the center of the garden.

The Secunder Bagh or "Garden of Alexander the Great" was built for one of the former kings of Oudh as an animal and bird sanctuary and a residence of his favorite mistresses; and it was a formidable-looking place, about a hundred and thirty yards square and thoroughly fortified, being the first and foremost obstacle commanding the approach to the Residency. The palace, with a central court, was surrounded by gardens and a double-thick brick wall about twenty feet high and flanked at the corners by circular bastions. There was only one entrance: a gateway on the South side, protected by a traverse of earth and masonry, over which was a two-storied guardhouse. (The opposite gateway and both wicket doors had been bricked up.) Close to the inner north side of the enclosure was a pavilion with a flat roof that had been parapeted and loopholed like the rest of the place, from which an incessant musketry fire was resumed as soon as we advanced again. Oddly but fortunately enough, there was no artillery in the place.

"Guns to the front! Action right front!" Sir Colin shouted. "Double! double!"

Captain Blunt galloped his three advanced guns out of the village and up the embankment of the road that ran past the Secunder Bagh and onto the level ground within eighty yards or point-blank range of the southeast corner of the enclosure, where his men unlimbered and loaded them and opened fire with solid shot. But it was an uneven contest; for Blunt soon found himself under a heavy fire from three different directions—not only from the Secunder Bagh but from the buildings in its immediate vicinity—so he had to point each of his guns in these three directions, so that it was no longer "action right front" but "action left and left front" as well. Needless to say, he desperately needed help—and fast!

Quick as they could, our men and the sailors manned the drag-ropes of the eight heavy naval guns; and these were run up over the embankment and onto the plateau to within a hundred yards of the walls. I myself assisted to drag them into position; and it is astonishing how any of us lived through the storm of bullets that rained down on us at such a close range, pelting and ricocheting from the big brass guns with a blood-chilling clangor. Certainly no bullocks or elephants could have survived it, being far larger targets than men, which was why we had to do the hauling.

What was now needed—and fast!—was infantry support; so as soon as the naval guns opened fire, the 4th Infantry Brigade (which was in front) was ordered to take shelter behind the embankment and then take steady aim and fire at every opening from which they could see the musket barrels of the enemy protruding.

Sir Colin and his staff now rode up onto the flat beside the horse-artillery guns, apparently indifferent to the enemy fire—the old chief every now and again turning round when a man was hit and calling out, "Lie down, 93rd! Damn you, lie down! Every man of you is worth his weight in gold today!"

"Never fear, Sir Colin!" a man replied, pointing to the bullet holes in his feather bonnet. "No doubt the boogers think our brains are higher up than other men's!"

Then, as fate would have it, a bullet passed through the head of a 93rd grenadier.

"So much for feather bonnets!" the old chief remarked, seeing that the grenadier's brains had been blown out. And when his staff then expressed their concern over his own recklessness in exposing himself to the heavy fire, he coolly replied that the rebels were such miserable shots that there was no danger and that he intended to ride (if possible) slower than before past the points of danger. "It's the chance shots, the random shots, the potshots—call them what you will—that are to be feared," he added. Just then, he himself was struck hard on the left thigh by a spent bullet after it had passed completely through a gunner, killing him on the spot. "I am hit!" Sir Colin exclaimed; but little harm was done except to his fierce dignity, and he escaped with only a severe bruise.

The mental strain caused by our restraint in the face of an unrelenting fire had its effect on many of us "red devils in petticoats," as the enemy called us, who believed that the way to escape death was to face it head-on; but none was worse affected than a private of my company named (paradoxically) Hope, who commenced cursing in such a manner that Captain Dawson (who commanded our company) reprimanded him, saying that foul and profane language was no sign of bravery. Hope replied that he did not care a "Goddamn" what the captain thought; that he would defy death, and that the bullet was not yet molded that would kill him; and he commenced exposing himself above the embankment behind which we were lying.

The captain was just about to order a corporal and a squad of men to take Hope to the rearguard as drunk and disorderly in presence of the enemy when Pipe Major Macleod, who was standing close to Dawson, said, "Don't mind the poor lad, sir. He's not drunk; he is fey!"—meaning doomed or fated to die soon. "It's not himself that's speaking; it's an evil sprite. He will never see the sun set."

The words were barely out of this Pipe Major's mouth when Hope sprang up on the top of the bank and a bullet instantly struck him on the right side, hitting the buckle of his purse belt, which diverted its course; and instead of going right through his body, it cut him round the front of his belly below the waistbelt, making a deep wound; and his bowels burst out, falling down to his knees. He sank down at once, gasping for breath, when a couple of bullets went through his chest and he died without a groan.

Macleod then turned and said to Captain Dawson, "I told you so, sir. The lad was fey! I am never deceived in a fey man. It was not himself who spoke when swearing in yon terrible manner."

Meanwhile, on the plateau, men and horses were being knocked over right and left; yet Captain Blunt's troop behaved very gallantly, and hard work they had to maintain their position. Blunt himself was thrown to the ground when his charger, a beautiful gray Arab, was shot dead under him; but freeing himself from the poor animal's dying struggles, he was up and at work again in an instant. Of the thirty men under his command, fourteen Europeans and six Indians were killed or wounded; and twenty of the twenty-four troop horses were also knocked over.

By this time, two of Captain Travers's 18-pounders of the Royal Artillery had (with considerable difficulty) been dragged up the bank and opened up on the southeast corner of the wall; and almost at once, Lieutenant Hardy (the commander) was killed and the junior subaltern wounded. Their fire, however, was not very effectual against the Secunder Bagh; but the first shots from our much-heavier naval guns—two 8-inchers and six 24-pounders—passed through the east wall of the Secunder Bagh, piercing it as though it were a piece of cloth and without knocking the surrounding brickwork away. It was from half to three quarters of an hour that these heavy guns battered at the thick wall, sending great clouds of dust into the air when each round struck. During this time, the sailors and artillerymen who were working them (without any cover except our infantry fire) were falling fast—over two guns' crews having been disabled or killed before the wall was breached. True: our men, who were lying down along the bank with their heads only exposed when they were ready to fire, did much to keep down the enemy's musketry; but still we were outshot by at least two to one.

However, after holes had been pounded through the enclosure in many places, large blocks of brick and mortar began to fall out; and then portions of the wall came down bodily, leaving wide gaps. In the meantime, another and smaller breach was made by the three remaining 18-pounders of Captain Blunt's troop, which were hauled up from the rear. This was about twenty yards to the left of the other gap, on the opposite side of the southeastern angle of the wall, and was made to enable a few men to keep up a crossfire through it till the stormers could get a footing inside the main breach. Told off for this important duty were Sergeant James Morrison and several sharpshooters from my company. The main breach could admit two men abreast, while this gap could only admit one at a time.

A terrific fire of musketry poured from the walls when Sir Colin and his staff, followed by some of the 53rd Light Infantry, rode round the southeast corner of the Secunder Bagh in order to direct the action of the upcoming horse artillery. The first man to fall was one of the wild Irishmen of the 53rd, who attempted to pass right under the turret at the angle of the wall and was severely wounded in the right hip; and he lay with bullets plowing up the earth all around him until Thomas Henry Kavanagh, a former government clerk who was guiding the column, leaped from his horse and dragged him by the arms into a hut close by—the poor fellow thankfully squeezing his hand. But when medical assistance arrived, he was beyond hope.

With that, Sir Colin ordered the 53rd to line the embankment that flanked the Secunder Bagh. A young and impetuous gentleman volunteer by his side, mistaking the order to mean an imminent assault, suddenly sprang forward on his native pony; and waving his sword, he called to the men of the 53rd to follow him—all the while exposed to a deadly-close fire.

The 53rd, who needed very little calling, let out an Irish cheer and were about to rush forward when Sir Colin checked them in a loud voice: "Steady, 53rd! Keep steady! Damn all that eagerness!" And then, to the young nobleman: "Come back, Lord Seymour! Come back! You have no business there! I did not order it!" And when this son of the Duke of Somerset rode back, rather shame-faced, the old chief said, "I witnessed your gallantry with great pleasure, but the 53rd have no need of it. Consider yourself, my Lord, as attached to my staff for the present. I admire your noble spirit and must take care of you!"

Meanwhile, the remaining horse artillery came up at a gallop and in superb style mounted the embankment with a single bound and unlimbered on the open flat. Having directed Captain Blunt to breach the south side of the southeast corner of the wells, Sir Colin (followed by his staff) rode on under the musketry of the enemy to see how things were faring on the left, where Colonel Hay and his detachment were engaged.

The fire from the south wall and towers of the Secunder Bagh increased in fierceness as the three companies of the 93rd, with a company of the ubiquitous 53rd, pressed forward to clear the sepoy huts in front of the 32nd Light Infantry barracks. The artillery with Hay immediately commenced a rapid and well-directed fire against the towers and the huts, the occupants of which were soon dislodged, allowing the infantry to rush upon the barracks before the guns could be moved forward in support. Consequently, they were met by a furious fusillade; and our impetuous men fell fast to the ground.

Coming upon the scene at this critical moment, Sir Colin spotted the "dead" wall at one end of the cross-shaped building; and having called on our pioneers to bring up some scaling ladders, he then shouted to the infantry, who were wavering in the ruins of the huts: "Forward with the ladders, 93rd! Go in at the roof! Tear off the tiles and go in through the roof, Highlanders!" By then, the artillery were up and busy keeping down the fire that held the infantry back.

Shouldering ladders, our men made a mad rush at the "blind" wall, up which they soon swarmed; and the old chief smiled as he saw them disappearing through the hole in the roof made by their bayonets and dirks and swords. The enemy did not wait to receive them, but fled out the other end of the building, where a couple of guns were entrenched. These they tried to turn on their pursuers, who (led by

Captain Stewart) furiously fell upon them and captured them, bayoneting and cutting down all those who stood in their way.

Satisfied that our left flank was now secure, Sir Colin rode back to examine the breach made by the horse artillery. There was almost a lull in the storm, which moments before was almost deafening and caused the earth to tremble beneath our feet. The old chief no sooner arrived than a corporal of the 53rd named Joe Lee called out: "Sir Colin, Your Excellency! Let the two thirds at 'em"—meaning the 53rd and 93rd—"and we'll soon make short work of the rascals!"

"Damn your impudence!" the old chief replied. "Do you think the breach is wide enough?" To which Lee answered, "Part of us can get through and hold it till the pioneers widen it with their tools to allow the rest to get in."

Sir Colin then turned to his chief engineer, Lieutenant Lennox, who declared the breach practicable—though a hole barely large enough for a single man was visible. So Sir Colin gave the honor of leading the assault on it to the 4th Punjab Infantry, who (as he said) were "like cats when it comes to getting into tight places."

Sir Colin then rode over and told Brevet Lieutenant Colonel John Ewart, who was in command of seven companies of the 93rd in the absence of Colonel Hay and the remaining three, to prepare to lead the assault on the main breach.

As soon as the bombardment commenced, Colonel Ewart had dismounted and stood exposed behind the embankment—not more than a hundred and fifty to two hundred yards from the Secunder Bagh—picking off the enemy on the top of the palace with one after another of several of the men's rifles, which he took and fired as quickly as they reloaded them, while making these men lie down. Tall as he was, it was said that he was protected by a miracle; and well he should have been; for he was singularly devoted to duty, careful and considerate, and attentive to the wants of his men in a way that made him the most popular officer in the regiment. There was a fierce glint in his eyes when the old chief said to him, "Colonel Ewart, bring on the tartan. Let my own lads at 'em!"

Then, after a few more rounds were fired from the guns, Sir Colin lifted his pith helmet and waved the 4th Punjabees on to the assault. They were as eager and ready as we were; for we had only to tighten our belts and fix our bayonets when Ewart shouted, "Attention, 93rd! Prepare to charge!" One of our buglers, who was in attendance on the

Commander in Chief, sounded the "advance." "Up, 93rd, and at 'em!" the Colonel shouted; and nearly eight hundred of us rose with such a roar of pent-up rage as I had never heard before nor since. It must have struck terror into the enemy, for they actually ceased firing; and we could see numbers of them through the breaches rushing from the outside walls to take shelter in that two-storied edifice in the center of the garden, the doors and windows of which they firmly barred. To add to their terror, Pipe Major John Macleod, with seven pipers—the other three being with their companies in clearing the ground on the left—struck up the Highland "charge," called "On With the Tartan!"

While we of the 93rd dashed from behind and over the embankment, the Punjabees on our right raced like mad with us for the breaches. It was a magnificent sight—a sight never to be forgotten, said all who witnessed it—that glorious race to be the first to enter the Secunder Bagh, the prize to the winner being certain death.

It has long been a disputed point who got into the enclosure first. A lean and long-limbed Sikh was first at the smaller breach and dropped in dead, shot by the snipers who were concealed in the vegetation. At least fifty bullets had penetrated him! Before the rest of the regiment was halfway across the flat, their temporary commanding officer (Lieutenant Paul) fell mortally wounded; and two others of their European officers (Lieutenants Oldfield and McQueen) were mortally and severely wounded respectively. (Only Lieutenant Willoughby, the remaining European, escaped unscathed.) This caused some of the men to waver, but they were instantly urged on by their native officers, who waved their tulwars and shouted, "Chullo, bhaee! Chullo, bahâdur! Humlah kurro!" (Come on, brothers! Come on, braves! Charge!) One of these officers—Soobahdar (Captain) Gokul Singh—got through the gap first, and survived, quickly followed by the others.

I believe the first man at the main breach was Lance Corporal John Dunlay of the 93rd, who stood for an instant in the gap before he fell forward inside, shot in the left leg. He was followed by Sergeant Major Murray, who was shot dead in the chest directly inside, and then by Captain Burroughs, who was severely wounded in a manner to be related later. (I should add that Murray—a fine active fellow— jumped through the opening like a harlequin, but had scarcely landed on the other side when he received the fatal shot.) Next came one of our drummerboys—a pretty, fair-haired lad, not more than fourteen years of age—who was shot down just inside the breach, with a bullet in his brain.

It was about this time that I got through myself, pushed in by Colonel Ewart, who immediately followed. My feet had scarcely touched the ground inside when a sepoy fired point-blank at me from among the long grass a few yards distant. The bullet struck the thick brass clasp of my waistbelt, but with such force that it sent me spinning heels over head. The man who fired was immediately cut down by Lieutenant Dick Cooper, who got through the breach abreast with me.

After Cooper had cut down several men in his path, a sturdy rebel officer came at him with a tulwar in his right hand and a shield in his left. They both cut at each other at the same time, but the rebel had lowered his shield while striking; and Cooper caught him directly on the head, splitting it like a melon. Still, the rebel sliced through Cooper's feather bonnet and deep into his scalp before falling dead; and immediately after, another swordsman took a swipe at Cooper that cut him right across the forehead and momentarily blinded him with blood and pain. Nevertheless, Cooper was able to cut open the rebel's head right down to his mouth—and through four folds of a turban. Cooper survived his wounds; and he owed his life, he said, to the fact that his sword was six inches longer than regulation. Indeed, regulation swords were little good but for show. They were too light, they broke easily, and their straight blades were fit only for giving point.

Colonel Ewart was followed by Captain John Lumsden, our interpreter and a large powerful man, who waved his sword and shouted, "Come on, men, for the honor of Scotland!" He instantly fell dead, shot through the heart; and his conduct was the more creditable because, being only an interpreter, he need not have joined the stormers. His exhortation was immediately taken up by the other officers, who shouted: "Scotland forever! Have at 'em! Charge! Give 'em the bayonet!" and "There they are! Go get 'em! Give 'em the cold steel! For the glory of Scotland!" and "Keep together, lads! Don't fire! At 'em with the bayonet!" and "Forward! forward, for the honor of Scotland!"

When struck down, I felt just as one feels when tripped up at a football match; and before I regained my feet, I heard Colonel Ewart say as he rushed past me, "Poor fellow, he's done for." I was but stunned; and regaining my feet and my breath too, which was completely knocked out of me, I rushed on to the inner court of the palace, the iron gate of which had been shot open, where I saw Ewart bareheaded—his feather bonnet having been shot off his head—engaged in a fierce hand-to-hand fight with several of the enemy, six of whom he had shot down with his revolver before having at the rest with his claymore. Those armed with muskets had allowed him to come within ten yards of them, when they fired a volley. Fortunately, they fired high; and only one ball pierced Ewart's bonnet, but with such force that it snapped his chinstrap and took off the bonnet. A tall rebel, armed with sword and shield, then dashed at Ewart and was the first to be shot dead by him. The five who followed were also dropped in quick succession by his high-caliber pistol, which says as much for Ewart's steady hand as for his deadly aim. He then proved himself as good a swordsman as he was a marksman by cutting down every man who opposed him.

By that time, the whole of the 93rd and the Punjabees had got in either through the breaches or by the outer gate, which had now been forced open; while the 53rd, led by Lieutenant Colonel Gordon of the 93rd (who was temporarily in command of the regiment), had got in by a barred window to the right of the outer gate; and Captain Walton, who was the first inside, was severely wounded. They did this by digging out the iron bars and smashing open the wooden shutters with their bayonets and rifle butts; and Lieutenant French, who was awarded the V.C. with four of his men, was seen chopping away with a pioneer's hatchet when a number of bayonets and stocks were broken in the process.

At the same time, a party of the 4th Punjabees rushed the traverse in front of the gateway, which was full of mutineers; and having been driven out of the earthwork, the enemy made for the gateway, the heavy wooden doors of which were being closed behind them when a Punjabee named Mokurrub Khan pushed his left arm (on which he carried a shield) between the doors, thus preventing their being shut. On his hand being badly wounded by a sword cut, he drew it out, but instantly thrust in his other hand, which was then all but severed from the wrist. But he gained his object. Another Punjabee behind him then thrust his rifle barrel into the opening, and the doors were soon forced open altogether; whereupon the Punjabees swarmed into the gatehouse, shouting "Wah! Shabash!" (Hurrah! Bravo!) and "Jai

Punjabeon ko! Mar Bengaleon ko!" (Victory to the Punjabees! Death to the Bengalees!). For his devoted action, Mokurrub Khan was awarded the Order of Merit: the Indian equivalent to the Victoria Cross.

The rebels were now completely caught in a trap—the only outlets being those through which our troops continued to pour—and so they fought with the wild despair of men without hope of mercy, and were determined to sell their lives as dearly as they could, shouting back at their attackers: "Jai Mujahedeen ko! Mar Kuffar ko!" (Victory to the Crusaders! Death to the Infidels!) and to each other: "Mar feringeon ko! Mar dalo belaitee shaitan!" (Death to the foreigners! Kill the foreign devils!).

There was a very narrow winding staircase on each inner side of the gateway, leading to the upper story of the gatehouse, which was well packed with the enemy; but without a moment's hesitation, the Punjabees mounted these corkscrew-like stairs and were soon in the midst of the enemy, cutting them up with their tulwars and hurling them out of the open windows. Few British soldiers would or could have done this, and yet their loss was small in consideration of the ferocity of the fighting. Only sixty-nine native officers and men were killed or wounded, while hundreds of the enemy perished in that small area.

All those rebels in the garden having been killed or driven into the palace, the inner court was then rapidly filled with dead and wounded by our unrelenting onslaught; and all the latches and hinges of the doors of the lower story were shot or battered off and the window shutters smashed or blown open, and the desperate combat then commenced to rage in the chambers of the palace.

Two officers of the mutineers were fiercely defending with their tulwars a regimental colors inside a dark room when Colonel Ewart rushed in on them to seize it; and although severely wounded twice in his sword arm, he not only captured the colors but killed both the officers who were defending it. This he did with only one stroke each of his claymore. By this time, opposition had almost ceased. A few only of the defenders of the Secunder Bagh were left alive, and those few were being hunted out of dark corners—some of them from below heaps of slain.

Colonel Ewart, seeing that the fighting was virtually over, left the scene to present his trophy to the Commander in Chief. But whether it was that Sir Colin considered it beneath the dignity of a field officer to expose himself to needless danger, or whether it was that he was angry at some other thing, I do not know; but this much I know: that Colonel Ewart, although severely wounded—having several tulwar cuts and many bruises on his body—ran up to the old chief where he sat on his gray charger outside the gate of the Secunder Bagh, startling the poor animal with his sudden and frightful appearance, and called out excitedly: "We are in possession of the place, sir! I have killed the last two of the enemy officers with my own hand, and here is one of their colors!"

"Damn your colors, sir!" said Sir Colin, struggling to control his shying horse. "It's not your place to be taking colors! Go back to your regiment this instant, sir!"

Ewart looked rather dumbstruck. However, the staff officers who were with Sir Colin gave him a cheer; and one of them presented him with a cap to cover his head, which was still bare. Softening, and with his horse under control again, Sir Colin then said to Ewart, "I thank you for your zeal and gallantry, Colonel. But go back to your regiment!" (Accounts differ slightly as to what Ewart and Campbell said to each other, but the most curt of Sir Colin's reputed replies was "Damn you, sir! What business have you to be taking flags? Go back to your men!")

Ewart then turned back, apparently very much upset at the reception given to him by the old chief; but I afterwards heard that Sir Colin sent for him in the afternoon, apologized for his rudeness and thanked him for his services. I have often thought over this incident; and the more I think of it, the more I am convinced (from the wild and excited manner and appearance of Colonel Ewart, who had been by that time more than an hour without his hat in the fierce rays of the sun, covered with blood and powder smoke, and his bloodshot eyes still flashing with the excitement of the fight, giving him the look of a man under the influence of something more potent than the blue-ribbon tipple of the officers' mess table) that when Sir Colin first saw him, he thought he was the worse for whiskey or even "Indian weed," if not "tetched" by the sun.

Having survived close-range musketry and hand-to-hand combat, Ewart eventually lost his left arm at Cawnpore by a small roundshot striking him on the elbow and shattering the bones; and the last time I saw him was when I assisted to lift him into a litter on that unlucky day, the 1st of December 1857. But even this he survived, to become a General.

Ewart's only equal in swordsmanship was Captain Fred Burroughs, who was born in India but educated in Switzerland and France, which accounted for his strange accent and his nickname of "Wee Frenchie"—his height being under five feet. (The 93rd were all tall men, none being under five feet six inches.) Burroughs was reputed to be the smallest man in the British Army—smaller even than "Little Bobs" Roberts—but what he wanted in size he made up for in pluck and endurance, having made himself a master swordsman. He served throughout the Crimean War with never a day absent from duty, which was something of a record, and he had the proverbial nine lives of a cat. Four months later, when we recaptured Lucknow, he stepped on an enemy mine and was sent about a hundred feet in the air. But like a cat, he landed on his feet on the thatched roof of a hut and escaped with only one of his legs broken in two places below the knee. It was the skill of our good doctor—"kindhearted Billy Munro," as the men called him—that saved his leg, and he lived to be a General.

Burroughs was not the first one of the 93rd inside the Secunder Bagh, as has been claimed; but he was certainly the first to survive, although he was immediately attacked by an Oudh irregular armed with tulwar and shield, who nearly finished him off before he got properly on his feet after having been knocked down by the frantic press of men behind him. But quick as a cat, "Wee Frenchie" dodged the blow and made a cut at his assailant that nearly decapitated him. In the same instant, however, another irregular attacked him; and it was the wire frame of his feather bonnet that saved him this time. The rebel got a straight cut at his head, but the blade glanced off the bonnet (which was dented in like a bishop's miter) and nearly slashed off his right ear. However, Burroughs immediately gathered himself together—there was so little of him to gather!—and soon showed his tall opponent that he had for once met his match in the art of fencing. Before many seconds, Burroughs's sword had passed through the rebel's throat and out at the back of his neck.

Notwithstanding his severe wound, Burroughs fought throughout the capture of the Secunder Bagh, with the blood running down from his nigh-severed ear over his shoulder to his gaiters; nor did he subsequently go to have his wound dressed till after he had mustered his company and reported to the Colonel how many of No. 6 had fallen that morning.

Having disposed of the enemy at ground level, we then went after them in the towers and gatehouse and upper rooms of the enclosure; and by our keeping together, as ordered, the bayonet soon did the work. But it was during this part of the struggle that I had another narrow escape. Each man carried his greatcoat rolled up with ends strapped together across the right shoulder just over the ammunition-pouch belt, so that it did not interfere with the free use of the rifle but rather formed a protection across the chest. As it turned out, many men owed their lives to the fact that bullets became spent in passing through their rolled greatcoats before reaching a vital part. Now it happened that in the heat of the fight in the Secunder Bagh, my greatcoat was cut right through (where the two ends were fastened together) by the stroke of a keen-edged tulwar which was intended to slash me across the shoulder. Although the blow staggered me for a moment, the blade failed to wound me by a fraction of an inch; and one of my comrades instantly finished my assailant with his bayonet. (I should add that the feather bonnet, heavy and ungainly though it was, also saved many a man's life.)

The pandemonium in the Secunder Bagh was hellish in the extreme: blood-splattered and smoke-stained Europeans and Punjabees trampling over the dead and dying, whose screams and groans mingled with the grunts and curses of those who stabbed and clubbed and cut them down, with the continuous sounds of hacking and bashing and jabbing, and with the constant shrill of the bagpipes. When all was over and Sir Colin complimented the pipers on the way they had played throughout the fight—fearlessly following the soldiers from place to place, armed only with their peculiar instruments of war, which had a chilling effect on the enemy, who gave them a wide berth—Pipe Major Macleod said, "We thought the lads would fight better with the national music to cheer them." And so they did! The pipes also incited the Punjabees, who would adopt them after this day and form a kind of fraternity with us "ghagré walé" or "petticoat wearers."

As I said, there was no escape for the desperate masses of the enemy, who were driven and hunted from one place to another—in and out of rooms, up and down stairs—relentlessly pursued and losing their footing on marble steps and floors slippery with their own blood. With their backs to the walls, some threw down their arms and begged for mercy, clutching in despair at the weapons that pierced them; while others stoically and scornfully faced certain death; but most fiercely defended themselves, hurling their bayoneted muskets at us and then flinging themselves upon us with their tulwars and struggling (even when dying on the ground) to strike again.

Our rage was so great that we actually bent and twisted our bayonets by the fury of our thrusts when pinning the shrieking wretches against the walls, two or three at a time, and all the while the officers urged the men on with shouts of "Remember Cawnpore!" But though many a man uttered "God forgive me!" as he drove his bayonet home, nothing could restrain men infuriated by the thought of that slaughtered garrison.

Shuttered windows were smashed open, bolted doors battered down, and hand grenades tossed into rooms crowded with fugitives who rushed out onto the points of our swords and bayonets when they attempted to escape the fires started by these explosives. Their clothes ablaze, their bodies maimed, they rushed out hacking blindly—some with their swords in both hands, others guarding their heads with their shields—only to be forced back into the flames. Into the towers and onto the ramparts and roofs the pursued rushed, only to be hunted down with a vengeance and pitched dead and dying into the courtyard upon the heaps there writhing and simmering in the midday sun—those on top being moved up and down by the labored breathing of those suffocating below—from which fumed the fragrance of crushed flowers and the stench of sweat and blood and excreta, and of burning flesh and hair and clothing.

By the time the bayonet had done its work, our throats were hoarse with shouting "Cawnpore!"; and the amount of perspiration expended also made us almost mad with thirst; and in our heavy bonnets, coats, and kilts, and also weighted down with equipment, we felt the heat intensely—the sun now being directly overhead.

In the center of the inner court of the Secunder Bagh there was a large "peepul" or sacred fig tree with a very leafy top, round the foot of which were set a number of earthen jars full of cool water; and when the slaughter was almost over, many of our men sought the shade of this tree and to quench their burning thirst. A number of soldiers of the 53rd and 93rd also lay dead under this tree; and this peculiar fact attracted the notice of Captain Dawson, who (after having carefully examined the wounds) concluded that in every case the men had evidently been shot from above. He thereupon stepped out from beneath the tree and called to a private of his company named James Wallace, who was a "deadeye," to look up and tell him if he could see anyone in the top of the tree.

Wallace had his rifle loaded; and as though stalking game, he began to move about beneath the tree, carefully scanning the top, and almost immediately called out, "I see him, sir!" Cocking and raising his rifle, he took steady aim and then fired; and down fell a body dressed in a tight-fitting red jacket and rose-colored silk trousers; and the breast of the jacket, bursting open with the fall, showed that the wearer was a woman. She was armed with a pair of heavy old-pattern cavalry pistols, one of which was in her belt, still loaded; and her pouch was still about half full of ammunition; while from her perch in the tree, which had been carefully prepared before the attack, she had killed more than half a dozen men.

When Wallace saw that the person he had shot was a woman, he burst into tears, exclaiming: "If I had known it was a woman, I would rather have died a thousand deaths than have harmed her!"

"Chivalrous of you, man!" another retorted. "And I'm bloody well sure she'd have been equally obliging in putting you to one of those deaths!"

She was but one of about half a dozen female warriors who were killed in the Secunder Bagh, mainly because they could not be readily distinguished from the men. We did not care to war on women, and would have spared them if possible, though our friends the Punjabees assured us that they were worse than the men and deserved to die the death of dogs. I saw the body of one of them who was in men's garbs with a crossbelt and cartridge pouch on her, who had been shot; and lying by her side was a dead baby with two bullet wounds in it. The poor mother had tied the wounds round with a rag. Lieutenant John McQueen of the Punjabees told me he had seen one of our men bayonet another woman; and on his upbraiding him for such a brutal act, he said the fellow turned on him like a madman, and for a moment he almost expected to be run through with the bayonet himself!

Wallace's single shot was followed by a series of volleys as the remaining mutineers were disposed of while they stood or cowered against walls and in corners, and as they lay on the ground, wounded or not. All opposition had already ceased; but no prisoners were to be taken, and so this finishing blow had to be struck. It was left to our reserve—Major Roger Barnston's 1st Battalion of Detachments—and it was in accordance with Sir Colin's orders to Brigadier Hope: "The men employed in the attack will use nothing but the bayonet. They are absolutely forbidden to fire a shot till the position is won."

Thus, when mouths were dry and black from biting cartridges, over two thousand of the enemy lay dead within the Secunder Bagh. The troops were then withdrawn; and the muster roll of the 93rd was called just outside the gate, when it was found that two officers and twenty-three men had been killed and seven officers and sixty-one men wounded out of a total of forty-eight officers and nine hundred and thirty-four men. ("Many of the wounded," said Dr. Munro, "came staggering out with the most terrible sword cuts I ever saw in my life.")

The roll of the 53rd was also called alongside of us, and Sir Colin then rode up and addressed both regiments: "53rd and 93rd, you have bravely done your share of this morning's work; and Cawnpore is avenged. There never was a bolder feat of arms than the storming of the Secunder Bagh! It was done in the most brilliant manner, and the loss inflicted on the enemy was immense! I shall inform His Excellency the Governor General, and through him Her Majesty the Queen, that I have never seen troops behave better."

The 93rd were grimly silent; but one of the 53rd shouted, "Three cheers for the Commander in Chief, boys!", which was heartily responded to by the wild Irish.

"There is more hard work to be done," the old chief said, "but unless as a last recource, I will not call on you to storm any more positions today. Your duty will be to cover the guns after they are dragged into position. But, my lads, if need be, remember I depend on you to carry the next position in the same daring manner you carried the Secunder Bagh."

With that came the usual response from Private John Scott of the 93rd: "Aye-aye, Sir Colin; and needs be we'll do that!"

But immediately after, someone from the ranks of the 53rd called out: "Will we get medals for this, Sir Colin?" To which he replied, "Damn your medals! You fight for the honor, not honors, of your country."

"Well, beggin' yer pardon, sir," another piped up; "but is that why ye accepted the K.C.B.?"

The old chief's stern, puckered face was now red with indignation. He answered: "I accepted the K.C.B., you ignorant bogtrotter, to show that the son of a carpenter was as good as the son of a peer!" He then simmered down, saying, "I can't say what Her Majesty's Government may do about medals; but if you don't get them, lairds and clodhoppers alike, all I can say is you have deserved them better than any troops I have ever seen under fire. Parade dismissed!" (I should add that Sir Colin was once heard to say: "I am wifeless and childless—a lone man. The peerage will bring me no satisfaction. Rank and honors give me no satisfaction. I would have been happier in command of a brigade." So much for the slur that he would have sacrificed anything for a peerage!)

All the time the rolls were being called, there was perfect silence around us—the enemy evidently not yet being aware of what had happened in the Secunder Bagh, for not a soul escaped from it to tell the tale. In fact, the silence was so great that we could hear the pipers of the 78th Highlanders playing "The Campbells are Coming!" and "On With the Tartan!" inside the Residency compound as a welcome to cheer us all.

I have heard various estimates of the number of rebels slain— between two and three thousand, and even the droll figure of exactly 1,857—but I can say for a fact that the muster rolls and parade states of the defenders of the Secunder Bagh on the 16th of November were discovered among other documents in a chamber which had been their general's quarters and orderly-room; and from these it was learned that a brigade of four separate regiments, numbering about two thousand five hundred men, had occupied the place. (One of them, the 71st Bengal Native Infantry, was a crack corps of the Company's army; and many of the sepoys, all of whom wore their uniforms, had medals from the Punjab campaigns on their breasts. They also fought under their old colors, and it was these that Colonel Ewart captured.) It was also estimated, from their appearance, that a large number of "budmashes" or bad characters from the city were present, thus increasing the total of slain to about three thousand. Over two thousand of these lay inside the rooms of the main building and in the inner court, while the rest lay in the outer court and garden and its pavilion, where they were left to burn and rot and be devoured by the carrion birds and beasts; for it was with the greatest difficulty that men could be spared to bury our own dead, let alone those of the enemy. (This was the practical reason why we took no prisoners.)

As for this morbid emphasis on the number of slain: I don't suppose that in modern times any such great number of men were killed in action on such a small space of ground and in such a short period of time.

8

YOU MUST TAKE IT— AT ALL COSTS!

Ensign Charles Devereaux of the 5th Fusiliers, who described some of the action on November 15, also told of his experiences fighting in the Secunder Bagh on the 16th:

We arrived just at the moment when the Secunder Bagh had been taken by storm; and we found the place a mass of dead and dying, many of them on fire. It was the most horrible scene I have ever witnessed. Not a square foot clear of fallen bodies could be seen. Hundreds of mutineer sepoys lay in piles of three and four deep—a burning, smoldering, suffocating mass—while upwards of fifty of our men lay among them, showing how fierce the battle must have been. The palace was in flames, and the stench arising from the burning bodies and the growls of the dying formed a scene that made me fancy I was in another world—the infernal one, perhaps.

But there was no time for reflection; for an urgent message to Sir Colin Campbell from the artillery, saying that the musketry fire from an untaken portion of the palace was picking their men off fearfully, followed by an order from Sir Colin that the position must be taken in five minutes and that no sepoy must be left to fire another musket after that time, had us in action at once.

Up the stairs we went and made a charge at one of the doors and knocked it in; and as we rushed into the room, we were met by a volley, which killed two of our men and a volunteer named Benson, who was going to meet a brother in the Residency. The mutineers then bolted up the narrow stairs to the flat roof and stood at the top, defying us to come on; but as only one man could get up at a time, we were momentarily at a standstill.

Piling up some of the furnishings in the room, we then lit a fire at the bottom of the stairs and got up in the smoke, driving the sepoys out onto the roof, where we went at them with a vengeance; and the first man fell by a bullet from my revolver, and the second got my sword clean through his stomach and out at his back—right up to the hilt. We killed eighty-four sepoys there, and we were so furious that we flung them all over the parapet and balustrade of the roof and gallery and down into the courtyard on top of the others, and immediately sent word to Sir Colin that it was done.

But a melancholy occurrence closed this glorious day's work. A powder magazine, unknown to us, was in this same corner of the building; and the place being in flames on all sides, it blew up and killed upwards of twenty of the Queen's 84th who were looting there. Two of them were shot by our own men, who took them for sepoys, so blackened were they and appeared just like them as they came rushing out of the flames, yelling like mad. But it wasn't the first time, nor the last, that we shot our own men by mistake in this maddening conflict.

Later, when we were resting in the garden, a bullet came from a tree overhead and killed a Sikh officer. We looked up; and there was a sepoy, loading his musket again. We soon brought him down with our revolvers, and were astonished at the feminine regularity of his features. Someone suggested it was a woman in disguise, and so it proved. She died cursing us.

Lieutenant Arthur Lang of the Bengal Engineers also described the action in the palace:

Every room, every staircase, every corner of the towers was contested. Quarter was neither given nor asked for. Finally, at each tower, a few desperate men held out; and lives were being thrown away in attempting to force the narrow winding staircases and small dark rooms.

As soon as I had blown open a bolted door with a bag of powder, I had a bayonet thrust out at my chest from behind the doorway; and back I sprang, you may be certain! I was then hit for the first time by a bullet, which sent me spinning from a stinging crack on the left shoulder. I thought I was done for, but was highly delighted when I found I didn't drop and when a soldier called out that the bullet had hit the wall behind me. It was a sharp glance off my pouchbelt, and the only effect was to make my shoulder and arm bruised and stiff for a couple of days.

The men in that room held out for two hours; and when their ammunition was gone, they went onto the roof and with fury hurled their tulwars and bayoneted muskets down at us, then fell to their deaths amidst a volley of bullets.

Lieutenant Fred Roberts of the General Staff, who entered the Secunder Bagh soon after the storming parties, recounted what he saw:

As we neared the gateway, where heaps of slain covered the ground in terrible confusion, Captain the Honorable Augustus Anson (Brigadier Sir Hope Grant's aide-de-camp) was knocked off his horse by a bullet, which grazed the base of his skull just behind the right ear and stunned him for a moment. The next moment, however, he was up and mounted again, acting as if nothing had happened, but was hardly in the saddle when his horse was shot dead. "I guess I'm meant to walk!" he remarked with a laugh. And as we were about to pass through the gateway, over more heaps of the dead and dying, Captain Harry Norman (the Assistant Adjutant General) received a violent blow on the head when a dying rebel was thrown from the top of the gateway by some Sikhs.

The enemy had obstinately contested the ground inside the gateway, where the dead and dying lay in heaps; but inch by inch they were forced back to the garden pavilion and into the space between it and the north wall, where they were all shot or bayoneted. I never saw such a sight! There they lay in a heap as high as my head, four or five feet deep—a heaving, tangled mass of dead and dying—with the fire of the burning woodwork of the pavilion slowly creeping over them, twisting their limbs into hideous contortions. It was a sickening sight: one of those which even in the excitement of battle and the flush of victory make one feel strongly what a horrible side there is to war, and especially a war of this kind. Such was the crush that the wounded men could not get clear of their dead comrades, however great their struggles, and those near the top of this ghastly pile of writhing humanity vented their rage and disappointment on everyone who approached them by cursing him and saying, "If we could only stand, we would kill you." Anson, for one, responded by plucking a bunch of trampled flowers from the garden and tossed them on the pile as a kind of funeral offering.

The firing and fighting did not cease altogether for some time after the main body of the rebels were destroyed. Now and then, a stray shot came from some poor wretch yet able to pull a trigger. A few barricaded themselves in the guardroom above the gateway and had to be blown out by artillery shells; others sought shelter in the bastions, where they had to be smoked out; but only one or two escaped the vengeance of our soldiers by dropping over the wall on the city side, where they were killed and robbed by native scavengers armed with clubs. And sixty-four of them, who had surrendered without a fight, were drawn up against a wall and shot and bayoneted to death with yells of "Cawnpore!" and "God forgive us!"

Early next morning, some of our Sikhs called up to three or four of the enemy who had spent the night in a corner tower, ordering them to come out. The evening before, long after the fighting was over, these men had kept up a fire upon all who entered the garden and had wounded several of our men. They came out as ordered, looking rather meek; for I presume they had had no food or water for many hours. The Sikhs made them kneel down, and having asked them a few questions, killed them with their tulwars by cutting off their heads, which they then took to show their comrades as tokens of the last of the rebels in the Secunder Bagh.

Considering the tremendous odds which those who first entered through the breaches were exposed to, and the desperate nature of the fighting, our losses were astonishingly small—less than two hundred—while the enemy lost more than two thousand.

But the day's fighting was not over, as related by Corporal Mitchell of the 93rd Highlanders

When the number of the slain in the Secunder Bagh was reported to Sir Colin Campbell, he turned to Brigadier Hope and said, "This morning's work will strike terror into the rebels—it will strike terror into them!"

He was sadly mistaken. It only infuriated them. The roll-call parade was no sooner dismissed than word reached them of the annihilation of their comrades; and a perfect hail of roundshot assailed us from buildings on our left, our direct fronts and especially from the Shah Nujjuf on our right front.

The Shah Nujjuf or "King of the Hill," so called from its location on a small hill on the riverbank, was about six hundred yards west of the Secunder Bagh and two hundred yards to the right of the road leading directly to the Residency. Surrounded by jungles and cottages, and enclosed by a walled garden, it was the massive white-domed tomb and mosque of the first King of Oudh. Besides being strongly fortified and defended, it had been converted into a powder magazine, thus making it an extremely dangerous as well as formidable position. (Ironically, Sir Henry Lawrence had ordered his troops to "spare the holy places"; and yet the enemy did not spare them, although theirs was a "holy war," because desperation made desecration necessary in defense of faith.)

As soon as that terrible fire was opened on us in an effort to bar our advance on the Residency, Sir Colin gave the order for us to man the dragropes of Captain Peel's naval guns for an immediate attack on the Shah Nujjuf; and the order was obeyed with a cheer. Then, at the word of command, Captain Middleton's heavy four-gun battery of the Royal Horse Artillery dashed forward with loud cheers—the drivers waving their whips and the gunners their caps as they passed us and Peel's guns at full gallop.

For more than seven hundred yards, the two 8-inchers and six 24-pounders were dragged along by our men and the sailors in the teeth of a hailstorm of lead and iron from the enemy's batteries; and it was a wonder that any of us survived, except that the storm blew mostly overhead. (If the rebel gunners had one fault, it was that they failed to depress their guns and generally overshot us.) In the middle of the march, however, a poor sailor lad (just in front of me) had one of his legs carried clean off above the knee by a roundshot; and although knocked head over heels by the force of the shot, he sat bolt upright on the roadside grass, with the blood spouting from the stump of his limb like water from the hose of a fire engine, and shouted, "Here goes a shilling a day, a shilling a day!"—meaning a crewman's pay. "Pitch into 'em, boys—pitch into 'em! Remember Cawnpore, 93rd—remember Cawnpore! Go at 'em, me hearties! Give 'em a Cawnpore dinner!"—meaning bayonets in their guts. And he then fell back in a dead faint, and on we went. I afterwards heard that the poor fellow was dead before a doctor could reach the spot to bind up his limb. During an attack, it was forbidden for anyone else to stop and help a wounded man; otherwise it might fail from lack of men and momentum.

Our attack on the Shah Nujjuf was vividly described by the Commander in Chief in his dispatch; "The 93rd and Captain Peel's guns rolled on in one irresistible wave, the men falling fast; but the column advanced till the heaver guns were within seventy yards of the walls of the Shah Nujjuf, where they ware unlimbered and poured in round after round against the massive walls of the building—the withering fire of the Highlanders covering the Naval Brigade from great loss. But it was an action almost unexampled in war. Captain Peel behaved very much as if he had been laying his frigate, the *Shannon*, alongside an enemy's ship."

It was at the beginning of this action that Midshipman Martin Daniel was killed instantly by a roundshot which tore away the right side of his head, scattering his brains over those near him. He was in command of an 8-inch howitzer; and Captain Peel had just asked if his gun was ready and he replied, "All ready, sir," when Peel said, "Fire the howitzer"; and Daniel was answering, "Aye-aye," when he was struck dead. His men later buried him where he fell.

After the naval guns were dragged into position, the 93rd took up whatever shelter they could get on the right and left of the guns; and I, with several others, got behind the walls of an unroofed mud hut, through which we made loopholes with our bayonets and dirks on the side fronting the Shah Nujjuf and were thus able to keep up a covering fire on the enemy.

Some time after the attack had commenced, we noticed Lieutenant Fred Alison (Sir Colin's aide-de-camp) and his horse in a heap together a few yards behind where we were in shelter. His sword had been shivered in his hand by a bullet while he rode up with our storming party to the Secunder Bagh, but he now had an even more narrow escape: his horse was struck in the head; and he himself was struck in the breast by a musket ball which glanced off round his ribs and came out at his back instead of passing through his heart.

I must now relate a service rendered by Sergeant "Mick" Findlay, of my company, which was never officially noticed nor rewarded. This was as he wished it, for he merely considered that he had done his duty; but it was because he had abandoned his post without orders, and the only saving grace was that he did so for the sake of a General-Staff officer, although even that was forbidden. However, Sergeant Findlay rushed out at once, got the severely wounded officer clear of his dead horse under a heavy shower of bullets and roundshot, and carried him to the shelter of the walls where we were lying. He then ran off in search of a surgeon to treat his wounds, which were bleeding very profusely; but the surgeons were all too busy—in fact, were overwhelmed with work, attending to the wounded in the thick of the fire—and Sir Colin was most strict on the point of wounds being attended to. Officers, no matter what their rank, had no precedence over the enlisted men in this respect. In fact, Sir Colin often expressed the opinion that an officer could be far more easily replaced than a well-drilled private.

Anyway, there was no surgeon available; so, since every soldier (when going on active service) was supplied with lint aid bandages to have handy if needed in such an emergency, Sergeant Findlay used his own, stanched the bleeding, and dressed Lieutenant Alison's wounds in such a surgeon-like manner that when Dr. Menzies of the 93rd eventually came to see him, he thought that Alison had been attended to by a doctor. When he did discover that it was Findlay who had done the job, he expressed his surprise and said that in all probability this prompt action had saved Alison's life. Dr. Menzies then applied to Captain Lawson to get Findlay into the field hospital as an extra assistant to attend to the wounded, but Dawson was reluctant to lose such a good noncom. "Besides," he said, "Findlay disobeyed the standing order regarding helping the wounded in face of the enemy; and his punishment will be to continue serving as a combatant rather than what his tender heart now fancies himself."

Alison later thanked Findlay for saving his life; but even he had no influence in making him a hospital sergeant, for which he seemed better suited. As Sir Colin said, "Findlay must be made an example of that we must play this game of war by the rules or risk being the losers." He was right, of course, but I must remark that I have known men get the Victoria Cross for incurring far less danger than Findlay did in exposing himself to bring Alison under shelter. The bullets were literally flying round him like hail—several passed through his clothes—and his feather bonnet was shot off his head. When he had finished binding up the wounds he coolly remarked: "I must go out and get my bonnet for fear I get sunstruck." So out he went for it; and before he got back, scores of bullets were fired at him from the outer walls of the Shah Nujjuf; but he had a charmed life, sure enough.

Those who have never been under the excitement of a fight like this may think that such coolness as Findlay displayed is an exception or an exaggeration. It is not so. If familiarity breeds contempt, then continual exposure to danger breeds coolness—and, I may add, selfishness and callousness too. Where all are exposed to equal danger, little sympathy is (for the time being, at least) shown for the unlucky ones who are "knocked over," to use the common expression in the ranks for those who are wounded or killed. General Sir Hope Grant regarded "the indifference to human life that war tends to engender" as a necessary evil whereby soldiers maintain their fortitude and discipline, adding that "although warfare (especially of the nature we were then engaged in) tends much to blunt men's best feelings, it also develops the noblest that men are capable of." Witness Sergeant Findlay.

Sergeant Dan White was also one of the coolest and most fearless in the regiment; only unlike Findlay, he looked on the drama of war with the eyes of an actor; and it has been my experience that some of the best officers are the most dramatic, which is how they inspire men to follow them anywhere. And their sense of humor helps you maintain your sanity. To give you an example: In the force defending the Shah Nujjuf, in addition to the regular troops, there was a large body of archers on the ramparts—former guardsmen of the late King of Oudh—armed with longbows and long steel-barbed arrows, which they discharged with great force and precision; and on Sergeant White raising his head above the wall of our hut, an arrow was shot right into his feather bonnet. Inside the wire cage of his bonnet, however, he had placed his forage cap, folded up; and so, instead of passing right through, the arrow stuck in the rolls of the cap. He coolly pulled it out; and looking at it, he exclaimed, "Bows and arrows! Why, the sight has not been seen in civilized war for nearly two hundred years! Ah, that I should be able to tell in the Salt Market of Glasgow that I had seen men fight with bows and arrows in the days of Enfield rifles! Well, well, Jack Sepoy—since bows and arrows are the thing, here's at you!" And with that, he raised his feather bonnet on the point of his bayonet above the top of the wall; and immediately another arrow pierced it through, while a dozen more whizzed past a little wide of the mark.

Just then, one poor fellow named Penny (of No. 2 Company), raising his head for an instant a little above the wall, got an arrow right through his brain—the shaft projecting more than a foot out at the back of his head. As the poor lad fell dead at our feet, Sergeant White remarked, "Boys, this is no joke; we must pay them off." So we all loaded and capped, then raised our bonnets on our bayonets; where-upon a whole shower of arrows went past or through them. Then up we sprang and returned a well-aimed volley from our rifles at point-blank distance, and more than half a dozen of the enemy went down. But one unfortunate man named Montgomery, of No. 6 Company, exposed himself a little too long to watch the effect of our volley; and before he could get down into shelter again, an arrow was sent right through his heart, passing clean through his body and falling on the ground a few yards behind him. He leaped about six feet straight up in the air, like a wounded buck, and fell stone-dead.

One of the rebel sharpshooters on the ramparts was causing con-siderable loss among the bluejackets, and so Captain Peel called out that anyone who would climb up a tree which was close at hand and shoot the fellow should be recommended for the Victoria Cross. Lieutenant Nowell Salmon and two gallant crewmen immediately rushed forward. One sailor fell dead at the foot of the tree, then the other, while Salmon clambered up with his rifle, but was severely wounded before he could use it; and Peel, seeing his men dropping fast around him, sent an aide to Sir Colin to say it would be necessary for him to retire. (Salmon was awarded the V.C. for his pains.)

By this time, the sun was getting low; a heavy cloud of smoke hung over the area; and every flash of the guns and firearms could be clear-ly seen. The enemy in hundreds were visible on the ramparts of the garden wall, yelling like demons, brandishing their swords in one hand and fiery torches in the other, shouting at us to "chullo" (come on). But little impression had been made on the double-thick solid-masonry walls by our artillery, the exposed men of which were still dropping. Lieutenant Alison's elder brother, Major Archibald Alison (Sir Colin's Military Secretary), while mounted a little in advance of the old chief in hope of shielding him from the enemy's fire, was struck in the left elbow and wrist by three bullets fired from a swivel gun on a parapet of the garden wall. (His shattered arm was subsequently amputated, but he survived to become a General.) The horse of Captain Henry Norman, our Assistant Adjutant General, was hit in three places almost simultaneously, but stoutly kept his rider in the saddle for at least half an hour; and nearly every other staff officer with the Commander in Chief was wounded or had his horse shot in two or three places. Brigadier the Hon. Adrian Hope and his aide-de-camp, and then his Brigade Major, were thrown to the ground, their horses shot dead by the shrapnel from one of our own prematurely exploding shells, but they were fortunately only bruised; and the same shell which had done this mischief exploded one of our ammunition wagons, killing and wounding several men.

Altogether, the situation looked dismal and critical when Major Barnston and his battalion of detachments were ordered to storm. This 600-man battalion was made up of wings of several of the European regiments then besieged in the Residency—the 84th and 90th Queen's and the Madras Fusiliers—and were therefore the most determined in rescuing their comrades-at-arms. But it was a desperate attempt—indeed, a forlorn hope—for although our heavy cannonade had crumbled portions of the outer layer of the wall, no breach had been made in the inner layer; and so the stormers would have to scale it with bamboo ladders; a course of action as difficult as it was dangerous. But they advanced bravely to the assault in skirmishing order, covered by our rifle fire and by the artillery, one of the defective shells from which mortally wounded Major Barnston by prematurely bursting in his path. (The fault was evidently with the fuses, but our limited supply of ammunition prevented our gunners being particular.)

The command then devolved on Captain "Joe" Wolseley, of the 90th Light Infantry, who made a most determined effort to get into the Shah Nujjuf; but the ladders were no sooner placed against the wall, which was still almost twenty feet high in spite of our shelling, than they were ignited by the enemy's torches; and any men who dared to mount them had to face fire and steel of several kinds. Indeed, they were raked with a perfect hail of missiles—grenades and roundshot and live shells hurled by hand and from swivel guns, spears and arrows, firebrands and brickbats, stones and stinkpots, red-hot shot thrown with tongs, shovelfuls of red-hot embers, burning bundles of oil-soaked rags and cotton—and even boiling water and oil was dashed down on them.

In the twilight, with all the smoke and flame and clamor, the scene would nave made a very good representation of Pandemonium. "At them! At them!" our officers were shouting, waving their swords; while those on the wall were shouting their war cries: "Deen! Deen!" (Faith! Faith!) and "Jai! Jai!" (Victory! Victory!) All but a double ladder collapsed, tumbling the stormers down, when ignited; and up this several officers scrambled, firing their revolvers as they went, protected only by their turban-wrapped leather helmets. Two of them reached the top of the wall, where they brought their swords into play; and a brief but furious hand-to-hand fight occurred, in which both officers were all but hacked to pieces before they fell. That settled it for the others.

The stormers were driven back, leaving many dead and wounded at the foot of the wall. Seeing this, Sir Colin turned to his Assistant Adjutant General (who was still mounted, though on a wounded horse) and exclaimed, "Norman, go after them! Stop them! What a disgrace! It's better that every man of them should lie dead on the field than that they should turn their backs on the enemy!"

Captain Norman rode off, shouting at them: "Go back! Go back! Will British soldiers run from sepoys?" But to no avail. They had had enough, and could not be shamed into further action.

When they had taken refuge with us in the nearby huts and walled gardens, Captain Wolseley went to report to the Commander in Chief, who shook his fist at him and said, "Sir, your men have disgraced the name of the British soldier! But I will not hold you accountable, but will put it down to the untimely loss of their commander by an accident likely to demoralize the best of men; and I will give them a chance to redeem themselves." He then ordered Wolseley to clear the ground around the Shah Nujjuf by setting fire to the thatched huts and patches of jungle and then withdraw his men out of range of the enemy.

Wolseley did as ordered, but returned a short time later; and before he could speak, Sir Colin exclaimed, "You have not half burned the huts, sir! Why have the men fallen back again?"

"Because, sir," Wolseley replied, "the fire was too hot."

"Damn your eyes, sir!" the old chief retorted. "I will not allow you or any other man to tell me that the fire is too hot."

Major General William Mansfield, Sir Colin's Chief of Staff, then spoke up: "I think the officer means the fire of the burning huts."

"All right, sir," Sir Colin conceded. "All right. It was my mistake. Go back to your men."

"This is very mortifying," Brigadier Hope then remarked to Sir Colin. "Pray, sir, let the 93rd have at the place before we retire. If we're to die, let us die like men, not sheep."

We of the 93rd, of course, had already been withdrawn; and Sir Colin now called on our Colonel to form us up for a final attempt on the Shah Nujjuf. As soon as we were ready, the old chief addressed us: "93rd! I had no intention of employing you again today, but that building in our front must be taken before dark! The artillery can't drive the enemy out, so you must—with the bayonet!" And as usual, he was answered at once from the ranks: "All right, Sir Colin—we'll do it!" and "Aye; we'll bring the women and bairns out of Lucknow or leave our own bones there!" To which he replied: "Very well, 93rd! Remember, I depend on you! Our friends in Lucknow have food only for five or six days, and the effort must be made to save them at any cost! Only you can do it, and I will lead you myself!"

"God bless the Commander in Chief!" cried another. "We'll follow him to Hell!" (I'll never forget what Mr. William Russell, *The Times* correspondent, wrote of us: "The Highlanders are very proud of Sir Colin, and he is proud of them. They look on him as if he belonged to them, like their bagpipes—a property useful in war.")

Sir Colin waved down the cheering and said, "Remember, men: the lives at stake inside the Residency are those of women and children, and they must be rescued! Remember also what I said to you at Balaclava: 'There is no retreat from here! You must die where you stand!' So I say to you now: It is not 'Will you take that place?' or 'Can you take it?' It's 'You must take it—at all costs!'"

A reply burst from the ranks: "Aye-aye, Sir Colin! We stood by you at Balaclava and will stand by you here! But you must not expose yourself for our sake! We can be replaced, but you cannot! You must remain behind; we can lead ourselves!"

The old chief smiled at this, and his gray eyes glistened with emotion; but tightening his lips, he abruptly drew his sword and swung his horse around and said to Colonel Hay, "The 93rd will advance—quick march." And so we did, cheering, with the pipers playing "The Cock of the North" and the colors flying in front of the center company, as steady as if we were on parade.

By that time, the battalion of detachments had cleared the front; but the enemy on the walls were still yelling at us to come on and piling up missiles to give us a warm reception. Captain Peel had meanwhile brought his two "infernal machines," known as a rocket battery to the front; and he sent a volley of rockets through the crowd on the ramparts. "I don't know what effect they'll have on the enemy," he remarked, "but they scare the deuce out of me!" (Peel later said to Mr. Russell of *The Times*: "If the enemy are only half as much afraid of them as we who fire them they are doing good service."

The effect was wonderful. Like dozens of flying demons, these erratic projectiles went hissing and shrieking high into the sky, then went whirling down, hurling their explosives at the ramparts in a spectacular succession of blasts. Not a man remained on the walls after this "salvo from Hell."

"Double! Double!" Sir Colin shouted; and we broke into a run, cheering wildly.

Just at that moment, Sergeant John Paton of my company came running down the ravine on the left of the Shah Nujjuf; and though completely out of breath at first, he soon told us that he had gone up the ravine at the moment the battalion of detachments had been ordered to withdraw and had discovered a breach in the northeast corner of the ramparts, next to the river. It appeared that most of our shot and shell had gone over the south wall and blown out the wall on the other side in this particular spot! Paton then told how he had climbed up to the top of the ramparts without difficulty and seen right inside the place without detection, as the whole defending force had been called forward to repulse the assault in front.

Captain Lawson and his company were at once called out of line; and while the others (on command) opened fire on the wall in front of them as a feint, we dashed down the ravine—Sergeant Paton showing the way. (He was awarded the V.C. for his exploit, though it was done without orders; but it was not like Findlay's escapade.) However, the enemy detected our intended diversion; and as soon as they saw that the breach had been discovered and that their well-defended position was no longer tenable, they fled en masse out the back gate.

If we of No. 7 Company had got in behind them and cut off their retreat, it would have been the Secunder Bagh over again! As it was, by the time we got through the breach, we were able to catch only about a score of the fugitives, who were promptly bayoneted. The rest fled pell-mell into and along the Goomtee, and it was then too dark to use our rifles with effect on the flying masses. However, by the great pools of blood inside the place and the number of dead floating in the river and scattered on the bank, it was plain to see that they had suffered heavily; and so the well-contested position of the Shah Nujjuf was ours at last. And as it was Captain Dawson and his company who had first entered the breach, to them was assigned the honor of holding the Shah Nujjuf, which was now one of the principal positions to cover the projected retreat from the Residency.

By this time, Sir Colin and those of his staff remaining alive or unwounded were inside the place; and a hearty cheer was given the old chief. Both he and we were too tired for any more speeches, and that night he lay down with us in his clothes—none of us having had our clothes or accouterments off since the 10th of the month, nor would we for another fortnight! And thus ended the terrible 16th of November 1897.

In his General order of the 23rd, Sir Colin let us know that "all ranks of this force have compensated for their small number by fighting as hard as it ever fell to the lot of the Commander in Chief to witness, and it is with the greatest gratification that His Excellency declares he never saw men behave better. The storming of the Secunder Bagh has never been surpassed and rarely equaled in daring, and the success of it was most brilliant and complete."

9

SECOND TO NONE IN
THE WORLD

*The decisive action on November 17, which resulted in a meeting of
the advanced forces of the relief column and the Lucknow garrison,
was described by Captain Garnet Wolseley (later Field Marshal Lord
Wolseley) of Her Majesty's 90th Light Infantry:*

Our right front being clear by the taking of the Shah Nujjuf, we began
by pressing back the enemy on our left front so as to secure that flank
of the column, which was moving forward towards the Residency. The
great point to be attacked was what had been the officers' messhouse
of our 32nd Regiment, which had long formed the most important
part of the Lucknow garrison before the Mutiny. We knew it was surrounded by a masonry-reveted ditch having two drawbridges over
it—one towards us, the other towards the city. It stood on high ground
in the middle of a large garden enclosed with unbaked-brick walls in
a dilapidated condition, and both it and the garden were held in force
by the enemy.

When Sir Colin Campbell had pounded it for a considerable time
with all his available guns, he sent for me and made quite a flattering
little speech, saying he had selected me for this attack and describing
what he knew of the messhouse defenses. He added that if I found I
could not take it, I was to place my men under cover and return myself
to tell him what I had seen and done. All he said conveyed to me the
impression that he did not think we should succeed at our first
onslaught, which was an unpleasant reminder of what had happened
the day before, but I suppose he wanted to give us a chance to redeem
ourselves for that fiasco. However, I was in the seventh heaven of
delight and extremely proud at being thus selected for what Sir Colin
evidently deemed a difficult and dangerous duty; and I was also

159

pleased beyond measure with the kind expressions he used towards me, considering what he had said the day before.

But I must confess that running then through the back of my brain was the suspicion that my company was to be employed upon a perilous attempt which, although it might not succeed, might yet open the way for the Highlanders. We all suspected that he wished his dispatch to announce that one of his old Crimean Highland Brigade regiments—the so-called "thin red line" at Balaclava—was the first to join hands with the besieged garrison. And being the eldest son of a Glasgow carpenter, and one who rose by merit rather than money, it was expected that he would show the kind of favoritism that would have been beneath the dignity of a "gentleman." (His battle cry, "We'll have none but Highland bonnets here!", during the assault on the Russian-held heights of Alma, was oft-quoted.) Anyhow, thoughts such as these may have been unworthy of the great and splendid soldier to whom they applied; but after all, the conviction that inspired them stimulated all in my company at the moment and made them determined that "no britchesless Highlanders" should get in front of them that day. In fact, I overheard many of them express that determination in very explicit Anglo-Saxon. And I should add that it is this intense feeling of regimental rivalry that is the lifeblood of our army and makes it what it is in action—second to none in the world—but speaking for myself, it is unbecoming a gentleman-officer to encourage such feeling, which is better left to the sergeants; so I said nothing to my men about the "kilties."

Having front-formed my company, I started with them at a good steady double for the messhouse; and close behind us came our supports: the company of Captain Irby, who was (as usual) smiling and using strong language to all around him. I steadied my men and "whipped" them in at the broken-down garden wall as we easily scrambled over it and then made for the open doorway of the messhouse itself. It was a fine, strongly built square building; and as I reached the masonry-reveted ditch round it, I rejoiced to find the drawbridge down and quite passable. It had suffered, however, from the heavy bombardment we had kept up so long upon the position generally; and it was broken at places, so we had to watch our step. As I ran across it, no enemy was to be seen anywhere! In fact, not a shot had yet been fired at us.

I ran through to the corresponding door on the opposite side of the empty house and could see the enemy as they scuttled off from the bullets some of my men were firing to help them on their way. The garden in that direction seemed fairly full of them. As ordered, my bugler sounded the 90th "call" and the "advance" as we crossed the other drawbridge; and I soon found my pal Captain Irby, with his company, beside me. With them also came a number of the 53rd Regiment, who seemed to be everywhere during all of the fighting. (No corps in India had a more deservedly high fighting reputation, nor one for more disorderly conduct and insubordination. It was mostly composed of reckless, daredevil Irishmen, who practically led themselves because few officers could be found willing to take them on.) They immediately went after the fugitives, though overwhelmingly outnumbered, and by sheer audacity drove them out of the garden and into other enclosures.

The enemy elsewhere opened a heavy fire upon the messhouse as soon as we got into it, obliging us to keep under cover till we decided what to do next. I had no orders as to what we should do if we succeeded in taking the place, probably because we were considered a forlorn hope; so, pointing to a very large and fine building to our left front, I said to my good cheery comrade, Captain Irby, who laughed and cursed at everything, "You go and take it, whilst I take the place to our right."

He laughed and cursed, as usual, but nodded agreeably. The building he and his men took (without much of a struggle) was called the Tara Kothee or "Star House," as it had once been the Royal Observatory of Oudh.

The building I selected to make for seemed an extensive one; but I did not know then that it was the Motee Mahul or "Pearl Palace," which joined the advanced position recently occupied by the besieged headquarters company of my own battalion in the Chutter Munzil or "Umbrella Mansion." Followed by my subalterns and men, numbering a little over one hundred in all, I got over the garden wall of the messhouse in the direction of the Residency. We were then in a broad road up which the enemy were firing pretty merrily from the Kaiser Bagh (Caesar's Garden) or main palace and neighboring buildings, so we passed them at a run to obtain shelter in an arcade outside the front wall of the Motee Mahul and close to the great gate into it.

This "Pearl Palace" was surrounded by a thick masonry wall at least twenty feet in height; and in front of the gateway was a high

brick wall, some fifteen yards in extent and well loopholed, which had
recently been built, as the mortar was still fresh. However, the defenders had failed to dig a ditch outside; so after they gave us their first volley, we manned the loopholes on our side of the brick wall; and there
we stood, the enemy on one side and we on the other, both striving for
the holes—a continuous poking and firing of weapons in and out.

I had a few men wounded and was consequently anxious to dig a
hole as quickly as possible through this newly constructed brickwork
whilst the mortar was still soft. Bayonets could have done the job, but
would have taken too long; so I sent my old "batman" or servant
(Private Andrews) back to those in reserve under the arcade, to have
them bring the crowbars and pickaxes we were provident enough to
bring with us. He came double quick, during which Andrews was
felled by a shot from a loophole. I ran into the road where he fell and
proceeded to drag him back under cover. Whilst I was doing so, another shot (coming from a loophole not ten feet off) went through him. I
soon had him under the arcade, however, where one of our assistant
surgeons patched him up temporarily; but, poor fellow, he was never
able to serve again. He was a pure Cockney—had served as my batman all through the Crimean War—and a braver or more daring soldier I never knew.

The tools were put to use at once, and in a short time we had a
hole big enough for a man to get through; so in we went, one after the
other, as fast as we could. In their haste to get out of our way, the
enemy left the gate open; so we charged on into the courtyard, along
one side of which a small number of the enemy took refuge in some
rooms, firing at us from the open doors and windows, whilst the rest
made for the rear gate. We made short work of those who remained,
going in after them with the bayonet; and I had a "close one" inside a
doorway when a man suddenly made a fierce cut at me with his tulwar, which nearly shaved my head as I just managed to avoid it. My
own sword was through him just as quickly. We then went after those
who bolted out the back, killing many of them, and had capital practice at the ones who attempted to swim across the river close by.

As this potting was going on, suddenly there was an explosion on
the west side of the courtyard; and out of the cloud of dust and smoke
that rose from it, there ran forward an officer and a number of British
soldiers from the direction of the Residency. To the astonishment of us
all, it was none other than Captain Tinling of our regiment with his

company behind him. They had sprung a mine to blow down the palace wall, to enable them to make a sortie in order to meet our relieving force. Thus, the first greetings between the relieved and the relievers were between two companies of the 90th; but this fact was not recorded in any dispatch. When Tinlin shook my hand heartily and asked how I was, all I could say was "Tolerable, but I lost a number of my men at those infernal loopholes."

Whilst we were in the courtyard, exchanging greetings, Brigadier the Hon. Adrian Hope (who had just arrived) took me aside and said, "I advise you to keep out of Sir Colin's way. He is furious with you for pushing on beyond the messhouse, for the capture of which his orders to you alone extended."

"Rather hard on me!" was my answer. However, I was fully compensated by the extremely kind and flattering terms in which Hope spoke to me of what my company had achieved. But I confess that I felt much hurt by what he told me of Sir Colin, though I fully understood the reason. I had upset his little plan for the relief of the Lucknow garrison by the 93rd Highlanders.

Brigadier Hope then said to me, "Your men must be tired. Take them back along the main road and halt upon it near the Shah Nujjuf. They will be sure of having a quiet night there, and they want it."

Rather sore—very sore indeed, I may say—at what my brigadier had told me, I marched my men off to the appointed spot, where they piled arms upon the side of the road; and all having had something to eat, we unrolled our greatcoats and lay down there without tents or cots for a good night's rest.

I don't know how long I had been in the land of dreams when I was roused by the angry voice of one of my subalterns: a "charming" man named Carter. As he was using strong language, I inquired what the matter was. He said that "some infernal son of a bitch" had put one of the legs of a cot right in the middle of his stomach. That was ominous! Who, other than a "big gun," would have had a cot? But I turned over and fell asleep again.

At the first streak of dawn, I awoke and sat up. My eyes lit upon the offending cot that Carter had condemned to the Devil. Its occupant woke up at the same moment, and to my horror I saw it was Sir Colin Campbell. He also had come back to that quiet spot on the road for some sleep, and someone had found a cot for him. In placing it on the road, he had accidentally planted one of its legs upon my subaltern

Carter's stomach. He then made the mistake of stepping on another man, who called him a "bloody bastard," thinking he was some other "blisterfoot." The whole situation under ordinary circumstances would have been intensely comical had it not been for what Brigadier Hope had told me the evening before.

Sir Colin saw me in a moment; and shaking his fist at me, with half a frown and a smile, he said, "How dared you attack the Motee Mahul without instructions? If I had but caught you yesterday!" His anger had left him, however, and no man ever said nicer or more complimentary things to me than he did then. He ended our conversation by telling me I should have my promotion to Major, in place of poor Barnston; so, in the matter of exceeding one's orders, I learned that "nothing succeeds like success."

The action of Wolseley's company of the 90th at the Motee Mahul had its effect on Dawson's company of the 93rd at the Shah Nujjuf as recounted by Corporal Mitchell:

About half an hour after our assaults on the messhouse and the Motee Mahul had commenced, a large body of the enemy (numbering at least six or seven hundred), whose retreat had evidently been cut off from the city, crossed over from the messhouse into the Motee Mahul in our front; and forming up under cover of some huts between the Chutter Munzil and the Motee Mahul, they evidently made up their minds to try and retake the Shah Nujjuf and thus cut off our rear and line of communications and retreat.

They debouched on the plain with a number of men in front carrying scaling ladders; and Captain Dawson, being on the alert, ordered all the men to kneel down behind the parapet loopholes with rifles sighted for five hundred yards and wait for the word of command. It was now our turn to know what it felt like to be behind loopholed walls; and we calmly awaited the enemy, watching them forming up for a dash on our position, having raised and set our backsights at five hundred yards. The silence was profound.

But we were thoroughly ready for them. We had just got a fresh supply of ammunition; and our Enfields had been well scraped and sponged out, which they sorely needed, because they had not been cleaned since the day we advanced from the Alum Bagh. They had, in fact, got so foul with four days' heavy work that it was almost impossible to load them. The paper cartridges frequently jammed in the barrels, causing misfires; the nipples became so clogged that the copper percussion caps could not detonate the charges; and even when firing was possible, commonly by using a smaller caliber of ball cartridge than that meant for the Enfield, the recoil had become so great that the shoulders of many of the men were perfectly black and blue with bruises.

Captain Dawson, who had been steadily watching the advance of the enemy and carefully calculating their distance, suddenly called out: "Attention! Prepare to fire! Five hundred yards! Ready! Present! One, two—fire!"

Over eighty rifles rang out, and almost as many of the enemy went down like ninepins on the plain. Their leader was in front, mounted on a finely accoutered charger, and he and his horse were evidently both hit. He at once wheeled round and made for the Goomtee, but horse and man both fell before they got near the river.

After the first volley, every man of us loaded and fired independently and rapidly; and the plain was soon strewn with dead and wounded. The unfortunate assaulters were now caught between two fires, for the force that had attacked the messhouse and the Motee Mahul commenced to send grape and canister into their rear; so the routed rebels threw down their arms and scaling ladders, and all that were able to do so bolted pell-mell for the Goomtee. Only about a quarter of the original number, however, reached the opposite bank; for when they were in the river, our men rushed to the corner of the ramparts nearest to them and kept peppering away at every head above water.

One tall fellow, I well remember, acted as cunningly as a jackal. Whether struck or not, he fell just as he got into shallow water on the opposite side and lay without moving, with his legs in the water and his head on the land. He appeared to be stone-dead, and so every rifle was now turned on those that were running across the plain towards the Badshah Bagh or "King's Garden" enclosure; while many others, who were evidently severely wounded and either on the ground or unable to move fast, were fired on (as our fellows said) "in mercy, to put them out of pain," just as if they were wounded game.

But to return to the fellow who was lying half-covered with water on the opposite bank of the Goomtee and who was ever after spoken of as "The Jackal," because jackals (like foxes) have often been known to play dead and wait for a chance of escape. After he had lain apparently dead for about an hour, someone noticed that he had gradually dragged himself out of the water, till all at once he sprang to his feet and ran like a deer towards the Badshah Bagh. He was still quite within easy range, and several rifles were leveled at him, but Sergeant Findlay, who was on the rampart and was himself one of the best shots in the company, called out: "Don't fire men! Give the poor devil a chance!"

So, instead of a volley of bullets, the men's better feelings prevailed; and "The Jackal" was reprieved, with a cheer to speed him on his way. As soon as he heard it, he realized his obligation. He halted and turned round; and putting up both his hands with the palms together in front of his face, he salaamed profoundly, prostrating himself three times on the ground by way of thanks, and then walked slowly away; while we on the ramparts waved our feather bonnets and clapped our hands to him in a token of goodwill. I have often wondered if he ever fought us again, or if he returned to his village to relate his exceptional experience of our clemency. Although this war was a brutalizing one for civilized men to be engaged in, and there was certainly nothing like it for putting all feelings of humanity and mercy out of the question on both sides, it did have its exceptional incidents.

Just at this time, we noticed a great commotion in front and heard our fellows—and even those in the Residency—cheering like mad. The cause we shortly after learned. The Residency garrison was relieved, and the women and children were saved; and every man in the relief force slept with a lighter heart that night. Such was the glorious issue of the 17th of November. But to accomplish this object, our small force had lost no less than eleven officers killed and thirty-six wounded, one hundred and twelve men killed and three hundred and ninety-three wounded, and five men missing—more than an eighth of our whole number. The brunt of the loss fell on the artillery and naval brigades (105 men), and on the 53rd (76), the 93rd (108), and the 4th Punjab Infantry (95). But if the cost was heavy, the gain was great. Over four thousand rebels were found slain; and about three thousand more, both wounded and dead, had been carried off by their comrades.

10

THE FIRE WAS MOST DEADLY

Although Campbell was able to do what Havelock and Outram could not—raise the siege—he wasn't strong enough (even with their help) to recapture and hold Lucknow, which was one vast fortress twelve miles in circumference and defended by an ever-increasing number of over fifty thousand men with at least fifty guns. Besides, his communications with Cawnpore (still the main base of operations) were threatened by the remnants of Nana Sahib's army and large reinforcements from the west. So, having safely evacuated the several thousand invalids and noncombatants in the dead of night by the route previously cleared and guarded for them, Campbell could but leave a token force of little more than four thousand men and thirty-five guns under General Outram at the Alum Bagh (that fortified garden enclosure south of Lucknow) as a warning that he would return some day with a force sufficient to finish the job.

Field Marshal Lord Wolseley (then Captain Garnet Wolseley of the Queen' s 90th) stated: "I do not know of any instance in military history where a General was called upon to face a more difficult or more dangerous problem than that which Sir Campbell had before him in the relief of Lucknow's beleaguered garrison. His task was rendered all the more critical and delicate by the large number of women and children and sick and wounded who had to be brought away safely and without a hitch—which was, I think, the best piece of staff work I have ever seen. All in all, it was a great military achievement."

"Not the slightest hitch occurred in the night's proceedings," declared Captain Francis Maude of the Royal Artillery. "So well, indeed, was the affair managed that the enemy actually kept up their fire on the Residency during the whole of the succeeding day, thinking we were still there. Thus, nearly seven thousand persons (of whom not

more than two thousand were effective combatants) were quietly withdrawn with all their guns from the heart of a hostile city without the loss of a single man, woman, or child."

For some, like Dr. Joseph Fayrer (the Residency surgeon) and Lieutenant George Barker of the Queen's 78th, it was with "a feeling of sadness" that they abandoned the place they had defended so long—what Maude called "the scene of desperate slaughter"— "that had cost us so much trouble and so many lives." And after nearly five months of cannonade and fusillade, day and night, the sudden stillness seemed "unpleasant"—even "appalling"—to those who needed to be let down to a quiet life by degrees.

At 9:30 of that fateful morning of November 24, General Havelock died a peaceful but inglorious death from dysentery at the Alum Bagh. He had just been knighted and promoted for his service to Queen and country, and he told Outram: "I die happy and contented. For forty years I have endeavored so to rule my life that when death came I might face it without fear." He was buried in the garden; and he had, in the words of General Campbell, "established a renown which will last as long as the history of England."

Like Campbell, Havelock rose by merit rather than influence; but that rise was slower than Campbell's—not only because he couldn't afford to purchase his promotions, as was then common, but because of his "unclubbable" personality." He was always as sour as if he had just swallowed a pint of vinegar," said one of his fellow officers, "except when he was being shot at. Then he was as blithe as a schoolboy out on a holiday." Worst of all, in the opinion of the clubmen, Havelock was foremost of the few pioneers of army reform at a time when boozing, whoring, and looting were prerogatives of the British soldier; and his unpopular pre-Victorian puritanism found vigorous expression in India, where debauchery was at its worst and where the many men he saved from it were known as "Havelock's Saints." He also had a brilliant military career there, rising to Adjutant General of the Bengal Army and adviser to Her Majesty the Queen; but although Governor General Lord Hardinge once said that if ever British India were in danger, the Government had only to put Havelock at the head of an army and it would be saved, an acerbic Anglo-Indian editor later commented (on learning that Havelock had been appointed to such a position to quell the Mutiny) that he was nothing but an old fossil dug up by the Commander in Chief and only fit to be turned into pipe clay:

allusions to his stuffiness and fussiness. But the "old fossil" soon proved that he was equal to the emergency, which was why the Duke of Cambridge (Commander in Chief of the British Army) characterized him as second only to the "Iron Duke" of Wellington in saving the British Empire.

It was now left to Outram to maintain the foothold in Oudh and thereby his reputation as "the Bayard of India." Meanwhile, Campbell and his twelve-mile-long column made a forced march of forty-seven miles in less than thirty hours, during which everyone suffered from the unseasonable heat, suffocating clouds of ankle-deep dust, excessive thirst, swarms of flies and gnats and galled and blistered ankles and feet—some so bad that when the soldiers later tried to take off their socks, their skin peeled off with them.

The twenty-four hundred men that Campbell had left to defend Cawnpore were now besieged by more than ten times that number of rebels; and when he and his staff arrived at the bridgehead opposite Cawnpore, the officer of the guard exclaimed, "Thank God you're here, sir! We're at our last gasp."

"Damn your eyes, sir!" Campbell retorted. "How dare you say that any of Her Majesty's troops are at their last gasp!"

The column crossed the pontoon bridge under heavy fire, but luckily without loss, and the convoy of invalids and noncombatants was lodged safely in the fort and later transported downriver to Allahabad. Then Campbell, with fifty-six hundred men, drove the enemy forces away from Cawnpore on December 6, capturing most of their baggage and artillery and ammunition, with a loss of only thirteen killed and eighty-six wounded.

For the next three months Campbell maneuvered the reinforcements that were steadily arriving from England and elsewhere in the Empire, clearing the country around Cawnpore and then making the final advance for the retaking of Lucknow; while Sir James Outram held his ground at and around the Alum Bagh against an estimated one hundred and twenty thousand rebels—almost the entire mutineer force of the Bengal Army—whose hit-and-run tactics, though causing few casualties, were (as Outram wrote) "excessively harassing to the troops, who I am obliged to turn out constantly and keep under arms."

"These rebels give us no peace by day or night," wrote one of the officers, "peppering away at a great pace; however, we are all jolly and have no sickness in camp." This, despite the fact that living conditions

were almost as oppressive in the vast encampment as they had been in the Residency. The violent and bitter north winds of winter blew clouds of dust and sand into the tents and huts, covering everything and everyone, and the worn-out summer clothing of many of the soldiers made picket duty particularly trying. But their perilous position made them all the more hardy; for they not only repelled several mass attacks but made several counterattacks, driving the enemy out of neighboring villages with heavy losses.

The most determined offensive was launched by the rebels on 25 February 1858; and it was described in part by Major James Robertson, the commander of the 2nd Battalion of the Military Train, an all-purpose corps of 250 European volunteers who acted as mounted infantry, irregular cavalry, horse-artillerymen, and land-transport guards:

On February 2, 1858, and only a few days before Sir Colin Campbell arrived with the intention of capturing Lucknow, Sir James Outram (who had already been reinforced by several regiments of cavalry) was informed by his native spies that the whole rebel army in Lucknow had resolved to come out before the arrival of Sir Colin and wipe us clean out.

On this occasion, we started at daylight and moved from the right of our camp—being the opposite direction from which attacks were generally made on us. We were leading the advance, Sir James riding with me; and when we got to a place which was thickly wooded and where we could see no distance in any direction for the trees, the General said, "Halt here till I send for you."

The rest of the force marched on; and we were left quite alone, forming in two squadrons at half distance, and there we waited patiently for a long time. We could neither see nor hear anything, but we were under the impression that the battle had not yet begun.

Suddenly, a staff officer came galloping up to me furiously and said, "There are two guns which have been annoying the Jellalabad Fort all the morning. You are to take them at once." (The fort was about a mile to the right front of the Alum Bagh, and we had a strong picket there.)

"Where are the guns?" I asked.

"I will show you," he said. I replied, "Come on."

We started off at once, first at a trot and then at a gallop, when suddenly (to our great astonishment) we found ourselves on the right flank of the rebel army—some thirty thousand strong—drawn up in a perfect line, as if on parade. The officer who brought the order led us right along the front or the whole of this force, and only about one hundred yards from them. Of course, the moment we appeared, a tremendous fire was opened upon us, which lasted the whole length of the line. (General Outram's calculation afterwards was that there were eleven infantry regiments in this line.) A terrific running fire and a perfect hail of bullets streamed over our heads; but miraculously, I may say, throughout the whole of this gallop, not a man or horse was hit; and the only casualty I could ascertain was occasioned by a musket ball through the Trumpet Major's trumpet.

When we arrived right at the other flank of the enemy line, the officer who was conducting us (and riding alongside of me) said, "There are the guns,"—pointing to two guns, which were then in the act of being loaded, and were being supported by a strong party of rebel infantry.

I gave the commands, "Squadrons, left wheel!" and "Charge!", and we rode right at them. A small party of the rebels was drawing water at a well which stood in front of us, and every man of them jumped into the well.

I was leading in front of everybody, in the hope of getting at the guns before they were loaded. The first man I encountered was a fat old native officer who evidently commanded the supports. As I came towards him, he made a fierce cut at me with his tulwar, but missed his blow; and as I passed him at full gallop, I drew my sword across his naked throat and the blood spurted right up to the hilt of my sword.

Instantly after this, a second man cut at me; but I caught the blows on my sword, dropped my point, and ran him through the throat, breaking six inches off the end of my blade when it struck his neckbone.

At the same instant, a man on the other side hit at me, fortunately missing his blow; and I struck him fair over the head, splitting his skull, and dropped him.

Just then, about ten yards in front of me, I saw a sepoy with his finger on the trigger of his musket, aiming directly at my chest. I swerved my horse sharp to the right and called out in Hindoostanee to the man, "Run away, and I won't hurt you!" For one instant he hesitated, with his finger on the trigger, then threw the musket on his shoulder and went off like a greyhound. He knew perfectly well that the moment he killed me he would have been killed himself by my own men, immediately behind. I always fought in an old blue quilted jacket over my uniform, and he evidently mistook me for a private soldier, and so I escaped his shot.

There was a short and sharp fight; and not many of the enemy was left alive, except those who saved themselves by flight. Fancy our astonishment when we saw almost the whole of this great army in full retreat back to Lucknow; and as we stood by the guns we had captured, we had the pleasure of seeing a magnificent charge by Hodson's Horse, who went galloping in among the flying sepoys, doing splendid execution. They evidently had dashed forward on seeing our charge, and were in good time to do some excellent work.

I had time to look about me as we stood by the guns; and I found that my second antagonist had cut clean through the pommel of my saddle and taken off the point of the toe of my right boot, without inflicting the slightest wound either on myself or on my horse.

Just then, Outram rode up to me, trying to look fierce; but I could see a bright twinkle in his eyes that said quite the reverse. "You are a pretty fellow," he said, "to go and fight a battle all by yourself and spoil my plans."

"Why, sir," I replied, "I only obeyed your orders!"

"My orders?" he retorted. "My orders, indeed!"

"Yes, General," I rejoined. "You ordered me to take these two guns, and there they are."

"Who dared to give you that order?" he asked.

"There, sir," I answered. "There is the gentleman"—pointing with my broken sword to the officer who had conducted us. Outram rode up to him at once, but what passed between them I never knew. I expect the officer got it hot!

One often hears people talk grandiloquently of the proudest day of their life, and I can safely say that that was the proudest day of mine; for as we returned to our camp, we had to ride right along the front of the line; and as we approached, someone called out, "Here are the Military Train! Here they come!"; and the men of the infantry regiments, whom we were passing at the time, came running out of their tents— some with towels in their hands, and some with handkerchiefs— cheering loudly, waving at us, and shouting, "Bravo! bravo, Military

Train!", patting our horses' necks axed escorting us into our own camp. It was a spontaneous display of admiration at our gallant charge, which they had seen while formed up in order of battle. Had the rebels been worth their salt, they ought to have killed every one of us.

I had one poor fellow mortally wounded in the final charge of the guns, who came to me from the 17th Lancers and rode in the celebrated charge at Balaclava. As he lay dying in hospital, he said, "It is very hard, after being through the Balaclava charge, to be shot by a traitor."

Our total loss that day was five men killed and five officers and thirty men wounded. The rebels lost between four and five hundred, and it was the last attack they ever made on our position.

Outram's official report expressed "cordial acknowledgments" to all those engaged—"especially to the Military Train, whose brilliant charge excited the enthusiasm of all who witnessed it." And as for the officer who had conducted us: "Colonel Berkeley, my able and zealous Military Secretary, whose knowledge of the ground was of great service in cutting off the enemy's retreat, was wounded while gallantly charging at the head of Hodson's Horse."

In a letter written at the time, I stated that "the moment that Hodson's Horse saw our charge, they dashed into the flying rebels, making one of the grandest charges that could be conceived; and as I sat on my horse beside the two captured guns, I could see them cutting and slashing in all directions. They are a splendid body of men, and behaved magnificently. I may add that the General ordered the two guns which we had taken to be planted in front of our camp as an honor."

Major Hodson wrote to his wife: "There has been a great fuss about the matter—Sir Colin having taken great and very just offense at its being reported to him that the cavalry were 'led' by Colonel Berkeley, a staff officer. He got wounded and then was officially reported to have 'led the cavalry.' Sir Colin denounced Colonel Berkeley's 'leading' as 'an insufferable impertinence,' called me up, and asked me before them all, 'Were you present with your regiment on the 25th?' And on my saying 'Yes,' he cried out, 'Now, look here! Look at my friend Hodson here! Does he look like a man that needs 'leading'? Is that a man likely to want 'leading'? I should like to see the fellow who'd presume to talk of 'leading' that man!'—pointing to me. I nearly went into convulsions; it was such a scene."

Lieutenant Hugh Gough, the adjutant of Hodson's Horse, told the story of his participation in the action:

On February 24th, 1858, we received an order to make a forced march of thirty-six miles from our camp at Oonao to the Alum Bagh to reinforce General Outram, who was threatened by a large body of rebels. We marched all that night and arrived at the Alum Bagh on the early morning of the 25th, when we received orders to be ready to turn out at a moment's notice.

We had just time to have a cup of tea and a poached egg or two on toast when the order came to turn out. A large body of rebels had come up during the night to threaten our right flank. It did not take us long to mount and be off.

This was my first day in action with Hodson's Horse as a complete regiment—I might almost call it a brigade!—for by Major Hodson's influence and the magic power of his name amongst the warrior tribes of the north, recruits from the Punjab and beyond had come flocking in; and I should say we were nearly a thousand strong.

No time was to be lost, as the enemy had already heard of the reinforcements which had come in during the night and were therefore in full retreat to Lucknow. When we now came in view of them, they were passing in rather a disorganized mass right across our front as we advanced. We could see they had a couple of field guns, one gun being about six hundred yards ahead of the other. The main body was almost entirely infantry; and all were mutineer regulars, arrayed in uniform, with banners flying.

Our rapid approach had a great effect upon them. They seemed to make no effort to rally and stand; and as we advanced and then charged, we got well into them, cutting right and left; and the whole affair seemed over almost at once. The rearmost gun was in our possession, and the enemy (as far as we had encountered them) in full flight.

But somehow, owing to the ardor of the siege and the pursuit, our regiment got quite out of hand, lost all formation, and scattered; and the enemy, seeing our condition and probably having a leader with a good cool head, rallied round their remaining gun, regained their formation as we lost ours, and pouring in volleys of musketry with discharges of grape from their gun, rendered our confusion worse confounded.

Our men, gallant and forward in pursuit or a charge, could not stand being hammered at a disadvantage and began to fall back. There was a din of shouting—officers doing their best to bring the men up and re-form them—but all to no effect, and it looked sadly probable that Hodson's Horse would in their turn retreat.

Hodson himself, at this crisis, managed to get a few brave spirits together—not more than a dozen. Well I remember him, with his sword arm in a sling from a wound he had received in a recent skirmish, brandishing a hogspear in his left hand and shouting to the men to follow him as he made an attempt to charge. He and I were riding close together; and as we advanced with our small following, I saw his horse come down with him; and the next instant my own charger, my beloved "Tearaway," reared straight up and fell dead.

The fire was most deadly—the range was short and just suited to the point-blank discharges from the smoothbore muskets to which we were exposed—so that nearly every one of our small party was killed or wounded. Fortunately, I fell clear of my horse; and catching one whose rider had just been killed, I speedily mounted, and as good luck would have it, was able to rally our men to a certain extent. Seeing our supports (the 7th Hussars and Military Train) coming up, they now came on with a will and a vengeance, and charging the remaining gun, scattered the enemy in all directions, cutting down as many of them as they could.

My temporary charger—a small gray country-bred mare—carried me well; and we followed the enemy in pursuit, the British cavalry also cutting in. But it was no easy matter, as the enemy had got amongst trees and low jungle and were guarded by a village, where cavalry were not of much use.

In the ardor of pursuit, I had got well ahead of my men, when I came upon a couple of sepoys on their way to the village. They had their bayonets fixed, and seeing me unsupported, stood defiantly—one in my direct front and the other on my right. I made for the one in front, but the one on the right took aim at me as I passed and shot me clean through the thigh—the bullet going through my saddle and my horse, striking her dead. Fortunately, I fell clear, though helpless. My opponents were just coming up to finish me off when they were sabered by a couple of troopers of the Military Train.

The affair was now over. Our casualties were three men and five horses killed; one officer (myself), six men, and twenty-three horses wounded. But the enemy suffered severely and were driven back into Lucknow; and we returned to camps and I was much pleased to think that our men had repaired their previous discomfiture. I believe that their temporary funk was really due to their having got out of hand after their first charge and not having time to rally before they had again to face the enemy's heavy musketry fire. The steadiest cavalry in the world might have found it difficult; and to an absolutely newly raised regiment, the position was a very trying one.

Hodson had been unable to remount after his horse was shot, so I had the honor of leading the final charge—for which he gave me much credit; but he was greatly annoyed at the behavior of the men and especially the native officers, and taking some of them round to my litter when I was being carried back to camp, accused them of being the cause of my being shot. But I gladly forgave them all, for they were really gallant fellows and had shown their good qualities on many a former occasion.

My wound placed me out of action for some time. However, I made a rapid recovery, and before very long, could limp about on crutches. The wound had been a very clean one, and the shot fired so close that it had scorched my breeches—the bullet carrying the torn cloth right through my leg. My other leg barely escaped injury by a shot through my scabbard, and a shot through my sun helmet missed my head by mere hair space.

11

CLOTH AND LEATHER AND FLESH AND BONE

The army that Sir Colin Campbell assembled for the recapture of Lucknow and the pacification of Oudh was the largest Indo-European force ever to take the field in India: thirty-one thousand troops and a hundred and sixty-four guns. But awaiting him in the most formidably fortified city in India were approximately a hundred and thirty thousand rebels with at least a hundred and thirty guns. However, dividing his force and effecting a pincer movement, he was able to drive his opponents out of the city by striking their flanking defenses and bombarding and storming his way through each connecting fortification in such a way as to prevent them from outmaneuvering him.

"We are engaged in a very rare operation," wrote William Russell, special correspondent of The Times; *"for seldom, indeed, has a besieging force ventured to bore its way into an enormous city, heavily fortified and defended by an immense regular army and a hostile armed population, by sapping through the adjacent enclosures, which facilitate our operations and cover us from the enemy's fire, as we bombard and storm each position at a time."*

On the 6th of March 1858, a division of six thousand men under Sir James Outram was sent northward across the Goomtee and then westward along the riverbank directly opposite the city. "The objective of our flank movement was not to attempt to capture Lucknow from the north," wrote Lieutenant Vivian Majendie of the Royal Horse Artillery, "but to assist in its being taken from the south by diverting the enemy's attention and then by establishing batteries which should enfilade and take in flank and reverse their line of defenses, which were chiefly erected at right angles to the river, and thereby render them untenable. Thus was our army divided into two great divisions: the one under General Outram on the left bank, the

other under Sir Colin Campbell on the right, both moving in the same
direction and parallel to the other, but the former always so far in
advance of the latter as was necessary for the establishing of the bat-
teries which were to drive the enemy out of their fortifications. After
this had been accomplished, Sir Colin would push forward his troops,
capturing position after position in regular succession."

The first phase of the operations on the right or south bank of the
Goomtee was described in part by Lieutenant Alfred Mackenzie of the
1st Sikh Irregular Cavalry:

On the 2nd of March, 1858, when our forces attacked and captured
the high ground at the Dil-Koosha Bagh or "Heart-Expanding
Garden" (a former hunting castle and deer park of the kings of Oudh,
several miles northeast of the Alum Bagh), I found myself in command
of the advanced party of the advance guard; for that was the position
of my troop that day. Immediately in rear of it was a squadron of the
9th Lancers, followed by more cavalry and by horse artillery.
Cautiously and steadily we felt our way between the Alum Bagh and
the Dil-Koosha Bagh, covered by half the troop in extended order,
commanded by Lieutenant Sandeman, who summarily brushed out
of our road sundry small bodies of hostile horsemen whom he encountered.

My half-troop was in support; and when the skirmishing began,
we pushed on and joined in the fun; and then was seen as pretty a bout
of swordplay as ever rejoiced the heart of a horseman. Through
orchards and plantations, with occasional open fields, an intermittent
series of little fights was kept up as we continued our advance. No
attempt at keeping order was possible or even necessary. As the rebels
scattered, so did we—each man singling out his victim. Clang! clang!
went sword against sword, then the sharp and dull sounds of blades
thrusting and slashing through cloth and leather and flesh and bone;
the shrieks and groans of men, the cries of horses, the spurting and
splattering of blood. The slaughter of the enemy was considerable, the
losses on our side trifling.

Suddenly, just as we emerged from a grove of trees onto an open
plain, a distant puff of smoke, followed by a loud report and then by
the familiar hiss of a roundshot as it tore through the air above us,
gave unmistakable notice that the ball had begun.

"Close up and take order!" I shouted. "Rein in and re-form!"

Another shot fell short, hit the ground in front of us and then ricocheted over our heads to the rear. Another and another, in quick succession, passed harmlessly.

While this was going on, I had instinctively wheeled my line and taken ground to the right, to make room for the troops which I knew would be pushed forward. The squadron of the 9th Lancers followed my example; a troop of horse artillery thundered up from the rear; more cavalry galloped out to the left of the guns; and. like magic, a line was formed to the front—the guns in the center, with cavalry on both flanks.

Up rode a staff officer with orders, and then the commands rang out: "Attention! Prepare to advance! Draw swords!" (Our sabers instantly flashed into light, gleaming menacingly in the rays of the rising sun.) "Carry swords! Slope swords! Forward at a walk—march! Trot march! Gallop ho!"

A trumpet sounded the "advance " and the "gallop"; and away we swept over the plain, straight for the enemy's positions under a furious fire—too furious and rapid, fortunately, to do us much mischief. One roundshot, however, smote a man of the 9th Lancers full in the face. His head disappeared into space, leaving a small red cloud that sprinkled those in its path.

In a few moments, we were within a hundred yards of the enemy, who were still frantically blazing away at us. Here, as ordered, we came to a halt; and our own guns, with the astonishing swiftness which is the admiration of all other branches of the army, unlimbered and came into action. Very different was their practice from that of the rebel artillery. Equally rapid, but with calm regularity, working like parts of a perfect machine, gun after gun, carefully and accurately laid, pounded away at the opposing battery with an almost instantaneously overpowering effect. A very few rounds and the fire of the enemy slackened away and soon nearly ceased altogether.

While this artillery duel was going on, I had a good opportunity of observing the effect of what is popularly known as "blue funk" on a young recruit. He was in the rear rank, and while the excitement of galloping to the front lasted, had kept his place among his comrades; but to sit still within a hundred yards of guns belching out smoke and noise and roundshot was more than his nerves were equal to, and he began—half unconsciously, I dare say—to pull on his horse's head and gradually back him out of the ranks.

This would never do! Example is catching; so I galloped round behind him and used language calculated to bring him to his senses, but without effect. With his mouth half open and his eyes starting out of his head, he continued to stare at the terrifying guns, greeting each explosion with a groan; and all the time, he kept backing his horse on to me.

I was obliged to put an end to this. In another moment, he would have bolted and disgraced us all—possibly infected some of his comrades with his own panic. So, for the last time, I shouted that I would run my sword into him if he did not "dress up."

He took no heed, and I then lunged at him with all my force. But his luck saved him. He had a small buffalo-hide buckler hanging from his left shoulder; and instinctively he twisted half round and caught the point of my sword in it, and there it stuck. The more I pulled and the worse language I used, the less would it come out—and I am afraid the string of words with which I expressed my disgust must have been far from discreetly chosen—when behind me a voice exclaimed: "Who commands this party?"

Upon my looking round, the unfortunate recruit's panic was nothing to what mine became when I saw the stern face of the Commander in Chief, Sir Colin Campbell. Caught in the act of trying to kill one of my own men, visions of a court martial—of the loss of my commission—swam before me as with one despairing effort I wrenched the blade out of the buckler and, dropping its point in salute to the Chief, stammered out my defense: "I really couldn't help it, sir! He was showing the white feather. I was afraid he would bolt."

To my intense relief, the grim features relaxed into a smile. "Never mind," said Sir Colin. "You were quite right. Look!"—pointing ahead—"they are trying to carry off some of their guns to the right front. Gallop after them and catch them."

It may be imagined I lost no time in carrying out that order and placing as great a distance as possible between me and His Excellency! My young recruit came too, and afterwards behaved very well. He turned out a good soldier after that "baptism of fire," and needed only to be startled out of his funk.

A hard gallop soon brought us up with the flying enemy, who were "scotched" by a big ditch, where they abandoned the guns and took to their heels, but too late to save themselves. Here I had a rather narrow escape from abruptly ending my military experiences. Two

Oudhian gunners, whom I was pursuing, suddenly turned round and stood at bay and almost simultaneously lashed at me with their tulwars as I charged between them.

The man on the right brought his sword down on my head—fortunately protected by a thick "pugree" or turban, many folds of which it divided and then glanced down onto my horse's shoulder, inflicting a long and deep wound. At the same moment, I delivered a swinging cut on his own cranium, which was covered by a small skullcap. That settled him effectually; but I had barely time to throw my sword round and receive on it a sweeping blow from the fellow on my left, which partially overpowered my guard and landed on my ribs—luckily much diminished in force, so that I escaped with a trifling flesh wound. He did not get another chance, for I dropped the point of my blade and ran him through the body.

I was well out of that scrimmage, but my unlucky horse was quite disabled; so I had to dismount, and entrust him to the care of one of my men, whose animal I borrowed for the rest of the day. A few minutes afterwards, another adventure of a touch-and-go nature befell me.

In a second melee with the fugitives, a brother officer had singled out a rebel foot soldier and was hotly striving to cut him down; but his antagonist, with bayonet fixed, kept him at bay and had just brought his musket to his shoulder to fire when most luckily, in the very nick of time, I saw what was going on and charged the sepoy, who (disconcerted by the sudden attack) hurriedly attempted to shift his aim onto me, but ineffectually. When he pulled the trigger, his bullet sped harmlessly past my face; while I brought the edge of my sword down on his skull with such good will that it clove in two, and he fell dead.

I must say that in the campaigns of the Mutiny, in which our native irregular cavalry was so freely used and played so important a part, hand-to-hand conflict was much more frequent than in ordinary wars. In fact, every officer of that branch had numberless opportunities of testing his skill at arms; for skirmishes were often of almost daily occurrence, and in each skirmish he carried his life literally at the point of his sword. That meant that there were many great sword-fighters in India at that time, but none greater than Major Hodson of Hodson's Horse. Whenever he encountered a rebel in single combat, he would ride round and round him, grinning, laughing, taunting him in the choicest language, parrying every blow as easily as if he were swatting flies, and deliberately playing cat and mouse with him, until at last he would catch him off-guard or blindside him with a fatal thrust or cut. Two or more opponents he would equally bewilder with his masterly horsemanship, his bravura, and his slick swordplay; and he never failed to kill his contenders.

I should add that the rest of our cavalry charged and took the rest of the enemy's guns immediately they were silenced by our own, and the first round in the contest for Lucknow was won by us.

Captain Octavius Anson of the 9th Lancers wrote on March 3:

When we got to the Dil-Koosha Bagh, we found that the enemy's batteries commanded the place all round. We were under fire all day. Colonel Little was struck by a musket shot which went through his left elbow joint (the difference of an inch or two in the direction of the bullet would have sent it through his heart); Trooper Turner, of G Troop, lost half his jaw and tongue from another shot; and one roundshot killed two of the Naval Brigade, about fifty yards from us, but there is something very exciting in being so near the enemy and hearing the roar of artillery going on all day.

And the Reverend James Mackay, chaplain of the 9th Lancers, noted in his journal on March 2:

As we approached the Dil-Koosha Bagh, over grassy ground on which were scattered many skeletons of rebels killed some time ago, a poor Lancer was brought to the rear in a litter, with his lower jaw horribly shattered (his chin knocked off) by a roundshot. Later, two of Captain Peel's Naval Brigade were terribly (and, I fear, mortally) wounded by another roundshot. One had his forehead shot off. A comrade jumped up and stuck it on again—a large piece of skull and brains; and the unfortunate man is still living, though in a hopeless state. The other had his right thigh frightfully smashed by the same roundshot.

General Outram encountered very little resistance except on March 9 at the Chukker Kothee or "Round House," a large yellow rotunda by the Lucknow racecourse, which was the northeast outpost of the enemy. A battery of the Royal Horse Artillery managed to drive most of the defenders out, whereupon they were pursued and savaged by Outram's cavalry, but what happened next was described by Lieutenant Vivian Majendie of the artillery:

In the lower story of this structure were some twenty of the enemy, who had either not been aware of their comrades' departure or had purposely remained behind with the fanatical determination of dying in defense of it; but whatever the reason, they were desperate men for whom there was now no escape.

While they held the rooms in the lower story, our soldiers occupied the rest of the place; and many an attempt was made to drive them out. But in spite of every effort, they held their own and succeeded in killing two officers and seven men and wounding five others who advanced with more courage than caution into the dark rooms in which they were located and where (from the fact of their entering from the outdoor glare) the intruders were comparatively blind and had fallen an easy prey to those whose eyes were accustomed to the partial darkness.

Shells with long fuses were then thrown through holes dug in the floors of the upper story and into the rooms they occupied, but with little result; as by moving from room to room, they were easily able to avoid them.

An attempt was then made to burn them out, which partially succeeded—one man being burned to death; while some others, driven out by the fire, were shot as they bled. Two or three also had been killed by the exploding shells; but a dozen more were still remaining, defying every effort to dislodge them.

Captain St. George of the 1st Bengal Fusiliers, accompanied by one of his subalterns, then entered the place and immediately shot two of the rebels with his revolver as they were lurking in the hallway. Passing on from room to room, he found them all unoccupied by any more live sepoys, until at last he came to a small and very dark chamber, which he incautiously entered, when two men (one on each side of the doorway) fired; and a ball struck him in the lower part of the chest. He staggered back into the arms of his subaltern, but at once recovered himself and walked out unassisted—looking giddy and sick, however, with eyes glazed and heavy—and feebly unbuttoned and helped to remove his own coat, when it was found that the ball had passed almost completely through his body from his chest to his back, whence it was afterwards cut out, being found buried very little below the surface. It was of course imagined that he was mortally wounded—no hopes whatever being entertained by the doctors of his recovery because of the internal injury and bleeding—but I am happy to say that he eventually went home with every prospect of ultimate recovery.

A young and much-admired officer of the Sikhs, named Anderson, was also killed with two of his men in the Chukker Kothee while endeavoring to expel the desperate occupants; and so at last General Outram, thinking that enough lives had been sacrificed in this manner, ordered some of our horse-artillery guns to be brought again to bear on the building. Five accordingly came into action and fired about twenty shells in quick succession at the windows and doorways; and as the smoke of the last round cleared away, Lieutenant Anderson's company of the Sikhs (who had been held in readiness for the purpose) received the signal, and dashing forward entered the house en masse.

It was most exciting to see them racing up to the place where (when they reached it) there was for a moment a confused scrambling at the doorways, then the sharp sounds of a few shots from within, then shouting and scuffling, then again bang! bang!; and finally there burst from the building, with triumphant yells, a crowds of Sikhs, bearing among them the sole survivor of the steadfast defenders. How many had survived the shelling and the Sikhs had killed I do not rightly know—and more, I heard, than two or three—but this one, alas for him! they had dragged out alive, perhaps knowing that he was the killer of Lieutenant Anderson (in whose honor they had been sent to storm the building) or of one of their dead comrades. And now commenced one of the most frightful scenes I ever witnessed.

Infuriated beyond measure by the deaths of their officer and comrades, the Sikhs (encouraged, I regret to say, by some Englishmen) proceeded to take their revenge on this one wretched man. Suffice it to say that they tortured him and then roasted him alive.

That few attempted (in vain) to stop this atrocity is hardly to be wondered at when you consider the number of our helpless sick and wounded who were tortured and burned to death in their litters nearly six months before, and when you consider that like many another war (such as our internecine conflicts in Britain, in which untold numbers perished in the same manner as this sepoy), this war of the Mutiny had most naturally assumed all the brutalizing features of a war of mutual retaliation and extermination. Besides, the whole thing was done so quickly and with such noise and confusion that to me, who beheld it from a short distance, it seemed almost like a dream—till I rode up afterwards and saw the incinerated remains.

So the Chukker Kothee was now ours.

12

NO QUARTER WAS SOUGHT OR GIVEN

The progress of General Campbell's operations on the south bank of the Goomtee was detailed by Sergeant William Mitchell of Her Majesty's 93rd Sutherland Highlanders:

After leaving Cawnpore, our infantry division—the 2nd, under Brigadier General Sir Edward Lugard—marched to the Dil-Koosha Bagh or "Heart-Expanding Garden," a palace and park barely beyond reach of the enemy's heavy guns, where we settled down for the siege and capture of Lucknow.

On the 9th of March, our division was under arms, screened by the Dil-Koosha Bagh palace and the garden walls round it; and Captain Sir William Peel's bluejackets were pouring shot and shell, with now and then a rocket, into the Martinière as fast as ever they could load. (This large and elaborate building was formerly a boys' college, founded by a French adventurer named Martin, and was now an outpost of the enemy, about fifteen hundred yards downhill from the Dil-Koosha Bagh, near the banks of the Goomtee. Its students and instructors had bravely served in the Lucknow Garrison.)

Peel's six-gun battery was constructed on the left front of the Dil-Koosha Bagh. In bringing up his ordnance, he might have gone directly into position; but with characteristic coolness, and with contempt for the enemy, he marched all the way round from the right and in full view of the foe. Mr. William Russell, the special correspondent of *The Times*, wrote: "It would have been a pretty sight, had it not been a matter of life and death, to see how solidly the bluejackets marched, with Peel and their officers among them, and how the sepoy artillerymen plumped shot after shot right across the line of their march—always contriving, however, to strike the spot over which a gun had just passed or that to which a gun was just coming. It was a terrible game of cricket, and we were all relieved when we saw the men and the guns safe behind their battery parapet."

Naval Cadet Edmund Watson, Captain Peel's fifteen-year-old aide-de-camp, also wrote: "It is quite a sight to see the Captain under fire, he is so cool. He was leaning on a gun one morning, looking through his telescope, when a shell came and burst quite close to us; and he never even lifted his head, but kept looking through the glass all the while. And when a man behind him exclaimed that the bits were coming down like a shower of rain, he said, 'Nonsense, non-sense; it's only the dust and dirt.'"

But Peel tempted Providence once too often and suffered a strange fate for it. Captain Oliver Jones, R.N., wrote of the 9th of March: "Peel, with his usual indifference to danger, thinking only of the effects of his shot against the Martinière and taking no notice of the bullets which were buzzing about our ears, was standing upon a little knoll—a fair target to the rebel marksmen, whom we could see laying their muskets along the top of the rifle pit in front of the building; then puff—a little white smoke, then bang! and whiz!, then sput! against some stone as the bullet fell flattened close to our feet. At last, one bul-let (more true than the others) struck the Captain; and he fell, saying, 'Oh, they've hit me!' It passed almost through his left thigh, close to the bone. He was taken to the Dil-Koosha Bagh, where the bullet was extracted, and his only annoyance was that the wound was severe enough to keep him from his guns."

When Lucknow was captured and the Naval Brigade was ordered to return to their usual duties, one of the late King of Oudh's carriages was prepared for Peel, to convey him down to Calcutta. However, he declined to make use of it, saying that he would prefer to travel in a litter like one of his bluejackets. As fate would have it, the litter in which he was placed had been used by a smallpox patient. He got as far as Cawnpore, where he was attacked by the disease; and on the 27th of April, his gallant soul ingloriously fled.

About two o'clock P.M. on the 9th of March, after a hearty bom-bardment of the Martinière, the order was given for the advance—the 42nd Royal Highlanders to lead and the 93rd to support; but we no sooner emerged from our shelter than the orderly advance became a rushing torrent, the better to minimize our losses. Both regiments dashed down the grassy slope abreast; and the earthworks, trenches, and rifle pits in front of the Martinière were cleared in a flash—the enemy flying before us as fast as their legs could carry them. We pursued them right through the gardens, capturing their first line of defenses along the canal in front of Major Banks's bungalow and the Begum's palace.

The next day, after our heavy guns cleared the building and grounds, we occupied the premises of Banks's house without a struggle; and thus we slowly and methodically advanced, taking position after position, step by step. For this, our old chief got the nickname of "Sir Crawlin' Camel" from the hotspurs among us; but he did not care to make the mistakes of the past, and by that he kept our losses at a minimum.

The house of Major Banks (the late second in command of the original Lucknow garrison), though in ruins, had a large compound surrounded by high mud walls. There we halted for the night in some outbuildings and set about preparing some food, our heavy guns and mortar batteries being meanwhile advanced from the Dil-Koosha Bagh to breach the Begum Kothee or "Queen's Mansion," which was actually an immense block of palaces and other structures, courtyards, and walled gardens—all heavily fortified and defended by more than five thousand men—immediately in front of and covering the Kaiser Bagh or "Caesar's Garden," which was the main citadel of Lucknow. Thus, the Begum Kothee was the key of the enemy's position along the canal, forming the southern point of the second line of defense, and its capture would facilitate the taking of every other stronghold.

While we were eating, the enemy pitched some shells into our position; and one burst close to a private of my section named Tim Drury, a big stout fellow, killing him on the spot. His body lay where he fell, just outside our hut, with one thigh nearly torn away; but you must not for a moment think that such a sight took away our appetites in the least. Having seen so much of death, we could now look upon the dead body of a comrade with as much indifference as if it were a pariah dog; and the only thought in one's mind was: Well, it's his turn now; and it may be mine next; and there's no use in being downhearted!

In the wee hours of the morning of the 11th of March, the Naval Brigade commenced bombarding the outer defenses of the Begum Kothee with five 68-pounders, nine 8-inch howitzers, and eight 5.5-inch mortars. Soon after daybreak, when the effect of their fire could be clearly seen, one of those unfortunate accidents of war occurred when Midshipman Garvey was sent on horseback to deliver messages to each of the three batteries. While passing in front of the row of mortars at a gallop, he did not see that the quick matches were alight until it was too late for him to stop; and the charges igniting, one shell struck him in the head, causing instant death. The horse he was riding escaped unhurt.

Mr. Russell of *The Times* wrote of this incident: "I heard an exclamation of alarm from the men at one of the mortars. As the smoke of the gun cleared away, I saw the headless trunk of a naval officer on the ground. It was a horrid sight. He had been killed by a shell which had been discharged just as he rode before the muzzle." Elsewhere he wrote: "Of all horrid sights, I know none so bad as seeing a man's brains washed out like froth by a cannonball!"

Our bluejackets then brought two of their heaviest guns to within fifty yards of the walls; and after about fourteen hours of steady battering, two practicable breaches were finally made in the outer and inner defenses.

It was now about half past four o'clock P.M. This hail barely finished our evening meal when we noticed a stir among the staff officers and a consultation taking place between our division commander (General Lugard), our brigade commander and former colonel (Brigadier the Hon. Adrian Hope), and the chief engineer of the army (Colonel Robert Napier).

Suddenly the order was given to the 93rd to fall in and form up in two battalions or quarter-distance columns of about four hundred men each. This was quickly but quietly done—the officers drawing their swords and holding them in the "carry" position; the men tightening their belts and pressing their bonnets firmly on their heads, examining the ammunition in their pouches and seeing that their bayonets were tightly fixed.

Thus we stood in grim silence for a few seconds, when the tall form of Brigadier Hope appeared and passed the signal for the assault on the Begum Kothee by waving his right hand to our two battalion commanders. Behind us, in support, were eight hundred of the 4th Punjab Rifles and a thousand Goorkhas or Nepalese soldiers; but we stormers never needed them and had the job all but done when they were ordered to advance. However, once inside the stronghold, they did great service by disposing of those who escaped us and by covering the bodies of our killed and wounded and preventing the fleeing enemy from mutilating them. And I must also commend Lieutenant Commander John Vaughan, R.N., who brought forward a dozen of the best rifle shots of the Naval Brigade and covered our advance and kept the breaches clear by firing at the windows and loopholes occupied by rebel marksmen. Captain Jones wrote that "Vaughan was shortsighted and always wore an eyeglass, yet was a capital shot and as cool when under a shower of bullets as if there was no such thing as gunpowder and lead."

I must say that before we stood to arms, two men of my company—Johnny Ross and George Puller, with some others—had been playing cards in a sheltered corner of the garden wall and in some way quarreled over the game. When the order was given for the fall-in, Puller and Ross were still arguing the point in dispute; and Puller told Ross to shut up. Just at that very moment, a spent bullet struck Ross in the mouth, knocking in four of his front teeth. Johnny thought it was Puller who had struck him and at once returned the blow, when Puller quickly replied, "You damned fool, it wasn't I who struck you! You've got a bullet in your mouth!" And so it was that Johnny Ross put up his hand to his bloody mouth and spat out four front teeth and a leaden ball. He at once apologized to Puller for having struck him, and added: "How will I manage to bite my cartridges now?"

"Well," Puller replied, "I reckon you'll have to pinch off the ends with your fingers, like the bloody sepoys were told to do!" (The powder ends of our muzzle-loading greased-paper cartridges had to be torn open with the teeth and the powder poured into the barrel before being reversed and then rammed home, and it was this procedure that was thought to be defiling by the mutineers. The pinching process, however, was considered "effeminate" and equally unacceptable; and for all practical purposes, you couldn't easily hold a rifle and pinch off a cartridge end at the same time.)

Just before the signal was given for the assault, Captain Charles Macdonald (whose company I had joined after my promotion to sergeant) stepped aside and plucked a rose from a bush close by, as we were then formed up in what had been a beautiful well-kept garden; and going up to Dr. William Munro, our surgeon (who was busy giving directions to his assistants and arranging bandages, etc., in a litter), he gave him the flower, saying, "Good-bye, old friend. Keep this for my sake."

I have often wondered if poor Charlie Macdonald had any presentiment that he would be killed. Although he had been a captain for some years, he was still almost a boy. He was wounded with a severe bruise in his right arm early in the day by a splinter from a shell; but he refused to go to the rear and remained at the head of his company, led it through the breach, and was shot down just inside—two bullets striking him almost at once, one right in his throat just over the breast-bone—as he was waving his claymore and cheering on his men. After the fight was over, I made my way to where the dead were collected and cut off a lock of his hair and sent it to his mother. When I went to do this I found his soldier-servant crying beside the lifeless body, wringing his hands and saying, "Oh, but it was a shame to kill him!" And so it was! I never saw a more girlish-looking face than his was in death. His features looked strangely like those of a wax doll—which was, I think, partly the effect of the wound in the throat.

When we got the signal, Captain Clarke (who commanded the leading company of the left wing) rushed forward impetuously, waving his sword and shouting, "Come on 93rd!" We followed with a roar. "It was not a cheer," said Dr. Munro, "which has a pleasant ring in it, but a wild piercing cry, which had an angry sound that almost made one tremble. I never heard the like before and never since." (He must not have heard our shout at the Secunder Bagh!)

Anyway, we rushed forward, bounding over the battered garden wall and through the gateway and across the short stretch of ground to the Begum Kothee; and about twenty yards inside the breach in the outer rampart, we were stopped by a ditch nearly eighteen feet wide and at least twelve to fourteen feet deep. It was easy enough to slide down to the bottom; the difficulty was to get up on the other side! However, there was no hesitation; the stormers dashed into the ditch; and running along to the right in search of some place where we could get up on the inside, we met part of the Grenadier Company, headed by Lieutenant Ned Wood (an active and daring young officer), who were also looking for a way out.

Mr. Wood then got on the shoulders of one of his men and somehow scrambled up, claymore in hand. He was certainly the first one inside the inner works of the Begum Kothee; and when the enemy saw him emerge from the ditch, they fled to barricade doors and windows to prevent us getting into the buildings. His action saved us, for the whole of us might have been shot like rats in the ditch if they had attacked him instead of flying when they saw the tall and broad-shoul-dered "bearded lady from Hell" with a two-edged broadsword in hand.

As soon as he saw the coast clear, Mr. Wood lay down on the top of the ditch and was thus able to reach down and catch hold of the men's rifles by the bends of the bayonets; and with the aid of those below pushing up from behind, we were all soon pulled out of the ditch.

When all were up, one of the men turned to Mr. Wood and said, "If any officer in the regiment deserves to get the Victoria Cross, Sir, you do; for besides the risk you have run from the bullets of the enemy, it's more than a miracle that you're not shot by one of our own rifles. They're all on full cock!" And so it was!

Seizing loaded rifles on full cock by the muzzles, and pulling more than a score of men out of a deep ditch in the presence of the enemy, was as reckless as it was a dangerous thing to do; but no one thought of the danger in the desperation of the moment; nor did anyone think of even easing the lock to half cock, much less of firing his rifle off before being pulled up. However, Mr. Wood escaped every rush on destruction.

By the time we got out of the ditch, we found every door and window of the palace buildings barricaded and every loophole defended by an invisible enemy. But one barrier after another was forced—at first by ducking and holding up our bonnets on the points of our bayonets until the enemy had fired, and then shooting and smashing in the barriers with our rifles and rifle butts before they could reload, and at last by the use of heavy explosives; and men in small parties, headed by the officers, eventually got possession of the main square, where the enemy in large numbers stood ready for the last desperate struggle after having been routed out of the buildings. But no thought of unequal numbers held us back. The command was given: "Keep well together, men, and use the bayonet! Give them the Secunder Bagh and the sixteenth of November over again! Now, go at 'em!"

The fight raged for about two hours from room to room and from gallery to gallery and from court to court, which resounded with the cries of the wounded and dying, the shouts of our soldiers, the shots of the rebels, and the shrilling of the war pipes—our Pipe Major, Jock Macleod (having been among the foremost stormers), playing the pibrochs inside the scene of slaughter as calmly as if he had been walking round the officers' mess tent at a regimental festival. And as in the Secunder Bagh, the enemy must have stood in awe of him as one possessed of a demon—and a formidable instrument of war; for he strode about untouched, piping lustily. When all was over, General Lugard complimented him on his coolness and bravery. "Ah, sir," he replied, "I know our lads would fight all the better when cheered by the bagpipes." And so they did!

No quarter was sought or given; and by nightfall, over eight hundred and sixty of the enemy lay dead in the center courtyard alone, while many hundreds more were killed in the different enclosures and buildings. But the finishing stroke in the main square was easy work compared with the "ratting out" through dark narrow passages and rooms, where you risked being shot by unseen foes, and the series of separate fights that occurred all over the detached structures of the main palace.

Captain MacDonald being dead I joined a party of sixteen men under his successor, Lieutenant Sergison; and while we were breaking in the door of a room, Mr. Sergison was shot dead at my side with several of the men. I then took command.

When we had partly broken in the door, I saw that there was a large number of the enemy inside the room, well armed with swords and spears and firearms of all sorts; and not wishing to be either killed myself or have more of the men who were with me killed, I divided my party, placing some at each side of the door to shoot every man who showed himself or attempted to rush out. I then sent two men back to the breach, where I knew Colonel Napier with his engineers were to be found, to get a few bags of gunpowder with slow matches fixed, to light and pitch into the room. Instead of finding Napier, however, the two men found the redoubtable Major William Hodson, who had accompanied his old friend Napier as a volunteer in the storming of the palace.

Hodson, who should have been with his own regiment but who was never behind when fighting was to be done, did not wait for the powder bags; but after showing the men where to go for them, he came running up himself, saber in hand. "Where are the rebels?" he asked. I pointed to the doorway of the room; and Hodson, shouting "Come on!", was about to rush in. I implored him not to do so, saying, "Don't! It's certain death! Wait for the powder. I've sent men for powder bags." But Hodson took a step forward; and I put out my hand to seize him by the shoulder and pull him out of the line of the doorway when he fell back, shot through the right side of the chest. He gasped out a few words, either "Oh, my wife!" or "Oh, my mother!"—I cannot now rightly remember—but was immediately choked by blood.

At the time, I thought the bullet had passed through his lungs; but I later learned that it passed through his liver. However, I assisted his Sikh orderly to lift him into a litter; for by that time the bearers had got in and were collecting the wounded who were unable to walk, and I sent him back to where the surgeons were at work, fully expecting that he would be dead before anything could be done for him. As it was, he lingered on till about half past one o'clock P.M. on the following day, when (as his doctor said) "he died most quietly, without a struggle." He was buried that evening in the grounds of the Martinière; and even Sir Colin wept at the funeral, declaring that Hodson had been "one of the finest and most brilliant officers" under his command and one whom he was proud to call his friend.

I should add here that Brigadier Hope was just as reckless as Hodson, which resulted in his also being shot dead later in the Oudh campaign, and that he had the same effect upon the enemy as Lieutenant Wood. Seeing a narrow window on the side of a building, higher than those in front but not barred, he had a couple of strong men give him a hand. Hoisting him up by the feet, they shoved him headlong through the opening and into a room full of malingering rebels. This big, tall, red-bearded Celt suddenly tumbling in upon them, sword and pistol in hand, was too much; and they fled without a fight.

Shortly after I had helped to lift poor Hodson into the litter and had sent him away in charge of his orderly, the two men who had gone for the powder came up with several bags, with slow matches fixed in them. These we ignited, and then pitched the bags in through the doorway. Two or three bags very soon brought the enemy out—some eighteen or twenty of them—and they were all bayoneted down without mercy.

One of those who were with me was Private Rule, a powerful young man of the Light Company. He rushed in among the ousted rebels, using both bayonet and butt of his rifle, shouting, "Revenge for the death of Hodson!"; and he killed more than half the enemy single-handed.

By this time, almost all opposition had ceased within the buildings, the dead occupants of which were later heaved out into the courtyards by the Punjabees and Goorkhas; and many of the remaining rebels had gathered in the center square and at the gates. Lieutenant and Adjutant "Willie" Macbean encountered a "havildar" or sergeant, a "naik" or corporal, and nine sepoys at one gate and killed the whole eleven, one after the other, with his claymore, which is a heavy two-handed and two-edged broad-blade weapon, best for hacking rather than jabbing. Thus, he disposed of his opponents by blocking their bayonet thrusts and then chopping them down—at least two of them almost completely in half, from the shoulder to the groin, and another from side to side, and beheading the rest.

The havildar, who wielded a tulwar, was the last victim and nearly escaped; but by the time he got out through the narrow gateway, several men or the 93rd came to Macbean's assistance from the other side. However, he called to them not to interfere: "Stand back, boys! Fair play for the havildar!" And so he and the desperate havildar went at it with their swords, Macbean obliging his opponent by wielding his claymore like a tulwar. At length, Macbean made a feint cut, but instead gave the point and put his sword through the chest of his opponent.

For this exploit, Macbean got the Victoria Cross—mainly, I believe, because General Lugard was looking down from the ramparts above and saw the whole affair. I don't think that Macbean himself thought he had done anything extraordinary. He was an Inverness-shire plowboy before he enlisted, and rose from the ranks. Wielding that plow had made his wrists strong enough to wield that claymore like a tulwar. Anyway, during the regimental parade which was held for the purpose, the decoration was pinned to his breast by our division commander, who said to him, "This cross has been awarded to you for the conspicuous gallantry you displayed at the assault of the enemy's position at Lucknow, on which occasion you killed eleven of the enemy by whom you were surrounded. And a good day's work it was, sir!"

"Tush!" Macbean replied, unmindful of the moment. "It didn't take me twenty minutes!"

There were three brothers of the name of Ready in the 93rd called David, James, and John. They were all tall, powerful men in the prime of life. David was a sergeant, and his two younger brothers were privates. When we were falling in for the assault, John Ready took off his Crimean medal and gave it to his brother David, telling him that he felt a presentiment that he would be killed in that attack and that David had better keep his medal and send it home to their mother. David tried to reason him out of his fear, but to no purpose. John replied that he had no fear and that his mother should know that he had died doing his duty.

Well, when the assault took place, one of the inner courts of the palace was held by a regiment of dismounted irregular cavalry, armed with swords as keen as razors and circular brass shields; and the party of the 93rd who got into that court were far outnumbered, as in fact we all were everywhere else. On entering, James Ready was attacked by one of these "sowars" or troopers; his feather bonnet was knocked off; and the sowar then got one good cut at him, right over his head, which severed his skull clean in two—the tulwar cutting right through his neck and halfway down through the breastbone. John Ready sprang to the assistance of his brother, but too late; and although his bayonet was driven home with a fatal thrust, he came within the swoop of that terrible sword, wielded by the powerful arm of a tall man; and he was cut right through the left shoulder diagonally across the chest, and his head and right arm were clean severed from the body. The sowar having delivered his sword stroke at the same moment that he received the bayonet through his heart, both he and John Ready fell dead together. David Ready, the sergeant, then seized the tulwar that had killed both his brothers and used it with terrible effect, cutting off heads of men as if they had been mere heads of cabbage.

When the fight was over, I examined that sword. It was of ordinary weight, well balanced, curved about a quarter circle, as sharp as the sharpest razor, and the blade as rigid as cast iron. Now, my experience is that none of our very best English swords could have cut like this one. A sword of that quality would cut through a man's skull or thighbone without the least quiver .

I must also mention the case of Cornet Bankes, of the 7th Hussars, who was terribly cut up in charging through a band of "ghazees" or zealots. His right leg was lopped clean off above the knee, his right arm sliced off, and his left thigh and left arm both cut through the bone—each wound produced by a single stroke from a sharp, curved tulwar. The young fellow was reported to be still alive, and even cheerful, when we marched from Lucknow; but he did not long thereafter survive the unsanitary conditions of our field hospital.

I saw the regulation sword of one officer which was so twisted that he could not get it into the scabbard again. It was one of Wilkinson's best; but when it struck a rebel's breastbone, it lost its shape. I saw others that were bent while trying to penetrate the thick cotton-padded jackets that many of the enemy wore. One of our regulation blades had even been cut clean in two by a single slash from a tulwar, and another was also broken—literally smashed in its owner's hand—in an encounter with a tulwar. Lieutenant Osborn Wilkinson of the General Staff—and no relation to the swordmaker, he was quick to point out—told me that his own Sollingen-steel blade twisted and failed when he was merely giving point and that thereafter he joined other officers in providing themselves with native swords, which are of the finest temper—like our best claymores—having been made in Toledo, Ferrara, and Damascus. Indeed, many of these swords are so durable that they date back to the Middle Ages!

By the time darkness set in, all active opposition had ceased in the Begum Kothee; but there were still numbers of the mutineers hiding in the bedrooms and closets, and these had to be dislodged by throwing in bags of gunpowder with slow matches fixed to them. When these exploded, they set fire to clothing and furniture, etc.; and the consequence was that in the inner apartments of the palaces there were hundreds of dead bodies half burnt; many wounded were burnt alive with the dead; and the stench from such rooms was horrible. However, owing to the nature of the conflict, it was virtually impossible to have prevented such accidents. Our object was to drive the enemy out, not burn them to death, but despair made many of them prefer fire to steel. Historians tell us that Charles the Ninth of France asserted that the smell of a dead enemy was always sweet; but if he had experienced the incendiarism in Lucknow, he might have had cause to modify his opinion.

I should add that some of those who barricaded themselves in the buildings saved us the trouble by killing themselves or each other; while others, maddened with fear at the explosives thrown into their lairs, rushed out and perished on our bayonets; and it was impossible to draw water from the wells because of the number of men who had jumped into them to escape what they considered a worse fate.

Sir Russell of *The Times* wrote that, "The scene was horrible. The rooms in which the dead sepoys lay heaped on top of each other, gashed by blades and torn by bullets and mangled by explosions, and burning slowly in their cotton-wadded clothing, with their hair and skin crackling and their flesh roasting literally in its own fat, whilst a light-bluish vapor of disgusting odor formed a veil through which the dreadful sights could be dimly seen, were indeed chambers of horrors ineffable."

Our loss was small compared with that inflicted on the enemy. The 93rd had one captain, one lieutenant, and thirteen rank and file killed; one lieutenant, one ensign, and forty-five men wounded. Many of the wounded died afterwards.

Our only regret was that Sir Colin Campbell wasn't at the scene of our hard-earned triumph; but he was detained by a reception in honor of the Maharaja of Nepal, who had come to our aid with nine thousand Goorkhas. However, suddenly the tall and handsome figure of Captain Hope Johnstone (the Deputy Assistant Adjutant General and aide-de-camp to Major General Sir William Mansfield, the Chief of Staff), covered with powder smoke and the dust and dirt of battle, strode up to the reception area and interrupted the ceremony by saying to the Commander in Chief, "I am directed by the Chief of the Staff, sir, to inform you that we have taken the Begum's Palace with slight loss to ourselves, and that we are now in possession of the adjoining buildings as well, and have killed over a thousand of the enemy." (As Sir Hope Grant wrote, "The effect was very remarkable and quite theatrical.")

Sir Colin jumped to his feet. "Who did it?" he asked excitedly.

"Why, the 93rd, sir," Johnstone replied.

"I knew it!" Sir Colin exclaimed, rubbing his hands together and jumping up and down like a schoolboy. "I knew they would do it! I knew my lads of the 93rd would do it!" And turning to those at the reception, he added: "It will strike terror into them! By God, it will strike terror into them"—meaning, of course, the rebels. He had said this after our capture of the Secunder Bagh, and was wrong; but this time he was right. The fall of the enemy's first line of defense made them less determined to keep their other strongholds, and only a limited number of desperadoes stood fast in our way.

Sir Colin later wrote in his dispatch: "The capture of the Begum's Palace was the sternest struggle which occurred during the siege, the attack having been one of very desperate character. The manner in

which the 93rd Regiment flung itself into the stronghold was magnificent."

That night we bivouacked in the courts of the palace, placing
strong guards all round. It was too dark and we were too tired to drag
out all the dead bodies, so we had puny "strange bedfellows"; and
when day broke on the 12th of March, the sights and smells were sickening. However, large parties of camp followers and coolies were soon
brought in to drag out the dead of the enemy (some of whom were still
slowly burning in their cotton-padded clothing) and throw them into
the ditch which had given us so much trouble to cross, and then cover
them with the earth which the enemy had piled up as ramparts. (They
had literally dug their own graves!) Meanwhile, our batteries were
advanced to bombard the Imam Bara or "Patriarchs' Mausoleum"
and the Kaiser Bagh or "Caesar's Garden."

During the forenoon of the 12th, I saw Mr. Russell of *The Times*
going round making notes; and I heard General Lugard telling him to
take care and not to attempt to go into any dark room, for fear of
being "potted" by concealed rebels. Russell wrote: "I saw one of these
fanatics, a fine old sepoy with a grizzled moustache, lying dead in the
court—a sword cut across his temple, a bayonet thrust through his
neck, his left thigh broken by a bullet, and his stomach slashed open
in a desperate attempt to escape. There had been five or six of these
fellows altogether who had shut themselves up in desperation in a
small room—one of many looking out on the court. At first, attempts
were made to start them by throwing in live shells. The use of a bag
of gunpowder was more successful; and out they charged, and with
the exception of one man, were shot and bayoneted on the spot. The
man who got away did so by a desperate leap through a window, amid
a shower of bullets and many bayonet thrusts. Others had exited
through upper windows and even from the roofs, but usually by being
thrown therefrom by their pursuers!"

Many such were hunted out during the day; and as there was no
quarter for them, they fought desperately. We had one sergeant killed
at this work, and several men wounded. And as in the Secunder Bagh,
we encountered a few armed and dangerous women, who fought as
fiercely as the men. I will mention one case in particular. A sepoy stood
at bay in a room, with a woman beside him—both of them firing at
whoever came near them. He was at last shot down by a man of the
93rd, when the woman leveled her own musket and pulled the trigger.

But it misfired, and her brains were dashed out the next moment by the soldier's rifle butt. When asked why he didn't just bayonet her, the soldier replied, "On account of she knocked my bayonet aside and said, 'Naheen, sahib! Golee, sahib—golee!'"—meaning, "No, sir! The bullet—the bullet!" "But as I wasn't loaded—and damned if I could be so in a twink! —I just brained her—which was a far worse thing than what she feared, I warrant!"

During the afternoon, a divisional order by General Lugard was read to us, in which he thanked "the officers and men of the 93rd, who exclusively carried the position known as the Begum Kothee. No words are sufficient to express the gallantry, devotion, and fearless intrepidity displayed by every officer and man in the regiment."

British troops storming Delhi's Cashmere Gate in September 1857.

The massacre of surrendered British soldiers at Cawnpore's boat landing in June 1857. Most women and children survived this day, only to be killed weeks later as a relief column approached.

The Ganges River at Cawnpore.

Delhi's Cashmere Gate after the British had retaken the city.

British and Sikh officers of Hodson's Horse. Some believe that the officer in the center is Hodson himself.

General Sir Henry Havelock led the first relief column to Lucknow, but after suffering heavy casualties in street fighting he could do no more than reinforce the beleaguered garrison.

William Hodson, commander of Hodson's Irregular Native Horse. At Delhi, he killed the princes of the last Mogul emperor, but was in turn killed during the final battle for Lucknow.

Sir James Outram accompanied Havelock's relief force in September 1857, graciously declining to assume command. The ambiguity of his role vanished after Havelock died during the siege.

General Sir Colin Campbell avoided the bloody route taken by Havelock and Outram, and in November was able to remove the women, children and wounded from Lucknow. He later returned at the head of the largest British army ever assembled in India.

Lieutenant (later General) Hugh Gough winning the VC at Lucknow.

Colonel John Ewart leads the 93rd Sutherland Highlanders in storming the Secunder Bagh (Alexander's Garden) during Campbell's first relief attempt.

The Secunder Bagh after the battle.

The Dil-Koosha Bagh served as a rebel strongpoint during the final assault on Lucknow in March 1858.

Mining, or tunneling, in order to place explosives beneath the enemy's positions was a tactic employed by both sides during the siege. Above, soldiers listen intently for the sound of digging.

British countermining techniques could be amazingly simple. Here, a soldier waits for rebels who are about to break through the wall.

The British Residency in Lucknow prior to the Mutiny.

The Residency after nine months of siege.

Part of Campbell's artillery arrives at Lucknow. The British used camels and oxen as well as elephants to move their heavy equipment.

British and loyal Indians after the siege. Seated at right center is Thomas Henry Kavanagh, who snuck through enemy lines disguised as a sepoy to inform Campbell of the best approach route to the Residency.

Lieutenant Francis Edward Farquharson of the 42nd Highlanders during the raising of the siege of Lucknow.

After the battle, Lucknow offered a contrast between symbols of splendor and utter devastation.

The Kaiser Bagh, or King's Garden, a key rebel stronghold.

The Residency's billiard room.

The main Residency building after the fighting.

A British cavalry assault on the outskirts of Lucknow during the final stage of the campaign. The siege, which had begun in July 1857, was lifted in March 1858.

13

A DESPERATE FIGHT NOW TOOK PLACE

The storming of the rebels' most formidable bastion in Lucknow, the Kaiser Bagh, was described by Captain John Gordon of the Ferozepore Regiment of the Sikh Infantry:

On the 14th of March, Major Brasyer easily captured the Imam Bara or "Patriarchs' Mausoleum" with one hundred Sikhs and two companies of the Queen's 10th Regiment. The second line of the enemy's fortifications had now been turned; and Colonel Harness, commanding the Royal Engineers, was recommended by Brigadier Russell (who commanded Brasyer's brigade of General Franks's division) to stop the further advance by continuing the sapping and mining and to obtain secure possession of the ground that they had passed over.

But the Sikhs could not be restrained. Some of them had followed on the heels of the flying foe and made their way into an outlaying court on the left of the Kaiser Bagh. From the roofs of the houses there, a party of them under the personal command of Brasyer, along with some men of the Queen's 90th Regiment whom Captain Havelock (Franks's adjutant) had led to the spot, plied with such destructive musketry the three nearest bastions of the entrenchment below them that the enemy abandoned their guns; and Brasyer, leading his Sikhs by a deserted bastion, then proceeded to clear the enclosures on the right of the Kaiser Bagh.

Havelock now called up the 10th to support Brasyer; and he made his way from house to house, driving out the defenders at the point of the sword and bayonet. The walls of the houses and the surrounding enclosures were pierced with loopholes through which the insurgents commenced a well-sustained fusillade; and at so short a distance, every shot told. They were under shelter, making return fire ineffectual; but our infantry pushed on, forcing the barriers and dislodging the enemy without firing a shot. Their ranks grew thinner and thinner, and men had to be left to keep possession of the places as fast as they took them; but at length, about fifty of them reached the Cheenee or "Chinese" Bazaar, which skirted the Kaiser Bagh and lay inside the third line of defenses. The enemy, seeing their small numbers, began to gather around both flanks, when Havelock with some Sikhs charged along the line of entrenchments, drove out the defenders, seized two adjoining bastions, and with their guns checked and scattered off a large body of rebels who, finding that the second line of defenses had been turned, were making for the Kaiser Bagh.

General Franks and Brigadier Napier (our Chief Engineer) now came up with strong supports, and a consultation was heard in a gateway as to what was to be done next. Sir Colin Campbell, the Commander in Chief, had been led to expect a desperate resistance at the Kaiser Bagh, which was the main palace and central stronghold of Lucknow, and had therefore determined that after due siege had been laid, it should be stormed next day by the Highlanders. But after a brief consultation at the gateway, Franks and Napier came to the conclusion that they were perfectly able to take it then and there. So more troops were sent for from the rear.

When Franks had been reinforced, he sent forward his stormers; and as soon as an opening had been made by them from the Cheenee Bazaar, they entered the courtyard of Nawab Saadut Alee Khan's mosque and mausoleum at the back of the Kaiser Bagh. The Sikhs, only 150 in number and led by Brasyer, along with some fifty men of the Queen's 97th Regiment, drove the enemy from their guns in the courtyard of the mosque and followed them so closely that they soon found themselves in the main square of the palace. There, a large body of the enemy were ready to oppose them.

Brasyer was vastly outnumbered, but he plunged his handful of men into them with the bayonet; and they forced them all the way up to the Badshah Munzil or "King's Mansion," the special residence of the former King of Oudh. However, the rebels now began to collect in their rear; while from the windows of the palace came gusts of bullets.

Slowly the small band fell back, loading and firing as fast as they could, till they reached the open gateway on the northwest side of the Kaiser Bagh, out of which they drove the men in their rear. Here they took refuge. But directly across from this gateway was another, in front of which the enemy had a gun protected by a crescent-shaped loopholed wall. The gun opened fire at them from an embrasure, and this sudden report was followed by a peal of musketry from the loopholes. Then, from the palace buildings in their front, the enemy plied them with continuous musketry. They were caught between two fires!

But before the gun could be reloaded, Major Brasyer and Lieutenant Cary dashed across the outer court and single-handedly burst open the closed embrasure in front of it, then jumped into the position, immediately followed by several Sikhs. The gun was captured in a brief but bloody struggle; and the remaining enemy were driven into the gateway, where they were kept in check till reinforcements arrived. Then the supporting regiments—a mixture of British soldiers and sailors, Sikhs and Goorkhas—fighting hard and fiercely, drove the rebels through courts as large as the Temple Gardens and filled with marble statues and fountains.

The opposing masses ware broken; but these scattered multitudes found refuge in the buildings, and every palace became a fortress. From the green jalousies and Venetian blinds covering the windows which lined the walls in double rows, a stream of bullets were poured into the square; and the marble pavement was stained with the blood of many a Briton, Sikh, and Goorkha. But building after building was taken at the point of the sword and bayonet, which accounted for every man in their path; and bloodthirst, revenge, and greed for loot drove the assailants mad. When night put an end to the slaughter and pillage, the Kaiser Bagh Palace had become a ruined charnel house, in which more than six hundred rebel corpses lay scattered and piled amidst shattered and torn decor.

The next day, the remaining rebels were driven out or killed. Then guards were placed in the palaces, and plundering and destroying were stopped by order of the Commander in Chief.

Sergeant Thomas Malcolm of Her Majesty's 10th Regiment of Foot, wrote of March 14:

By sunset, we drove the enemy from three miles of strong defenses and made their case completely hopeless.

The Kaiser Bagh or King's Palace, the very heart and core of all the enemy's fortifications, was defended by ten thousand rebel sepoys. Here the fighting was most desperate; but we succeeded in driving the defenders from their position, killing (I am sure) four or five thousand of them. In one open space, the rebels were very numerous and had no means of escape. They threw themselves down on their knees and prayed for mercy; but no mercy they gave to us, and I can assure you they got none; for they lay six deep in this one spot alone. All the sweepers in the army were several days employed in disposing of the dead sepoys.

Sir Colin Campbell, when he heard that we had taken the citadel, expressed surprise, saying he had not believed it could be taken so soon.

On March 24, Malcolm noted in his journal: "Lucknow is in our hands. We all felt we were engaged in desperate work. For nine days and nights we did not change our clothes. We were not allowed to take off our belts and boots. We were not even permitted to wash our faces, and we barely had time to eat and sleep, until the place was in our hands."

Lieutenant Arthur Lang of the Bengal Engineers, who accompanied four Sikhs of the 4th Punjab Infantry, related his experiences:

We advanced so rapidly that before we could realize the fact, we were in the Kaiser Bagh! Few as our troops were, on they pushed—the enemy never being allowed to turn and re-form. We deployed by sections in the maze of passageways, entering every room and court.

Presently came a volley of bullets, smashing on the walls about us, with shouts of "Maro kafir suer!" (Kill the infidel pigs!) from some of the enemy who were skulking about in a garden. This garden proved a cul-de-sac from which they could not escape.

After having shot some four or five of those we could see, we left a few men at the windows overlooking the garden and then went out to kill the rest. But while we were beating carefully through the high grass and shrubbery, one of our watchers came out to say that the remainder were killing one another; and so we found fourteen lying in a heap, dying in one corner, with their throats slashed or their hearts stabbed by their own bayonets.

Lieutenant Vivian Majendie, of the Royal Horse Artillery, stated:

Many accounts of the capture of that grand stronghold, the Kaiser

Bagh, have appeared in print; but there was another operation carried on this day that, though it involved a great amount of desperate fighting and was perhaps the severest struggle which took place during the whole siege, has nevertheless been hitherto entirely unhonored and unsung. I refer to the capture of the "Engine House" by Her Majesty's 20th Regiment.

There was a large building, surrounded by several smaller ones, situated between the Kaiser Bagh and the river, and occupied by the enemy, which it was necessary to clear; and two companies of the 20th, under Major Ratcliffe, were detached for this duty—the remainder of the regiment, with some of the Queen's 38th, being posted outside. The detachment was then divided; and the greater number, under Captain Francis, entered by a narrow passage at one side of the building; while the smaller party, with Major Ratcliffe, entered at the other side. Oddly enough, neither entrance was barricaded.

Francis's party, pressing along the passageway, in which they had two men killed by the fire ahead, were first to arrive at a small room filled with a motley collection of mutineers. Detachments of almost every native regiment in the Company's service seemed to have assembled here. The blue and white uniforms of the Bengal cavalrymen and artillerymen were mixed up with the red and white of the infantry, while others were dressed in the plain white cotton clothes usually worn by off-duty soldiers. Equally various were their weapons. Matchlocks, muskets, carbines, pistols, sabers, scimitars, daggers, and even lances and spears flashed before the eyes or our men as they entered and drove the rebels at bayonet point into another small inner room.

A fierce exchange of fire was now carried on through the open doorway, the men on each side watching for an opportunity to deliver a hasty shot round the doorposts without exposing themselves too much. This, however, could not last too long; and eventually, Captain Francis ordered all his men to load simultaneously. They then made a rush through the doorway, firing as they went; and in spite of two of them being shot and two more cut down, they succeeded in effecting an entrance. A desperate fight now took place.

The small room was so crowded by the enemy, who were as thick as standing corn, that there was hardly space to move—our men having literally to mow their way through this living mass, plying their bayonets furiously and unceasingly, till they had made for themselves standing room. It must have been an awful scene, with all that hacking and slashing and jabbing of men jammed and struggling together, with occasional shots breaking in upon the hideous chorus of shrieks and curses and groans which resounded in the air, till the floor became wet and slippery with warm blood, which spurted and splattered all over, and heaped with trampled bodies.

The remaining rebels at last made a desperate attempt to escape by fleeing from the small room into a large central storage chamber filled with engines, cranks, pipes, furnaces, boilers, and other appliances of machinery. Just as they entered it, however, they were met by another body of rebels, who were trying to escape from the party under Major Ratcliffe, which had fought its way through from the opposite side of the building in the same fierce manner as the other party.

And now, hemmed in on all sides, with all hope of escape cut off and with nothing left to them but to die, the rebels seemed to become perfectly paralyzed and helpless with terror and despair, and made no further efforts—or very feeble ones, if at all—to defend themselves from our men. From the doorway at the opposite end of the room, a leaden shower rained in upon them—our men then actually piling up in the doorway the corpses of those they had killed as a barricade against the shots, few and far between, wherewith some of the poor wretches who still lived feebly replied to those murderous volleys which were striking them down by dozens.

The scene of horror at last began to draw to a close. The shots from the enemy, becoming less frequent, told that the work of death was nearly over; while our men, exhausted and sated with carnage, were firing a few last shots down the pipes and among the machinery, to put an end to the small number of rebels who were attempting to hide therein.

Just then, as though to magnify this overwhelming accumulation of horrors, a fire broke out in the building—the beams and doorposts having become ignited from the constant discharge of firearms—and the flames, communicating with the clothes of the dead and dying men who lay piled on the floors, and spreading rapidly, soon reduced the whole to a sickening, smoldering mass of disfigured corpses. And when I add that there were several living men who had hidden themselves underneath the dead bodies of their comrades in the hope of so escaping the general slaughter, and that these wretched creatures were thus roasted alive, you may agree with me that it would be scarcely possible to imagine a more ghastly scene.

The number of enemy killed in these rooms amounted to about three hundred, while fifty or sixty more fell outside the building in endeavoring to escape—having fallen into the clutches of the remainder of the 20th Regiment and the two companies of the 38th, who were stationed round the place for that purpose. This carnage was accomplished, incredible though it may seem, with a loss to us of only about eight or nine killed and some fifteen or sixteen wounded.

In connection with it, I have also heard related a tragic anecdote. In one of the buildings adjacent to the "Engine House," another body of rebels was also holding out desperately; and one or two of our men had already been shot dead when General Franks (who had commanded the division on the scene) ordered that no further assaults should be made, but that other measures—such as shelling or setting fire to the place, should be resorted to in driving out the occupants. Thus, until such measures could be implemented, anyone seen approaching the building was warned off.

But a little drummerboy of the 38th Regiment, who had greatly distinguished himself in the morning at the capture of the Kaiser Bagh (where he had been given a round of grog by some officers who had witnessed his daring conduct, after which he had returned to camp and obtained more "firewater"), now made his appearance on the scene, flushed with pride and promises of promotion and dazzled by the vision of a certain bronze cross with the words "For Valor" embossed on it—to say nothing of "pot-valor." Before anyone could stop him, he drew his toy sword (for it was little else) and threw himself with a shout into the building the enemy occupied. His horrified comrades could not have saved him even if they had gone after him; for hardly had he set foot inside the building than he was cut down, and his small body was ruthlessly hacked to pieces where it lay.

Needless to say, the enemy were evicted by 8-inch howitzer shells and then shot down by volleys. So much for this day, the 14th of March.

14

IN ALL ITS RUINED GRANDEUR

Lieutenant Vivian Majendie depicted one of the last scenes of the Lucknow drama, which occurred while he was stationed at the north end of the iron bridge that spanned the Goomtee near the Residency compound:

About 10:30 A.M., March 16th, our attention was attracted by large bodies of the enemy moving out of the city across the stone bridge at the northwest corner of Lucknow. We immediately got our guns into action and blazed away vigorously, the riflemen on picket assisting us by keeping up a hot fire from the roofs of houses; but the range (about one thousand yards) was too great for us to do much more than frighten them, as our heavier guns were then trained on the city and we were left with the light ones to hold our end of the iron bridge. However, we could have accounted for most if not all of the fugitives had we been closer; but Sir Colin wanted to give the enemy this one escape route in order to take the pressure off his troops in the city, where our losses should have been much heavier and the siege prolonged indefinitely by encountering thousands of desperate men driven into a corner and forced into an inescapable position. Later, as scattered bands, they could and would be more easily disposed of elsewhere; but for now, the immediate objective was to rout them out and thus deprive them of their greatest military and political asset: the capital of the rebellion.

About noon, the 23rd Royal Welsh Fusiliers, the 79th Cameron Highlanders, and the 1st Bengal European Fusiliers of our division appeared a short distance downstream from us on the opposite bank, to which they had crossed that morning by a rough bridge of boats which had been hastily thrown across the river, then advanced rapidly and drove the enemy before them, killing large numbers as they went and capturing the south end of the iron bridge, where a brass 9-pounder fell into their hands.

We had two light field guns and one 18-pounder on our end of the bridge and were keeping up as heavy a fire as we could upon the stone bridge, across which the enemy continued to pass, and also upon the buildings which they still occupied on our side and the other side of the river, and the whole scene had become intensely animated and excited as our Enfields rattled out their never-ceasing shots, while our battery added to the ever-increasing uproar.

A furious fusillade was kept up on all sides across the river, where bodies of our troops could be seen constantly pushing and rushing forward along the narrow streets, driving the panic-stricken enemy before them. Smoke and flames were rising up from several quarters, heightening the tremendous effect of shot crashing through domes and walls and showering bricks and stones into the streets below; of shells bursting high in the air and sending their fragments spinning and whistling down and tearing through all in their path; of the blazing sun overhead, shedding a fierce glare and heat that seemed to defy the fumes and fire of battle.

The stone bridge presented a scene of wild confusion glorious to behold and enough to drive one mad with excitement as shot and shell terrorized the crowds of fugitives who were pouring over it from the streets in which running fights were going on from house to house, where clusters of desperate rebels shut themselves up and fought fiercely, necessitating a series of small sieges on our part to force them out.

At one house in particular, close to the iron bridge, six sepoys made a determined stand; but our men at last got in, killed three, and dragging the others (who had cried quits) into the street, placed them in a row against the outside of the building and fired at them. One man, hit in the chest, sank down in a half-sitting posture against the wall; and when I saw him, life was not quite extinct. His dull eyes were wide open and stared horribly into vacancy; and his head turned in a slow and ghastly manner from side to side, much like those mechanical waxwork figures with movable heads, as though he were mourning over his comrades, whose bodies (pierced with several bullets) lay at his feet—the whole making one of the most terrible scenes I ever saw. We got a soldier who was passing by to send a bullet through the poor wretch's head and so put him out of his misery. There were many sights this day of an almost equally awful description, but none which has remained so indelibly impressed on my memory as this one—especially as, immediately after the man's death, a crow and a hawk swooped down to pluck out his eyes and snatch up his brains.

Sepoys who had been dragged from their hiding places lay sprawled in the streets, with their throats cut from ear to ear and with every gaping wound exposed by the nakedness of their bodies, which had been stripped by human scavengers; while overhead and in the shadows, winged and four-legged scavengers awaited their chance to feast. Nearly every house had been the scene of some short but desperate tragedy; up every lane and turning lay at least two or three bodies, fought over by looters or by the carrion eaters; and frequently, on entering a house, did one stumble over and start back from the mangled remains of one of its miserable defenders. Heaps of debris were everywhere—shattered furniture, utensils, and dead bodies all mixed up together in the blood-splattered houses and streets. We killed between three and four hundred of the enemy in that quarter of the city, but lost a hundred of our own in doing so. Very strange, unreal and sad, does all this seem.

There, down the quiet stream, lazily floated black, bloated, distorted corpses, sometimes collecting together in gruesome companionship at bends of the river, or holding horrible reunions beneath the arches and against the buttresses of the bridge; while huge obscene birds, seating themselves upon them, tore off the flesh and plucked out the entrails, and then soaring away with these morsels, enjoyed uninterrupted their beastly meal. A couple of young naval officers of ours went down from their battery in the Residency to have a swim, but the river was so choked with sepoy corpses that they could not make up their minds to jump in.

Finally, the flames uprising from burning buildings, and now and again an exploded mine rolling its dense volume of smoke with loud and long-continued reverberations into the air and hurling burnt fragments of human bodies in every direction; the rugged shot holes through the parapets of the bridges, through the fire-blackened walls of roofless houses, through the gilded and painted domes and turrets of stately mosques and temples; battered minarets and magnificent palaces half destroyed and totally pillaged, ornaments smashed or ripped to pieces, gardens trampled, fountains broken, ponds black from the gunpowder cast into them, summerhouses choked with bodies charred and mangled by explosions, the sickening odors therefrom contaminating the air; our field hospital full of men maimed and scorched by explosions—many groaning in their agony, others calmly bearing their suffering, a few unconscious to pain, the death rattle in their throats; and the bursting into a room in the last palace by some of our troops and there finding the rebel Prime Minister of Oudh lying on the richly carpeted floor with his throat cut and just breathing his last, having been murdered by his deadly rival the Moulvie or religious leader of the rebels (who would later be shot and beheaded by a loyal Raja), marked the end of the siege and capture of Lucknow—in all its ruined grandeur, a city more vast than Paris and once more splendid.

The total British casualties were 19 officers and 108 men killed, 95 officers and 540 men wounded, and 13 men missing—less than the columns of both Havelock and Campbell had suffered in their prior battles to relieve the Residency garrison. Governor General Lord Canning declared: "That this great success should have been accomplished at so little cost of valuable lives enhances the honor due to the leader who has achieved it." The rebel loss was estimated at about 4,000 killed. Few of the wounded escaped.

The recapture of Lucknow enabled Lord Canning to issue a proclamation of amnesty for all those who would lay down their arms and were not guilty of murdering British subjects. Thus, most of the Lucknow fugitives (including conscripts and those sepoys who were forced into disloyalty by their comrades) returned peacefully to their houses; and General Campbell, now Lord Clyde, eventually dealt with the rest. The old Bengal Army was abolished along with the East India Company, but a new Indian Army was established under the Crown without the fatal flaws of the old.

Mop-up operations continued into the early part of 1859, but by July the Governor General was able to proclaim: "War is at an end, rebellion has been put down, order is reestablished, and peaceful pursuits have everywhere been resumed." This was achieved at a cost of at least fifty millions sterling and the loss of at least thirteen thousand soldiers of the Raj and forty thousand mutineers, or a third of both forces. Untold thousands of civilians also perished. And so ended what historian Sir George Forrest called "a struggle as furious and relentless as any recorded in history."

    Lord Clyde summed up the military situation in his General Order of 28 May 1858: "In no war has it ever happened that troops have been more often engaged. In no war has it ever happened that troops should always contend against immense numerical odds. And in no war has constant success without a check been more conspicuously achieved."

    "Assuredly," added William Russell of The Times, *"never was the strength and courage of any people tried more severely in any one year since the world began than was the mettle of the British in India in 1857; and yet, with all their courage, they would have been exterminated if most Indians had been hostile to them, had not helped and strengthened them, had not made possible and shared the glory of their desperate defense."*

Select Bibliography

The material for this book was gathered mainly from the vast periodical collections of the British Library and the National Library of India. A list of the hundreds of newspapers and magazines from which the narratives were derived would be too extensive, but one form or another of each of the primary sources was reprinted in one or more of the following selection of books; and numerous other books, besides the periodicals, provided similar and much additional information.

Alison, Archibald: *Autobiography* (1883).

Anderson, Robert: *Personal Journal of the Siege of Lucknow* (1858); in *Narrative,* q.v.

Anson, Octavius: *With H.M. 9th Lancers During the Indian Mutiny* (1896).

Atkinson, George: *The Campaign in India* (1858).

Ball, Charles: *History of the Indian Mutiny* (2 vols., 1858–59). Contains many letters, etc.

Barker, George: *Letters from Persia and India* (1915).

Bartrum, Katherine: *A Widow's Reminiscences of the Siege of Lucknow* (1858).

Birch, Frederick: in Inglis, q.v.

Blake, George: *Memoir* (1883).

Bourchier, George: *Eight Months' Campaign* (1858).

Case, Adelaide: *Day by Day at Lucknow* (1858).

Chalmers, John: *Letters from India* (1904).

Chick, Noah: *Annals of the Indian Rebellion* (1859).

Delafosse, Henry: in *Narrative,* q.v.

Devereaux, Charles: in *Narrative,* q.v.

Dodd, George: *Chronicle of the Indian Revolt* (1859). Contains many quotations, etc.

Duff, Alexander: *The Indian Rebellion* (1858).

Edmondstoune, John: in Inglis, q.v.

Ewart, John: *Story of a Soldier's Life* (2 vols., 1881).

Fayrer, Joseph: *Recollections of My Life* (1900).

Forbes, Archibald: *Havelock* (1891).

Forbes, Mrs. Hamilton: *Some Recollections of the Siege of Lucknow* (1905).

Forrest, George: *History of the Indian Mutiny* (3 vols., 1904, 1912). Contains many quotations, etc.

Frost, Thomas: *Complete Narrative of the Revolt in India* (1858).

Fulton, George: *Journal* (1858).

Germon, Maria: *Journal of the Siege of Lucknow* (1870).

Gordon, Charles: *Recollections* (1898).

Gordon, John: in Kaye and Forrest, q.v.

Gough, Hugh: *Old Memories* (1897).

Grant, J(ames) Hope and Henry Knollys: *Incidents in the Sepoy War* (1875).

Groom, William: *With Havelock from Allahabad to Lucknow* (1894).

Gubbins, Martin: *Account of the Mutinies in Oudh and of the Seige of the Lucknow Residency* (1858).

Hare, Edward: *Memoirs* (1899).

Harris, Geraldine: *A Lady's Diary of the Siege of Lucknow* (1858).

Harris, James: *China Jim* (1912).

Havelock, Harry: quoted in Forbes, Malleson, and Marshman, q.v.

Hodson, George: *Twelve Years of a Soldier's Life in India* (1859).

Hodson, William: in George Hodson, q.v.

Home, Anthony: *Service Memories* (1912); in Forrest, Gubbins, and *Narrative*, q.v.

Hunter, Charles: *Personal Reminiscences* (1911).

Hutchinson, George: *Narrative* (1859).

Inglis, Julia: *Letters* (1858); *The Siege of Lucknow: A Diary* (1892).

Innes, J(ames) McLeod: *Defence of the Lucknow Residency* (1883); *Lucknow and Oudh in the Mutiny* (1895); *The Sepoy Revolt* (1897).

Johnson, William: *Twelve Years of a Soldier's Life* (1897).

Jones, Oliver: *Recollections of a Winter Campaign* (1859).

Kavanagh, T(homas) Henry: *How I Won the Victoria Cross* (1860).

Kaye, John: *Lives of Indian Officers* (2 vols., 1867); History of the Sepoy War (3 vols., 1876–80). Contains many quotations, etc.

Lang, Arthur: *Diary and Letters* (1897).

Lowe, Edward: quoted in Forrest, q.v.

Mackay, James: *From London to Lucknow* (2 vols., 1860).

Mackenzie, Alfred: *Mutiny Memoirs* (1891).

Majendie, Vivian: *Up Among the Pandies* (1859).

Malcolm, Thomas: *Barracks and Battlefields in India* (1881).

Malleson, George: *History of the Indian Mutiny* (3 vols., 1878–80). Contains many quotations, etc.

Marshman, John: *Memoirs of Major General Sir Henry Havelock* (1860).

Maude, Francis: *Memories of the Mutiny* (2 vols., 1894).

Mecham, Charles and George Couper: *Sketches and Incidents of the Siege of Lucknow* (1858).

Medley, Julius: *A Year's Campaigning in India* (1858).

Metcalfe, Henry: *Memoir* (1882).

Mitchell (Forbest-Mitchell), William: *Reminiscences of the Great Mutiny* (1894).

Munro, William: *Reminiscences* (1883).

Narrative of the Indian Revolt (1858). Contains many letters, etc.

Outram, James: *The Campaign in India* (1860).

Ouvry, Henry: *Cavalry Experiences* (1892).

Parry, Sydney: *An Old Soldier's Memories* (1897).

Polehampton, Henry: *A Memoir, Letters, and Diary* (1858).

Rees, Leopold: *Personal Narrative of the Siege of Lucknow* (1858).

Roberts, Frederick: *Forty-One Years in India* (2 vols., 1897); *Letters Written During the Indian Mutiny* (1924).

Robertson, James: *Personal Adventures and Anecdotes of an Old Soldier* (1906).

Ruggles, John: *Recollections of a Lucknow Veteran* (1906); in Narrative, q.v.

Russell, William: *My Diary in India* (2 vols., 1860); in Ball, Dodd, and Narrative, q.v.

Swanston, William: *My Journal* (1858).

Thackeray, Edward: *Two Indian Campaigns* (1896); *Memoirs* (1912).

Tweedie, William: *A Memory of the Indian Mutiny* (1904); quoted in Forbes, q.v.

Verney, Edmund: *The Shannon's Brigade in India* (1862).

Vibart, Edward: *The Sepoy Mutiny* (1898).

Walker, Thomas: *Through the Mutiny* (1907).

Watson, Edmund: *Journal* (1858).

Wilberforce, Reginald: *An Unrecorded Chapter of the Indian Mutiny* (1894).

Wilkinson, Osborn (and Johnson): *Memoirs of the Gemini Generals* (1896).

Willis, Frederick: in Maude, q.v.

Willock, Henry: in Maude and *Narrative*, q.v.

Wilson, Thomas: *Defence of Lucknow* (1858).

Wise, James: *Diary of a Medical Officer* (1881).

Wolseley, Garnet: *Story of a Soldier's Life* (2 vols., 1903).

Wood, Evelyn: *The Revolt in Hindustan* (1908).

Young, Keith: *Delhi, 1857* (1902).

Index